Tourism and Retail

Tourists are drawn to explore new environments and peoples. What better way to interact with a locality than to seek out and roam its marketplaces? The nature of tourist shopping activity thus goes beyond mere functional purchasing into multi-sensory explorations of place and space. Awareness of the shifting nature of these attractions is crucial to retailers and place marketers, in this age of the Internet, in order that the physical space of the market continues to serve as meaningful social and cultural space.

This book offers new perspectives on the intersection between tourism and retail research that is liminal to both fields yet central to the tourist experience, standing as an important and illuminating realm of consumer behaviour. It features a selection of multidisciplinary researchers' perspectives on tourist retail format and formation attractiveness for consumers, from the economist to the fashion retailer. By reviewing selected developments in space, place and behaviours within leisure, entertainment and recreational shopping, encompassing travel points, retail centres, sensory/festival marketplaces, leisure/cityscapes, department stores and fashion, the book offers thought-provoking insights into the past, present and future of tourist retail across a variety of global locations.

Given the growing emphasis upon consumer experience in place and space study and the apparent importance of retail activities within the tourism sphere, this book will be valuable reading for all those interested in retail, tourism and wider socio-cultural leisure environments and behaviours.

Charles McIntyre is Senior Lecturer in Retail Marketing and Design and Head of the Retail Research group at the University of Bournemouth.

Routledge Advances in Tourism

Edited by Stephen Page
School for Tourism, Bournemouth University

1. The Sociology of Tourism
Theoretical and empirical investigations
Edited by Yiorgos Apostolopoulos, Stella Leivadi and Andrew Yiannakis

2. Creating Island Resorts
Brian King

3. Destinations
Cultural landscapes of tourism
Edited by Greg Ringer

4. Mediterranean Tourism
Facets of socioeconomic development and cultural change
Edited by Yiorgos Apostolopoulos, Lila Leontidou and Philippos Loukissas

5. Outdoor Recreation Management
John Pigram and John Jenkins

6. Tourism Development
Edited by Douglas G. Pearce and Richard W. Butler

7. Tourism and Sustainable Community Development
Edited by Greg Richards and Derek Hall

8. Tourism and Political Boundaries
Dallen J. Timothy

9. Leisure and Tourism Landscapes
Social and cultural geographies
Cara Aitchison, Nicola E. MacLeod and Stephen J. Shaw

10. Tourism in the Age of Globalisation
Edited by Salah Wahab and Chris Cooper

11. Tourism and Gastronomy
Edited by Anne-Mette Hjalager and Greg Richards

12. New Perspectives in Caribbean Tourism
Edited by Marcella Daye, Donna Chambers and Sherma Roberts

13. The Advanced Econometrics of Tourism Demand
Haiyan Song, Stephen F. Witt and Gang Li

14. Tourism in China
Destination, cultures and communities
Edited by Chris Ryan and Gu Huimin

15. Sustainable Tourism Futures
Perspectives on systems, restructuring and innovations
Edited by Stefan Gössling, C. Michael Hall and David B. Weaver

16. Advances in Tourism Destination Marketing
Managing networks
Edited by Metin Kozak, Juergen Gnoth and Luisa Andreu

17. Drive Tourism
Trends and emerging markets
Edited by Bruce Prideaux and Dean Carson

18. Tourist Customer Service Satisfaction
An encounter approach
Francis P. Noe, Muzzafer Uysal and Vincent P. Magnini

19. Mining Heritage Tourism
A global synthesis
Edited by Michael Conlin and Lee Jolliffe

20. Tourist Experience
Contemporary perspectives
Edited by Richard Sharpley and Phillip Stone

21. Sustainable Tourism in Rural Europe
Edited by Donald Macleod and Steven Gillespie

22. The Critical Turn in Tourism Studies
Creating an academy of hope
Edited by Nigel Morgan, Irena Atelkevic and Annette Pritchard

23. Tourism Supply Chain Management
Haiyan Song

24. Tourism and Retail
Edited by Charles McIntyre

25. International Sports Events
Impacts, experience and identities
Edited by Richard Shipway and Alan Fyall

26. Cultural Moment in Tourism
Edited by Laurajane Smith, Emma Waterton and Steve Watson

27. Contemporary Tourist Experience
Richard Sharpley and Philip Stone

Forthcoming:

Responsible Tourist Behaviour
Clare Weeden

Information Communication Technologies and Sustainable Tourism
Alisha Ali and Andrew J. Frew

Future Tourism
Political, social and economic challenges
James Leigh and Craig Webster

Human Rights and Global Events
Rebecca Finkel

Tourist Experience and Fulfilment
Insights from positive psychology
Sebastian Filep and Philip Pearce

Tourism and Retail

The psychogeography of liminal consumption

Edited by Charles McIntyre

Routledge
Taylor & Francis Group
LONDON AND NEW YORK

First published 2012 by Routledge

2 Park Square, Milton Park, Abingdon, Oxon OX14 4RN
711 Third Avenue, New York, NY 10017, USA

Routledge is an imprint of the Taylor & Francis Group, an informa business

First issued in paperback 2017

British Library Cataloguing in Publication Data
A catalogue record for this book is available from the British Library

Library of Congress Cataloging in Publication Data
McIntyre, Charles, 1955–
Tourism and retail : the psychogeography of liminal consumption / Charles McIntyre.
p. cm.
Includes bibliographical references and index.
ISBN 978-0-415-69358-5 (hbk: alk. paper) 1. Tourism—Economic aspects. 2. Tourism—Psychological aspects. 3. Retail trade. 4. Consumption (Economics) I. Title.
G155.A1M212 2012
338.4'791—dc23
2011032291

ISBN: 978-0-415-69358-5 (hbk)
ISBN: 978-1-138-08140-6 (pbk)

Typeset in Times New Roman by Prepress Projects Ltd, Perth, UK

Contents

Figures

Tables

Contributors

Sean Beer is a Senior Lecturer at the School of Tourism, Bournemouth University, UK. Sean is involved in local and national food marketing and research and has a passionate interest in the interactions between tourism, culture, the countryside and the food supply chain. Originally trained as an agricultural scientist in the UK and New Zealand, backed up with practical experience gained on the family farm and associated businesses, he is currently interested mainly in the nature of the authenticity of food.

Corinna Budnarowska is a Lecturer in Fashion and Retail Buying, and Retail Programme Leader at the School of Tourism, Bournemouth University, UK. Corinna has many years of practical experience in fashion and retail, running entrepreneurial businesses, both on the UK high street and online. She has also been heavily involved in e-marketing, online analytics and social marketing developments in education–business interactions, including projects such as the Bournemouth University Hub.

Daniel Ganly is the MBA Programme Director at The Business School, Oxford Brookes University, Oxford, UK. Daniel has worked for a number of blue chip retailers both across the UK and internationally, including Marks & Spencer, Clarks Shoes and Virgin Retail Europe, where he held a number of international and national roles in the area of operations, marketing and buying, before becoming a full-time academic.

Joe Goldblatt is the Executive Director of the International Centre for the Study of Planned Events at Queen Margaret University in Edinburgh, Scotland. Joe is the author, co-author and editor of 22 books in the field of planned events and was the first professorial educator to be inducted into the International Festivals and Events Association Hall of Fame. He has had a stimulating international career, moving to Edinburgh from the USA.

Christine Harris is currently a Senior Lecturer in Retail Management at the University of Bournemouth, previously with Wolverhampton University and the University of Manchester Institute of Science and Technology. Christine has been involved in researching consumer needs for commercial and charitable organisations, as well as investigating street traders in the UK and overseas and working with town centre managers to identify the needs of their visitors.

Charles McIntyre is a Senior Lecturer in Retail Marketing and Design, and is Head of the Retail Research Group at the School of Tourism, Bournemouth University, UK. He previously had director-level positions with HMV (UK) and Virgin Retail (Europe and Australia). In his academic career, he is particularly interested in liminal and cultural retailing, experience and design, publishing on tourist consumption, museum visits, music purchasing, cafés and consumer behaviours relating to mobile technologies, as well as consulting for local food brands.

Ruth Marciniak is a Principal Lecturer in Marketing and Communications at the Business School, London Metropolitan University, UK. Ruth is particularly interested in travel, fashion and e-marketing. Her research interests encompass theoretical and empirical enquiry into issues around strategy planning within the retail sector. She has published in academic journals including the *International Journal of Retail and Distribution Management* and the *Journal of Management and Decision*. She has presented academic papers at a number of national and international conferences, including the British Academy of Management.

Andrew Murphy is currently Associate Head of School, Communication, Journalism and Marketing for the Albany campus, Massey University, New Zealand, and teaches Consumer Behaviour and Retail Marketing courses. In an international academic career, Andrew gained his PhD at the University of British Columbia, Vancouver, on the institutional and consumptive implications of online grocery shopping. He has also lectured at the Universities of Southampton and Birmingham in the UK.

Robin Shepherd is a Principal Lecturer and Director of Hospitality and Tourism programmes at The Business School, Portsmouth University, UK. Robin has been a financial advisor for regional businesses and predominantly researches local food branding, slow food, local food cooperative movements and supply chains.

Colin C. Williams is Professor of Public Policy in the School of Management at the University of Sheffield, UK. His recent books include *Informal Work in Developed Nations* (2010, Routledge), *Rethinking the Future of Work* (2007, Palgrave-Macmillan) and *A Commodified World?* (2005, Zed). His research interests are in work organisation, consumption and livelihoods.

Acknowledgements

The editor would like to acknowledge the debates and contributions of many colleagues in tourism and retail that have helped contribute to the current text. Within Bournemouth University, particular thanks go to Professor John Fletcher, Professor Alan Fyall and Caroline Jackson for their belief, contacts and encouragement over what has been the long process between inception and completion of the manuscript. Outside Bournemouth University, thanks go to Professor Harry Timmermans, Head of the European Institute of Retailing and Services Studies (EIRASS) in Eindhoven University of Technology, the Netherlands, and Editor of the *Journal of Retailing and Consumer Service*; Professor Charles Dennis, Professor of Marketing and Retailing and Director of Research at Lincoln Business School, the University of Lincoln; Professor Margaret Sullivan, Professor of Marketing Communication, Columbia College, Chicago; Professor Dallen Timothy, School of Community Resources and Development, Arizona State University; Dr John Ensor, Head of School, Marketing, Tourism and Languages, Edinburgh Napier University; and last, but certainly not least, Dr Antje Cockrill, MSc Management Programme Director (Finance and Marketing), School of Business and Economics, Swansea University. To all these people, all the contributors and anyone I may have missed out – many thanks again!

Introduction

Tourism and retail: the psychogeography of liminal consumption

Charles McIntyre

A common question asked when teaching marketing is 'what is the difference between generic (product) marketing and retail (service) marketing?' The answer is usually around two dimensions of push–pull and product–place distinction. In the first process one is pushing a product *out* to the customer, serving a market wherever it can be reached, whereas in the second one is 'pulling' customers *into* a retail 'space' in order to create a distinct market 'place' by encouraging them to spend some time there. This concurs with the notion that 'if we think of space as that which allows movement, then place is pause; each pause in movement makes it possible for location to be transformed into place' (Tuan, 1977: 6).

In creating a market 'place' the main aim of retail, as with marketplaces from ancient times, is to attract and retain a sufficient density of people to support trade. An effective market space is therefore not purely about supporting economic transactions, but also about creating a sense of place suitable for encouraging and maintaining social and cultural interactions. By this distinction, it would seem obvious to consider retail and tourism together in terms of their place and space attractiveness or 'magnetic' qualities, including their social, cultural and economic spatial effects upon visitors. This orientation also incorporates both fields of study within the realms of psychogeography, as per Guy Debord's (1958: 52) situationist definition of 'The study of specific effects of the geographical environment (whether consciously organised or not) on the emotions and behaviour of individuals'.

In considering retail for tourists, we are dealing with a bordering, transitional – so called liminal – region, 'between the sacred and the secular, the mundane and exotic, and the local and global' (Goss, 1993: 27). In this, the study of the tourist realm crosses over into generic leisure study, with retail landscapes providing everyday escapes of socio-cultural entertainment, such as in the form of the shopping mall (the above definition being used by Goss in just such a retail geographical study). Tourist and leisure environments support the behaviours of the *flâneur* (the casual, urban stroller), and their associated activities of *dérive* (experimental transient passage through varied ambiances) and *détournement* (integrating pre-existing aesthetic elements within the construction of a milieu); all situated in the commercial, public spaces of a society of consumerist spectacle. These propositions and the study of them arose particularly following the retail innovations of Paris from the nineteenth century onwards (Aragon, 1994; Benjamin, 1973a,b, 1999; Bowlby, 1985; Debord, 1958; Zola, 1995).

In most tourist and leisurescapes to this day we will find retail strolling and shopping space investigation as key activities – around shops, stalls or other displays. Sometimes, retailers appear as secondary, more obviously *liminal* attractions, only loosely appended to the main reason for an outing (such as perhaps in museum, art gallery or even hospital visits). In terms of 'touristic' or recreational shopping, some have claimed that the advent of the shopping mall and the mix of leisure and shopping spaces they present is a postmodern development of social control and commodification, as per *the society of the spectacle* (Chaney, 1991; Debord, 2009; Shields, 1992: 6–7). However, although undoubtedly applicable to some constructs of modern retail and shopping mall influences, such as in the *Disneyisation* and *Macdonaldization* of society treatises (Bryman, 2004; Ritzer, 1996), it is hard to justify such a strictly modernist position to this, considering the historical importance of marketplaces and town centres as mixed social and leisure interactions. So, although the forms of supermalls and airport shopping that mix tourism and retail are relatively new, the chapters of this text will serve to show that there is a history to such mixed domains.

A direct link between tourism and retail can nevertheless be seen to be the case in many modern city-centre break destinations and events – the New York shopping trip comes to mind in the UK as a specific long-distance holiday event. Any recent analysis of Christmas movies and advertisements in the UK would confirm that New York is a key signifier of this season in popular culture, even though many recognising this may not actually have been there – and so retail myths and symbolic constructs are made by means of 'armchair travelling', as per Huysmans (1956: 21–22, 128–129). There can be no doubt that such mythologies of retail place attractiveness can pull tourists to a location as a – or *the* – key attribute within a location's place-brand or attractive image.

Since the publication of Pine and Gilmore's (1999) *Experience Economy* rallying-cry text for services study, the two fields of retail and tourism can be seen to be growing closer in focus. Retail studies are increasingly featuring an anthropological focus on shopping behaviours, blurring the previously discrete academic boundaries between retail, tourism and leisure (Baker, 2000; Falk and Campbell, 1997; Miller, 1998; Miller *et al.*, 1998; Murphy *et al.*, 2011; Shields, 1992; Timothy, 2005; Wrigley and Lowe, 2002).

In academic study, retail has sometimes been viewed in overtly negative terms, as an unwanted and parasitic intrusion of commercial opportunism into socio-cultural spaces and places. This orientation views shopping per se as politically controlled consumption of commercially produced product-objects and the symbolic aspects of their acquisition/exchange in a *hyper* rather than *real* or authentic space and process (Baudrillard, 1998; Bauman, 1996; Benjamin, 1973a; Clarke, 2003). Albeit relevant to an analysis of built modernist cathedrals of consumption, this would seem to ignore the evidence that shopping is an essential human activity of social and cultural (as well as economic) interaction, taking place within liminal and autonomous leisure realms that are situated between the public and the private, the individual and the social and the internal and the external domains, necessary for interpersonal trade. As opposed to basic, functional shopping events, this kind of retail involves a *shopping around* activity orientation rather than just a *shopping for* things (Falk and Campbell, 1997: 2–3). The shopping around paradigm is particularly applicable to leisure shopping forms, such as tourist retail, that cannot easily be replaced by online substitution, and is related to a shift from an *economic essentialism* towards *cultural essentialism* in retail studies, apropos of a growth in postmodern thinking (Williams, 2002). The importance and relevance that shopping can have to people's lives as a central concern of humanistic meaning whilst being out-in-the-world has also been argued from both a feminist and a humanist viewpoint by Douglas (1997) and Miller (1997), the latter taking an oppositional viewpoint to Benjamin's (1999) Parisien Arcades Project's apparently negative views on shopping activity as a female *flâneuse* and male *flâneur* controlled activity of little intrinsic value. Countering this reading, Benjamin (1973b) himself focuses on the deep pleasures that he derived from his own personally positive activity of shopping for books!

Yet the increased general anthropological importance that is now being assigned to retail activities within leisure is often at odds with broad leisure studies texts of the past, where retail has sometimes been missed out altogether, such as Michael Argyle's (1996) classic text *The Social Psychology of Leisure*, where neither retail nor shopping appears in the index or has a separate section in the text, unlike the subject of 'holidays and tourism'. The general psychogeographical orientation of this book will hopefully aid in altering this.

The book's initiation followed discussions when planning to relaunch the retail research group (RRG) at Bournemouth University (BU) on the Dorset coast of the UK. It became obvious that our little group of researchers was firmly embedded within the exploration of retail environments as part of the tourist experience. Bournemouth itself is an 'old world' tourist town, having been a tourist destination since at least Georgian times, and is one of the key remaining English traditional seaside resorts, encouraging boulevardian strolling along an extensive beachfront promenade that is linked to the main shopping streets by equally promenadian gardens.

Over the book's genesis period, contributions were recruited from friends and working colleagues both from within, and outside BU (moving between old-world and new-world perspectives, not only between but also within chapters). The aim was not to produce a comprehensive textbook approach, but rather to attempt to make an interesting and informative read relating to the subject of retail's attractiveness for tourists. This means we are offering a series of individual viewpoints, discussions and debates around interest areas that wrestle with the nature of the consumption process for tourists, exploring interrelationships within various psychogeographic realms of retail and tourism domains.

In the first part of the book the focus is on retail place regarding the *formations*, groupings or agglomerations of retail that may make up socio-cultural tourist realms, asking how retail could be integral to, and synergistically a part, of the tourism space and place experience.

In Chapter 1, it is extremely pertinent that Professor Colin C. Williams, Professor of Public Policy at the Management School, University of Sheffield, has agreed to contribute his views on the text's subject, as he is the author of a key earlier conceptual piece (Williams, 1997) that firmly cemented my own academic interest in the area of retail as a primary economic 'magnet' and value creator. He continues to comment on this theme here, noting the conceptual *retail turn* towards a positive economic magnet role for retail, with a particular focus on the visibly large, physical formations of regional shopping centres (RSCs), from the point of view of an extremely respected, socially and environmentally oriented economist. Professor Williams presents a thoroughly refreshingly positive view of the role of retail in the development of space and place's primary attractiveness, in contrast with a more generally accepted negative orientation towards retail and consumerism in tourism and travel studies. As part of this, he begins to examine the role of 'entertainment' in retail formations such as RSCs, forming a visitor-attracting, value-creation viewpoint towards retail venues. This theme will be further developed in many of the succeeding chapters.

In Chapter 2, Christine Harris, the resident retail historian at BU, then comments upon the theme of the changing mix and character of the UK high street over time (its US equivalent being 'main street'). Her approach is critical of the 'clone' towns' emergence in UK high streets and their unappealing lack of local differentiation for visitors for short- or long-term tourist attractiveness. This illustrates a more negative viewpoint towards certain retail consumerist formations, such as out-of-town (and in-town) major RSC developments and their potential new-world contribution towards a process of degrading old-world city and town centres. This orientation forms a contrast with the overall positive, regional developmental effects of such retail developments argued in Chapter 1, instead considering modern out-of town developments as one of many contributing factors to making towns and cities less attractive. She therefore argues for a holistic approach from those in charge of town centre development in order to avoid tourist leakage and centre degradation.

In contrast to Christine's 'old world' versus 'new world' dynamics of in-town versus out-of-town UK tourist attraction, in Chapter 3 Professor Joe Goldblatt gives a very personal view upon the current state of innovative retail developments across both new and old world environments, and the excitement that can be generated by some recent developments. Professor Goldblatt is the executive director of the International Centre for the Study of Planned Events at Queen Margaret University, Edinburgh, Scotland. He is the author or editor of over 20 books in the field of events management and began his career producing events in retail shopping centres throughout the United States. His model of a sensual temporal marketplace focuses upon the changing nature of retail formation experiences in providing a diversity of entertaining retailing innovations and events. This includes consideration of the changing nature of markets and the place of pop-up stores and the Internet in creating motivation for place visits and long-term experience associations. The role of the Internet introduced here becomes another theme arising from many of the chapters in the second 'format' part of the book. In this chapter Professor Goldblatt gives pointers for possible future development of new kinds of tourist retail formations.

For the last chapter of Part I, I attempt to expand on the specific nature of the tourist consumer and to consider some aspects of the theoretical nature of tourist retail place and space across the retail literature. Included here is a focus upon retail in holiday resorts as well as the previous main focus upon cityscapes and large commercialised formations. This chapter's spatial perspective on tourist retail focuses on some key conceptual issues around tourist retail attractiveness and effects, further alluding to ideas that can be seen to be inherent in parts of the other chapters in Part I. These include theoretical concepts relating to 'healthy' consumerism of tourism retail formations as part of leisure environments, including the concepts of 'active'/(co)creative retailing and biophilic response, as well as considerations of 'third place' and flow theory. And so in Part I we cover several major aspects and viewpoints of tourist retail formations of cities, resorts, high streets and out-of-towns, including RSCs. Although they are a part of the discussions in many of these chapters, we have chosen not to particularly focus upon shopping malls or cultural souvenir shopping to any great extent as these are areas of the subject that can easily be seen to have been covered expansively elsewhere.

In Part II of the book we then move towards an increased focus upon individual retail formats and outlet types. In Chapter 5, Ruth Marciniak of London Metropolitan University explores the relationship between travel and retail formats (travel retail being a subset of tourist retail). This is the most obvious manifestation, perhaps, of common ground in retail-based, tourism-oriented research, as the field of travel research has been extensively featured in tourist retail studies, predominantly in the form of the extremely well-developed (some would say overdeveloped) area of airport retailing. Starting with a historical perspective, Ruth considers current evident preoccupations of retail-based travel developments, including airport retailing, but shifts the attention to a case study upon St Pancras railway station in London – railway stations being notorious areas of *flâneurie* in past times but perhaps only more recently seeing commercial developments along the lines of the airport mall developments.

Food tourism is one of the areas of tourist retail that has also been covered extensively elsewhere (see Henderson, 2009, for a recent review). As a specific, retail-based psychogeographical project liminal to this area, in Chapter 6, Andrew Murphy, Sean Beer and Robin Shepherd, from Auckland, Bournemouth and Portsmouth Universities respectively, give their views upon the touristic attractions of the increasing sphere of farmers' markets and their changing format to characterise place and space in relation to local food qualities and cultural interactions. Chapter 6 ends with a case study on the developing role of farmers' markets in New Zealand as a form of visitor attraction with links to a perceived 'authentic' past, furthering a shift from old- to new-world issues.

In Chapter 7, Daniel Ganly from Oxford Brookes University and I discuss the tourist perspective from our shared background in international entertainment retail formats, primarily related to city-centre retailing as experienced in our joint previous industry-based days designing and operating megastores for Virgin across Europe in the early 1990s. The focus here is on entertainment aspects of retail as part of place attractiveness. The discussion brings in many disparate elements for experiential consideration including the sought-after tourist entertainments of department stores, theme restaurants, shopping malls, lanes, casbahs and even cruise ships. Another linking theme that can also be perceived as arising from previous chapters is the 'big store–little store' (or corporate and non-corporate) one applied to potential retail attractiveness, offers and mixes as appropriate for tourist consumption.

Finally, putting forward thoughts upon future retail formats that may be particularly relevant to young consumers, in Chapter 8 Corinna Budnarowka, the fashion specialist of the retail research group at BU, moves us from food to fashion. She considers various fashion formats and the upmarket–downmarket retail styles within an urban tourism perspective, giving a youthful orientation upon the role of 'street' and niche fashion retailers in particular and their potential for renewed local entrepreneurial activity related to the creation of differentiated, 'clustered' and non-corporate, servicescapes of an alternative lifestyle variety.

Speaking as the editor, as well as a contributor, I sincerely hope that any reader finds some areas of interest amongst the areas covered – perhaps even some surprise, illumination or areas of personal contention? The hope is that the text, by its focus across many varied aspects of the subject, will whet others' appetites for exploring it with gusto themselves. Personally I have found much entertainment and enlightenment in all the other contributors' chapters. Needless to say, however, although it is an honour to present the various contributions herein, any omissions or errors must be entirely taken as my responsibility, for which I can only apologise.

Charles McIntyre

References

Aragon, L. (1994) *Paris Peasant*. Boston: Exact Change.

Argyle, M. (1996) *The Social Psychology of Leisure*. London: Penguin Books.

Baker, A. (ed.) (2000) *Serious Shopping: Essays in psychotherapy and consumerism*. London: Free Association Books.

Baudrillard, J. (1998) *The Consumer Society: Myths and structures*. London: Sage.

Bauman, Z. (1996) From pilgrim to tourist: or a short history of identity. In Hall, S. and du Gay, P. (eds) *Questions of Cultural Identity*. London: Sage, pp. 18–36.

Benjamin, W. (1973a) *Charles Baudelaire: A lyric poet in the era of high capitalism*. London: New Left Books.

Benjamin, W. (1973b) *Illuminations*. London: Fontana.

Benjamin, W. (1999) *The Arcades Project* (trans. Eiland, H. and McGlaughlin, K.). Cambridge, MA: Belknap Press, Harvard University Press.

Bowlby, R. (1985) *Just Looking: Consumer culture in Dreiser, Gisseng and Zola*. London: Methuen.

Bryman, A. (2004) *The Disneyisation of Society*. London: Sage Publications.

Chaney, D. (1991) Subutopia in Gateshead: the MetroCentre as a cultural form. *Theory, Culture and Society* 7, 49–68.

Clarke, D. B. (2003) *The Consumer Society and the Postmodern City*. London: Routledge.

Debord, G. (1958) Situationist International #1. In Knabb, K. (ed. and trans.) *Situationalist International Anthology* (revised and expanded edition, 2006), Berkeley: Bureau of Public Secrets, pp. 47–61.

Debord, G. (2009) *Society of the Spectacle* (trans. Knabb, K.). Eastbourne: Soul Bay Press.

Douglas, M. (1997) In defence of shopping. In Falk, P. and Campbell, C. (eds) *The Shopping Experience*. London: Sage, pp. 15–30.

Falk, P. and Campbell, C. (eds) (1997) *The Shopping Experience*. London: Sage.

Goss, J. (1993) The magic of the mall: An analysis of form, function and meaning in the contemporary retail built environment. *Annals of the Association of American Geographers* 83(1), 18–47.

Henderson, J. C. (2009) Food tourism reviewed. *British Food Journal* 111(4), 317–326.

Huysmans, J.-K. (1956) *Against Nature* (trans. Baldick, R.). London: Penguin Books.

Miller, D. (1997) Could shopping ever really matter? In defence of shopping. In Falk, P. and Campbell, C. (eds) *The Shopping Experience*. London: Sage, pp. 31–55.

Miller, D. (1998) *A Theory of Shopping*. Cambridge: Polity Press.

Miller, D., Jackson, P. Thrift, N., Holbrook, B. and Rowlands, M. (1998) *Shopping, Place and Identity*. London: Routledge.

Murphy, L., Benckendorff, P., Moscardo, G. and Pearce, L. P. (2011) *Tourist Shopping Villages: Forms and functions*. New York: Routledge.

Pine, J. and Gilmore, J. (1999) *The Experience Economy: Work is theatre and every business is a stage*. Boston, MA: Harvard Business School Press.

Ritzer, G. (1996) *The Macdonaldization of Society*. Thousand Oaks, CA: Pine Forge Press.

Shields, R. (ed.) (1992) *Lifestyle Shopping: The subject of consumption*. London: Routledge.

Timothy, D. J. (2005) *Shopping Tourism, Retail and Leisure*. Clevedon, UK: Channel View Publications.

Tuan, Y.-F. (1977) *Space and Place: The perspective of experience*. Minneapolis: University of Minnesota Press.

Williams, C. C. (1997) Retailing and economic development. In C. C. Williams (1997) *Consumer Services and Economic Development*. London: Routledge, pp. 108–125.

Williams, C. C. (2002) Why do people use alternative retail channels? Some case-study evidence from two English cities. *Urban Studies* 39(10), 1897–1910.

Wrigley, N. and Lowe, M. (2002) *Reading Retail: A geographical perspective on retailing and consumption spaces*. London: Arnold.

Zola, É. (1995) *The Ladies' Paradise* (trans. Nelson, B.). Oxford: Oxford University Press.

Part I

Tourist retail place and space formations

1 Re-theorising the role of retail shopping centres as tourist attractions in economic development

Colin C. Williams

Introduction

For many decades, retailing and tourism were depicted as largely separate activities. Today, however, this is no longer the case. Given that 'retail tourism', whereby people go to particular places in order to go shopping, is becoming an ever more popular and prominent form of tourism, this chapter addresses how attractions are now being developed to capture such retail tourism.

In consequence, the chapter charts the transformations in thought and practice regarding the role of the retail sector in economic development. In contrast to the tourism industry, which for many decades has been widely recognised as positively contributing to economic development, not least by bringing external income into areas, retail ventures for a long time were negatively depicted as dependent, even parasitic, activities that rely on the wealth created by other sectors and contribute little, if anything, to economic development. In recent decades, however, this has begun to change. The intention of this chapter is to begin to unravel how and why retailing has started to be re-conceptualised.

To do this, the first section briefly sets out the changing size and structure of the UK retail sector, followed in the second section by a review of how the conceptualisation of the role of retailing in economic development has changed over time. This will unravel how for much of the twentieth century this sector was viewed as a secondary activity contributing little, if anything, to economic development and how, since the 1990s, it has started to be more positively depicted as a magnet for attracting external income and tourists, and a driver of local economic development, as captured in the trend of 'retail-led economic regeneration' (Lowe, 2005).

Given this re-reading of the role of retail ventures in local economic development, the third section then examines the particular case of regional shopping centres (RSCs). This will chart various waves of RSC development and how they have been increasingly recognised as honey-traps for attracting retail tourists, resulting in entertainment becoming integral to such developments. The final section then synthesises the finding that retail attractions are no longer viewed as dependent or parasitic activities but, rather, as magnets and drivers of economic development, and explores the future prospects for retail ventures in general, and shopping centres more particularly, by examining current thinking on the role of the retail sphere in economic development and how the on-going emergence of the triple bottom line of the economic, social and environmental impacts might change the practice of developing retail attractions to generate external income.

Size and nature of the UK retail sector

In the UK in 2008, nearly 3.2 million people were employed in the retail sector, which equates to some 11 per cent of the total UK workforce. Indeed, almost 8 per cent of gross domestic product (GDP) is generated by the retail sector; retail sales totalled about £265 billion in 2007, which was larger than the combined economies of Denmark and Portugal (British Council of Shopping Centres, 2008; Datamonitor, 2008).

Significant structural changes have also occurred in this large and expanding sector, especially in terms of the patterns of retail ownership. Until 1964, manufacturers could decide the price of their goods in the shops. Efficient stores, wishing to sell more, could not compete by charging their customers less. Large chain stores could not undercut village grocers. The abandonment of price fixing in the 1964 Resale Price Maintenance Act, however, meant that small amounts could no longer be bought from a manufacturer for the same price as bulk purchases. By bulk buying, chains could compete by cutting prices. A retail revolution resulted. The outcome was a shift from local to corporate ownership and an increasing concentration of retail capital. By 2006/7, the top four food and drink retailers (namely Tesco, Sainsbury's, Asda and Morrisons) had 78 per cent of total retail sales compared with just 74 per cent market share in 2003/4 (Mintel, 2008). Of these, Tesco is by far the largest with a market share of 33 per cent in 2006/7 (compared with 32 per cent in 2003/4).

Nevertheless, the UK retail market has witnessed ever greater competition from foreign-owned companies. On the one hand, foreign discount stores, such as Netto and Aldi, have entered the UK market, which has higher net profit margins than other EU nations (Guy, 1994, 2007). Indeed, by 2006/7, Aldi had become the tenth largest food and drink retailer in the UK, with a turnover of £1,322 million and a market share of some 1.3 per cent, whilst Netto had a turnover of some £627 million and a market share of 0.6 per cent. On the other hand, although US-owned 'warehouse clubs' (e.g. Costco) failed in their bids to enter the UK retail market directly, major US companies such as Wal-Mart eventually gained market share by directly acquiring British retailers (Asda in Wal-Mart's case). The long-term trend in UK retail ownership, therefore, is away from local indigenous ownership and towards national and international companies with multiple outlets, all of which result in an outflow of profits and income from the local, regional and national economy.

Re-theorising the role of the retail sector in economic development

Despite this restructuring and growth of the retail sector for much of the twentieth century, retailing received little, if any, attention from those involved in local, regional and national economic development. Indeed, retail planning and economic development were widely treated as separate and unconnected issues. The retail sector, that is, was commonly viewed as a dependent activity reliant on the wealth created in other sectors for its vitality and viability.

Why was this negative dependent depiction of retailing adopted? To answer this, it is necessary to understand 'economic base' theory, or what is sometimes called 'export base' theory, which for most of the twentieth century has been a principal conceptual tool used to formulate local economic policy and theorise local economic development (Haggett *et al.*, 1977). Assuming that an economy needs to earn external income to grow, this theory has viewed any economy as composed of two sectors: 'basic' sector industries, which generate external income and act as 'engines of growth', and dependent sector activities, which are said to merely circulate income within the area and are therefore viewed as 'parasitic' activities feeding off the wealth created in the basic sector industries. Grounded in this theorisation, local, regional and national economic development has traditionally sought to develop its basic sector.

What are considered basic and dependent sector activities, nevertheless, have changed over time. In the first wave of thought and practice, from the industrial revolution until the 1970s, the basic sector was viewed as composed of manufacturing, and services were seen as dependent activities. The focus in economic development was thus on developing and promoting manufacturing industry. Services were regarded as 'lollipop' jobs and of no real value to economic development. Indeed, this view perhaps persists. As Bachtler and Davies (1989: 168) point out, 'the view that the economy is solely manufacturing driven still has widespread currency. The view is that services are wholly dependent on manufacturing and that service jobs are not "real" jobs'. Indeed, in many local government economic development strategies, statements are still found such as that 'most services in the district are of an essentially local nature' (Kirklees Metropolitan Borough Council, 1991: 6). So too do the groves of academe remain littered with such views. Campbell (1996: 49), for example, claims that 'service activities depend on [manufacturing] for their survival and growth', and Peck and Tickell (1991: 36) believe that 'service industries are essentially "parasitic" in that they do not actually add to wealth in the economy, although they can help to realise the value of wealth created elsewhere'.

Retailing, in consequence, was widely depicted in first-wave thought and practice as a dependent (or parasitic) activity feeding off the wealth created by so-called basic industries. As Lowe and Crewe (1991: 345) state, 'the retail trade is typically seen as an insignificant backwater, a sector which is somewhat tangential to the "real" world of production'. This view is captured by Lackey and Eckenstahler (1995: 86) when they state:

> If you ask a room full of economic developers who their clients and prospects are, 100% would identify manufacturers. Many would talk about distribution facilities. Several would even discuss back office and corporate headquarters facilities. Few, if any, would talk about retail . . . yet each of their local

> economies may be losing tens-of-millions of dollars and thousands of jobs annually from lost retail sales – dollars being spent by the residents of their communities, outside these communities.

Since the 1980s, nevertheless, this simplistic dominant/subservient view of the relationship between manufacturing and services has been questioned, not least on account of the twin trends of de-industrialisation and tertiarisation in the advanced economies and the accompanying new international division of labour (Dicken, 1992; Sassen, 1991), with control and command functions located in a network of global cities in developed nations. This demise of the centrality of manufacturing resulted in a re-evaluation of the role of services in economic development in a second wave of thought and practice. Producer services (services sold to other businesses) were shown to export (Beyers and Alvine, 1985; Coffey, 1995, 2000) and therefore incorporated into the basic sector alongside manufacturing as a motor of economic development. The old 'manufacturing as engine of growth' and 'services as dependent' dualism of the first wave was replaced by a 'manufacturing and producer services as engines of growth' versus 'consumer services as dependent activity' dichotomy in the second wave. Retailing, in consequence, continued to be firmly located in the dependent sector living off the wealth created elsewhere in the economy.

Since the 1990s, however, a third wave of thought and action has emerged. This has shown that the major sector remaining entrenched in the dependent category, namely consumer services, also fulfils an external income-generating function (Williams, 1997a, 1999). Numerous studies have revealed how consumer services such as tourism, universities, sports facilities and events, cultural industries and retailing all perform a similar function to export industries in that they generate external income for areas by attracting visitors from outside to spend their money within the area (Williams, 1997a).

A direct outcome has been a 'retail turn' in economic development theory and practice. The retail sector has been recognised to play a positive role in economic regeneration. Indeed, it has often taken the lead role in economic regeneration in areas unable to attract other sectors, whilst in other areas it has been used to bolster the attractiveness of the area to other sectors. Today, therefore, not only is retailing viewed as a basic sector activity that attracts people from outside the area to spend their money (i.e. 'retail tourism' as opposed to tourism retail expenditure) but retail attractions also sometimes take a lead role in economic regeneration (Lowe, 2005; Williams, 1997b). Indeed, given that shopping is now the second most popular leisure activity, exceeded only by television watching (Goss, 1993), it perhaps makes sense that retail economic development in turn develops 'retail tourism', by which is here meant attracting tourist shoppers to a place in order to spend their money.

Given this re-reading of the role of retail ventures in local, regional and national economic development, the particular case of RSCs will now be analysed. This will reveal the various waves of regional shopping centre development and how RSCs have become increasingly recognised as honey-traps for retail tourists and therefore how entertainment has been integrated into their fabric in order to make them even more effective magnets.

Regional shopping centres and their impacts

Examining the history of the planned RSC in the UK, three broad and distinct waves of development can be identified, namely a first wave of new town, expanded town and in-town RSCs during the 1950s, 1960s and 1970s, a second wave of out-of-town RSCs during the 1980s and 1990s and a current third wave of in-town RSCs, which act as honey-traps for retail tourists and therefore as vehicles for retail-led urban regeneration. Each wave of RSC development is here considered in turn.

First wave of regional shopping centre development

The origins of the planned shopping centre lie in the work of Victor Gruen, an architect of the shopping mall during the 1950s in North America. Southdale in Minneapolis, which opened in 1956, was the world's first enclosed (fully covered) mall, which was then replicated across the USA (Friedan and Sagalyn, 1989). In the UK, although the American model of planned enclosed malls was adopted, the US model of building free-standing suburban facilities was not followed. Instead, in the UK, shopping malls were 'a vehicle for enlarging and modernising central area shopping' (Guy, 1994: 181).

In the 1960s and 1970s, that is, many shopping malls were constructed in UK towns. Examples include the original Bull Ring in Birmingham (1964), the Dolphin Centre in Poole (1969), Luton's Arndale Centre (1972), the Victoria Centre in Nottingham (1972), the Arndale Centre in Manchester (1976), Newcastle's Eldon Square (1976) and St David's Centre in Cardiff (1981). The only exceptions to the in-town emphasis in the UK during the 1960s and 1970s were the major out-of-town shopping centres built in planned new and expanded towns. Such shopping centres included Shopping City in Runcorn (1971), Telford Centre in Telford (1973), Kingfisher Centre in Redditch (1973), Central Milton Keynes in Milton Keynes (1979), Eastgate in Basildon (1980) and Queensgate in Peterborough (1982). However, beyond these strategic shopping centre developments, the 1960s through to the 1980s was characterised by regional-sized malls being accommodated within existing town centres. Indeed, the only regional out-of-town centre constructed in the UK outside the established shopping centre hierarchy prior to the 1980s was Brent Cross in north-west London, opened in 1976 (Miller *et al.*, 1998).

During this wave of shopping centre development, there was little conceptualisation that shopping centres might act as motors of economic development by attracting external income. Instead, the widespread perception was that these developments would provide a required service for local people and/or make the area more attractive to basic sector industries.

Second wave of regional shopping centre development

The second wave of RSC development, from the mid 1980s onwards, was different in form and viewed in a different manner. These RSCs were all edge-of-town purpose-built developments of at least 500,000 square feet of retail floorspace with a wide range of commercial establishments, usually including catering and leisure facilities, which are designed, planned, managed and marketed as a unit (Williams, 1994).

Driven in large part by growing consumer expenditure and a property boom (itself fuelled by the ready availability of finance) and facilitated by a laissez-faire approach towards retail planning, some 54 applications were made between 1982 and 1991 to build new edge-of-town or out-of-town RSCs (Reynolds and Howard, 1993). The outcome was that planning permission was granted for a batch of out-of-town RSCs which directly mirrored for the first time their American counterparts. These included Merry Hill (Dudley, West Midlands) opened in 1989, Metrocentre (Gateshead) opened in 1986, Meadowhall (Sheffield) in 1990 and Lakeside (Thurrock, east of London) in 1990. Indeed, it was only because of the onset of recession, a slow-down in consumer expenditure and increased interest rates at the end of the 1980s, together with a move towards tightening government regulation regarding out-of-town retail development through Planning Policy Guidance Note 6 (PPG6: Department of Environment, 1993, 1996), that the many other planned regional-level edge or out-of-town RSCs were never constructed.

Nevertheless, this did not stop a second wave of out-of-town RSCs, all granted permission in the very different regulatory environment of the 1980s, but opened in the late 1990s and early 2000s. This second wave of out-of-town RSCs included Bluewater Park in Dartford, the Trafford Centre in Manchester, Braehead in Glasgow, Cribbs Causeway in Bristol and the White Rose Centre in Leeds.

Since these were constructed, no more have been developed. This is not for lack of demand. It is because ever more stringent conditions have been set for allowing the building of new RSCs (Department of Environment, 1993, 1996), including Planning Policy Guidance Notes PPG6 and PPG13 in 1996, part L PPS2 and PP26. This is because such complexes are asserted to suffer from three problems. In terms of their social impacts, they are perceived to be poorly accessible, especially for deprived social groups; in environmental terms, they are argued to have negative impacts, especially with regard to 'greenfield' sites and CO_2 emissions; and in economic terms, RSCs are viewed as parasitic activities, which have a negative effect on overall job numbers and destroy city centres, by diverting trade away from existing retail facilities.

Recognising the potential of RSCs as vehicles for economic development, however, a number of studies have challenged both the evidence and logic used to support these assertions, especially the last assertion that they are parasites (Williams, 1992a,b, 1993, 1994, 1995). First, and on the issue of their social impacts, RSCs have been shown not to suffer from poor access. Indeed, RSCs are rated by shoppers as highly on the issue of 'ease of access' as other shopping centres, and they have invested heavily in public transport infrastructure to such an extent that customer profiles reveal that lack of access to a car makes no difference to whether RSCs are visited, resulting in a clientele that is relatively representative (Howard and Davies, 1992). Indeed, some perceive social integration, rather than social exclusiveness, as the principal function of RSCs (Glennie and Thrift, 1992). Second, and on the issue of their environmental impacts, not only have RSCs been shown to be built on 'brownfield' rather than 'greenfield' sites, but the only data on the resource consumption and pollution impacts of RSCs is revealed to be that constructed for public inquiry purposes for a consortium of local authorities opposed to the building of the Trafford Centre in Manchester (Williams, 1995).

The economic argument against RSCs, meanwhile, is that they are parasitic activities that have a negative effect on overall job numbers and destroy existing city centres by diverting trade away from current retail facilities. However, both the empirical data and the logic underlying these notions are highly questionable. The only evidence mustered in a literature review of their negative employment impacts is derived from forecasts of RSC proposals (Whitehead, 1993). None is a 'real' statistic of what has happened in practice. Similarly, the data used to reveal that RSCs transfer jobs rather than create them are controversial. One study uses employment change in large and small grocery retailers, which are asserted to be predominant in RSCs and city centres respectively (Whitehead, 1993). Nevertheless, few RSCs contain large grocery stores, and the notion that small grocery retailers are predominant in city centres is based more on a longing for some past golden age than on the reality of the High Street today. Hence, the data are inappropriate for the task.

Not only are the data inadequate but so too is the logic. According to PPG6, the key issue for a new retail development was whether it would deleteriously effect the 'vitality and viability' of existing facilities (Department of Environment, 1993, 1994a, 1995). Retail impact studies thus analysed its trade diversion impacts (e.g. Howard, 1997). This was the principal policy focus because it was deemed that retailing was merely a 'dependent' activity, circulating money within a locality. It is clear, however, that RSCs are not. They create jobs in the same way as any other basic sector activity, namely by generating external income so as to stimulate growth in the local economy. As such, there is little reason for using different economic impact assessment methods to those applied in other sectors, as one hopes the following cases will demonstrate.

Case studies

In a bid to assess the economic impacts of the MetroCentre in Gateshead, rather than use retail impact assessment techniques, which provide little scope for evaluating the more positive outcomes of such developments, the standard economic impact assessment techniques are here employed, which measure the direct, indirect and intangible impacts are applied to this RSC.

Case 1: The MetroCentre and its impacts

The MetroCentre in Gateshead opened in 1986 on a site previously used for dumping ash from the local power station. To provide a preliminary and tentative measure of its contribution to the local economy, the degree to which it induces income into the locality, and thus jobs, and prevents the seepage of income out of the locality can be analysed. The finding is that this RSC is not a dependent activity, merely circulating money within the local economy. Instead, the MetroCentre attracts 78 per cent of its trade from people whose home is greater than 5 km from the MetroCentre (Howard and Davies, 1987) and thus outside Gateshead. The amount of external income induced into Gateshead by this RSC is therefore £156–187 million (Williams, 1997a). Concomitantly, since there are 7,490 full-time equivalent jobs in the MetroCentre (Robertson and Fennell, 2007), approximately 5,850 are extra jobs which would not otherwise have existed in Gateshead. Few manufacturing inward investment schemes, it should be noted, have generated this number of jobs in any locality in the UK.

These, however, are only the direct jobs created within the RSC. This number does not include the many additional jobs created, the direct jobs in associated activities beyond the RSC but still attributable to it (e.g. from visits to nearby tourist attractions); the indirect jobs created in the supply chain; and the induced jobs resulting from successive rounds of expenditure from incomes produced from direct and indirect employment. No attempt is here made to calculate the gross number of jobs, nor the net employment impact of the MetroCentre for the region as a whole. This is for two reasons. First, even if a net job loss were to result, this is no reason for the MetroCentre to be opposed. This would be due to productivity rises in the retail sector which, if they occurred in other industries, would be widely applauded, not criticised and decried (Williams, 1996). Second, it is erroneous to criticise the job gains in Gateshead because of the losses elsewhere, as commonly occurs (e.g. Whitehead, 1993). It is logically inconsistent to celebrate endeavours to promote manufacturing growth poles, yet oppose a retail development which performs the same function. To reject retail job gains in Gateshead on account of losses elsewhere is not a relevant criticism when such interlocality specialisation is the norm in all other sectors of the economy. Parity of treatment is needed. The rationales for treating RSCs differently from other industries, and retailing differently from other sectors, are very flimsy indeed.

The MetroCentre, in consequence, has operated as an anchor in a 'growth pole' and attracted enterprise to cluster around it. On the one hand, this is due to its 'magnetic effect'. Additional businesses have established here to feed off both the RSC itself, in the form of goods and services provision, and its clientele. On the one hand, this clustering has also been due to its 'demonstration effect'. Its success has shown other businesses that firms can succeed in this area and given them greater confidence to relocate than would otherwise have been the case if the MetroCentre did not exist. An RSC which is built at a cost of £350 million and employs 5,500 people, putting an investment of approximately £64,000 per employee into an area, represents a considerable fixed investment – achieved, incidentally, with little or no public sector leverage. This bolsters confidence in the locality, resulting in an upward spiral of investment, as witnessed by a clustering of activity. The alternative would doubtless have been continued site dereliction involving a local eyesore, untreated contaminated land and a direct and visible sign of the area's lack of success and its community's impoverishment (Williams, 1997a). Moreover, since the MetroCentre symbolises the consumerist ethic that pervaded late twentieth-century Britain, this 'cathedral of consumption' has been used to make the area appear a more attractive place for consumers to live and/or visit. It is not just the MetroCentre, however, that can be construed in this manner.

Case 2: Meadowhall and its impacts

After some competition between Rotherham and Sheffield, Meadowhall was given outline planning permission in 1987 and opened in 1990 next to Junction 34 of the M1 on the site of the old Hadfield steelworks in the Lower Don Valley in northern England. Nine million people live within one hour's drive of this £230 million development. It is composed of 284 units, including 'anchor' stores such as Marks & Spencer, Debenhams, House of Fraser, Sainsbury's and Oasis, as well as having one of the largest open-plan food halls in Europe, with 1,000 seats.

Since opening, it has proved an immensely popular attraction to both Sheffielders and outsiders, with over 480,000 visitors each week (Taylor *et al.*, 1996). Howard and Davies (1992) find that, although relatively affluent social groups are slightly more likely to use Meadowhall than poorer social groups, the clientele is not biased towards the affluent. Indeed, what is important about Meadowhall is its all-inclusiveness, rather than the minor differences between particular social groups in their tendency to visit this complex (Howard and Davies, 1992). Neither is there poor access for those without private transport: 19 per cent of visitors use public transport (Howard and Davies, 1992). Indeed, consumer research reveals that, on the issue of 'ease of access', Meadowhall is rated as highly as other shopping locations within a 30-minute drive, and customer profiles show that lack of access to a car makes no difference to whether Meadowhall is visited (Howard and Davies, 1992).

What, however, have been the economic impacts of Meadowhall on Sheffield? Based on a sales turnover of £325 million per annum and the fact that 30 per cent of trade is drawn from those living over 30 minutes' drive time away (Howard and Davies, 1992), then at least £97.5 million is generated in external income. Given that there are 7,000 jobs at Meadowhall, approximately 2,100 of these will be extra jobs which would not have existed in Sheffield if Meadowhall had not been built. These are solely the jobs in the RSC. Excluded are the many indirect jobs created in associated activities and those induced from successive rounds of expenditure out of the incomes produced from the direct and indirect jobs. Its external income-generating function is not the only economic benefit of Meadowhall. This complex also prevents income from leaking out of Sheffield both by reducing the need for the local population to go elsewhere to shop (e.g. Chesterfield, Manchester, Leeds) and by encouraging consumers to shop in locally owned businesses, since

RSCs have a higher proportion of local tenants than the traditional high street (Williams, 1992a, 1995).

More intangibly, it can be argued that Meadowhall also impacts on the image of Sheffield to both potential investors and the local population. So far as the former is concerned, Meadowhall has had both a magnetic effect (functioning in much the same way as the key industry in a conventional manufacturing growth pole by encouraging other consumer business to relocate in its environs, resulting in a major consumer services growth pole) and a demonstration effect (displaying that businesses can successfully locate in the Lower Don Valley). It has also promoted civic boosterism. With the rise in shopping as a leisure pursuit, such icons make an area seem an attractive place in which to live, work and do business, not only to potential investors but also to the local population (Williams, 1992a, 1995). However, such intangible impacts are easy to assert but seldom measured or valued. Future studies will thus need to pay greater attention to assessing these intangible impacts.

Despite these direct, indirect and intangible impacts, Meadowhall is still perceived by some as a parasite that has decimated the city centre. Even before Meadowhall, however, the city centre was in a state of disrepair and in decline. If anything, the competition from Meadowhall has led to the rejuvenation of Sheffield city centre after years of neglect. Indeed, there is now an active town centre management team and there are significant improvements to the overall retail experience. This is more widely argued by Warnaby and Medway (2004), who examine the role played by place marketing as part of the competitive response by town centres to out-of-town retail developments. Similarly, Reeve (2004) highlights how town centre management owes much to the emergence of RSCs.

Neither has there been an outflow of stores to Meadowhall. All of Meadowhall's anchor stores are present in the city centre and many have undertaken extensive refurbishment of their premises, and those living in Sheffield know that there are many factors besides Meadowhall that have inhibited trade in the city centre, not least the construction of Supertram, a city-centre transportation causing much disruption in the building. In other words, the self-inflicted 'push' factors seem just as important to any exodus of people as the 'pull' factor of Meadowhall itself (Williams, 1995). Meadowhall, therefore, far from being a 'parasite', has been a key factor in the revitalisation of Sheffield. It has brought many new jobs and a better-quality shopping environment in Sheffield, and has helped to positively reconstruct the city's image.

With the rise in opposition to such edge-of-town RSCs, however, there has been a shift of regional shopping centre development back into the city centres since the turn of the millennium.

The third wave of regional shopping centre developments

Revised Planning Policy Guidance Note 6 (Department of Environment, 1993, 1996) together with PPG13 *Transport* (Department of Environment, 1994b) prioritised the vitality and viability of town centres. The 'sequential test' of new retail development incorporated into the 1996 revision of PPG6, following a recommendation by the House of Commons Environment Committee, further prioritised town centres and significantly increased the difficulty of obtaining planning permission for out-of-town shopping centres. For an out-of-town development, the developer needed to show, following a 1998 High Court Judgement, a 'need' for the retail space (Adlard, 2001; Guy, 2007) and that no more central sites were suitable and available. By 2000, moreover, it had become clear that the sequential test had been further strengthened by the adoption of a stricter 'class of goods' test (DETR, 2000), namely whether the goods sold out of town could be sold instead in town centre sites (Ouseley, 2000; Partridge, 2001a,b).

Given this regulatory tightening, and the shift towards environmental goals and a strong social inclusion agenda during the 1990s and into the new millennium, a shift of the development dynamic occurred away from out-of-town developments and towards city-centre sites. This third wave of RSC development, or what may in future be referred to as a first wave of in-town RSCs, includes The Oracle in Reading (opened in 1999), Buchanan Galleries in Glasgow (1999), West Quay in Southampton (opened in 2000), the Overgate Centre in Dundee (2000), Touchwood in Solihull (2001), The Chimes in Uxbridge (2001), Basingstoke's Festival Place (2002) and Birmingham's latest version of the Bullring (2003).

This has started to alter Britain's retail fabric. As Lowe (2005) points out, a new era of 'retail-led urban regeneration' has emerged in which the retail sector is acting as the motor for economic regeneration. In contrast to previous eras, when retailing was viewed as a parasitic or dependent activity in economic development, retailing is now being employed as a lead sector. Despite this new penchant for retail-led regeneration and using RSCs as an engine of growth, however, Sparks (2004) notes that few studies have been conducted of the economic social and environmental impacts of the new in-town RSCs. One exception is the work of Lowe (2005) on Southampton West Quay and the pioneering work of Walker (1995) on the economic impacts of Princes Quay in the centre of Hull, which clearly displays that third-wave in-town RSCs have economic impacts of a similar magnitude to second wave out-of-town RSCs. They are also perhaps more socially inclusive and environmentally sustainable than out-of-town RSCs, although this is at present more an a priori assumption than an evidence-based fact. Perhaps the most fascinating aspect of the contemporary RSC developments, however, given the subject matter of this book, is their explicit construction as retail attractions and magnets.

Retailing and RSCs as visitor attractions

Examining the recent waves of RSC development, it becomes quickly apparent that retailing is no longer seen as a dependent or parasitic activity. Instead, it is now frequently the lead sector. Indeed, the intention of contemporary RSCs is to act as a magnet or retail attraction for retail tourists. Given, to repeat, that shopping is now the second most popular leisure pursuit, after watching television, 'retail tourism', by which is meant the attraction of tourist shoppers to a place to spend their money, constitutes a large and perhaps growing segment of tourism expenditure. It should be noted that this is different from attracting tourism retail expenditure. Retail tourists are shoppers who travel to different shopping places to spend money on retail goods and services, rather than tourists who visit a place to do some other non-retail tourist activity and as a by-product make retail expenditures.

One prominent consequence of recognising the existence of retail tourism as distinct from tourism retail expenditure, is that entertainment and pleasure have become increasingly an integral component of the marketing strategies employed by RSCs to entice customers. Indeed, entertainment is viewed as a key tool for differentiating one shopping centre from its competitors and as a determinant of consumer patronage decisions. Entertainment is therefore pivotal to shopping centres because it induces an exciting or fun shopping experience, which in turn encourages consumer patronage (Haynes and Talpade, 1996).

Entertainment in shopping centres can be seen to be of two types, namely special event entertainment and speciality entertainment. The key distinction between the two is the length of duration or span of operation. That is, special event entertainment is offered on an occasional or seasonal basis for a short period of time, such as fashion shows, bridal fairs and taking pictures with Father Christmas. Conversely, speciality entertainment is of a longer duration and generally incorporated into the shopping centre's fabric, such as cinemas, food courts, ice rinks and video arcades.

Indeed, in order to display the importance of entertainment in the consumer patronage decision, Sit and colleagues (2003) identify six consumer segments of shopping centre patrons, labelled the 'serious' shopper, the 'entertainment' shopper, the 'demanding' shopper, the 'convenience' shopper, the 'apathetic' shopper and the 'service' shopper. For them, the entertainment and service shoppers are identified as the entertainment-seeking segments, of which the entertainment shopper comprised 22 per cent of shopping centre respondents they surveyed and tended to be mainly teenage single males with a low income. Service shoppers, meanwhile, representing a further 20 per cent of respondents surveyed, perceive both speciality and special event entertainment to be an essential part of the service rather than part of the entertainment of a shopping centre. They are young adults, often married, with an average income. A large portion of shopping centre patrons, in consequence, place an emphasis on entertainment as a key feature of shopping centre development.

El-Adly (2007) similarly examines shopping malls in the United Arab Emirates from the perspective of shoppers and unravels not only six mall attractiveness factors, namely comfort, entertainment, diversity, mall essence, convenience and luxury, but also three types of mall shopper, namely relaxed shoppers, demanding shoppers and pragmatic shoppers. Similarly to Sit and colleagues (2003), he asserts that entertainment is now a key measure of the attractiveness of shopping malls.

Entertainment, in consequence, has become a key aspect of contemporary shopping centre development in particular and retailing more generally. This is because it is a way of differentiating one retailing environment from another and engendering patronage. Indeed, studies have revealed a strong association between retail image and consumer shopping preferences (Ruiz, 1999), frequency of visit (Haynes and Talpade, 1996), money spent (Donovan and Rossiter, 1982), amount of purchase (Spies *et al.*, 1997), desire to stay (Wakefield and Baker, 1998) and re-patronage intention (Spies *et al.*, 1997; Wakefield and Baker, 1998). Recognising this, there is a blurring of the edges between entertainment and retailing. Retailing is becoming a tourist experience, with a heavy emphasis being placed on the consumer's enjoyment of the shopping experience, including its impact on customer's re-patronage intentions (Hart *et al.*, 2007). The outcome is that the retail strategy of integrating entertainment into a shopping centre's and retailers' marketing mix has gained in popularity over the past few years and is now becoming much more commonplace. Numerous major stores and shopping malls in the USA, for example, have been constructed with substantial square footages allocated to entertainment, such as Nike Town, Mall of America and River Falls Mall (Haynes and Talpade, 1996). Similarly, greater proportions of floorspace are being devoted to both special event entertainment and speciality entertainment in contemporary UK retail developments, not least cinemas, ice rinks, food halls, fashion shows, tea dances and so forth.

Conclusions and future prospects

This chapter has revealed how the role of the retail sector in economic development has been recast. In the past, it was seen as a dependent activity that contributed little, if anything, to economic development and simply fed off the wealth created by the other basic sector industries. In recent decades, however, retailing in general, and shopping centres more particularly, have been recast as basic sector industries that generate external income for the areas in which they are located, and even a lead sector for economic regeneration, which not only generates external income and prevents leakage of income out of an economy but also bolsters the attractiveness of areas to other industries.

Indeed, alongside this more positive reading of the contribution of retailing in general, and shopping centres more particularly, to economic development, has emerged the recognition that shopping is now one of the principal leisure pursuits, second only to watching television. The result is that 'retail tourism', by which is meant attracting shoppers to a place in order to spend money, has become a growing segment of the overall tourism industry. A growing share of all tourists, that is, visit places perhaps principally to go shopping; thus, retailing in general and shopping centres more particularly are therefore an important component of the tourist industry, especially when it is entwined with visiting entertainment facilities that are increasingly an integral component of shopping centres.

What, therefore, are the future prospects as far as concerns using retail attractions to promote economic development? Several reasons exist for suggesting that the use of regional shopping centres in particular, and retailing more generally, as drivers of retail-led economic regeneration may well have peaked and be coming to an end. To understand why this is the case, the ways in which economic base theory has been re-conceptualised in a fourth wave of thought need to be explained followed by a discussion of how this will impact on practice.

Based on the assumption that an area needs to generate external income in order to grow, economic base theory traditionally divided any economy into two sectors: a basic sector that generates external income and a dependent sector merely circulating income within the area. In the first wave of thought and practice, manufacturing was treated as the basic sector; in the second wave producer services were included; and in the third wave consumer services were added. The problem, however, is that all sectors had now become basic activities and none were dependent activities. This resulted in a new fourth wave of theorising the economic base, which argues that economic development and growth are not as strongly correlated with external income generation as the first three waves assumed. For an economy to grow, it contends that it is not a rise in external income per se which is needed, but rather, an increase in net income. Net income, to explain, is a product of the total external income, times a multiplier (which is larger the more self-reliant the economy), minus total external spending. Economic growth is thus dependent not only on attracting external income but also on preventing the leakage of money out of the area (Persky and Wiewel, 1994; Williams, 1997a,b, 1999).

The outcome is that preventing leakage of income is now seen as playing a crucial role in economic development. This strategy of reducing leakage is both socially inclusive, since it re-orientates retailing towards meeting local needs and wants rather than external desires, and also a more environmentally sustainable approach, since it seeks to reduce travel distances for retail purposes. Indeed, recognising this desire for more sustainable consumption patterns, some commentators have already begun to respond by arguing that retailing in general and shopping centres more particularly can be less environmentally degrading and resource efficient than has perhaps so far been the case. Al Waer and Sibley (2010) have recently analysed the economic, social and environmental sustainability of RSCs and developed an assessment model to evaluate the sustainability of future retail centres over their entire lifespan. In doing so, they foreground the emergent triple-bottom line thinking that seeks to understand the economic, social and environmental impacts of retail schemes. Future developments, it appears, will be more orientated towards preventing leakage and will include initiatives such as local sourcing of goods and services, local ownership and local production. It seems, therefore, that, even if recent years have seen a concerted shift towards seeking ‘retail tourists’ and external income generation through visitor spending, future years may well see a fourth wave of more ‘sustainable’ shopping centre development in the form of a more locally orientated approach which puts far less emphasis on such retail developments as magnets for external visitors.

The future of retail developments in general and shopping centres more particularly, however, is as always in major part what we choose to make it. The future, in other words, is in our hands.

References

Adlard, H. (2001) The 'need' for retail development. *Journal of Planning and Environmental Law* May, 522–534.

Al Waer, H. and Sibley, M. (2010) *Sustainable Regional Retail Centers: Tools for planning, design and assessment*. London: Earthscan.

Bachtler, J. and Davies, P. L. (1989) Economic restructuring and services policy. In Gibbs, D. (ed.) *Government Policy and Industrial Change*. London: Routledge, pp. 140–162.

Beyers, W. B. and Alvine, M. J. (1985) Export services in postindustrial society. *Papers of the Regional Science Association* 57, 33–45.

British Council of Shopping Centres (2008) *Response to Consultation in Draft PPS4: Planning for sustainable economic development*. London: British Council of Shopping Centres.

Campbell, M. (1996) The Leeds economy: trends, prospects and challenges. In Haughton, G. and Williams, C. C. (eds) *Corporate City? Partnership, participation and partition in urban development in Leeds*. Aldershot: Avebury, pp. 29–58.

Coffey, W. J. (1995) Producer services research in Canada. *Professional Geographer* 47 (1), 74–81.

Coffey, W. J. (2000) The geographies of producer services. *Urban Geography* 21(2), 170–183.

Datamonitor (2008) *UK Retail Futures 2011: Sector summary*. London: Datamonitor.

Department of Environment (1993) *Town Centres and Retail Development*. Planning Policy Guidance Note 6. London: HMSO.

Department of Environment (1994a) *Vital and Viable Town Centres: Meeting the challenge*. London: Department of Environment.

Department of Environment (1994b) *Transport*. Planning Policy Guidance Note 13. London: HMSO.

Department of Environment (1996) *Town Centres and Retail Development*. Planning Policy Guidance Note 6. London: HMSO.

DETR (2000) *The Government's Response to the Environment, Transport and Regional Affairs Committee Second Report: Environmental Impact of Supermarket Competition*. London: HMSO.

Dicken, P. (1992) *Global Shift: The internationalization of economic activity*. London: Paul Chapman.

Donovan, R. J. and Rossiter, J. R. (1982) Store atmosphere: an environmental psychology approach. *Journal of Retailing* 58(1), 34–57.

El-Adly, M. I. (2007) Shopping malls attractiveness: a segmentation approach. *International Journal of Retail and Distribution Management* 35(11), 936–950.

Friedan, B. J. and Sagalyn, L. B. (1989) *Downtown Inc.: How America rebuilds cities*. Cambridge, MA: MIT Press.

Glennie, P. D. and Thrift, N. (1992) Modernity, urbanism and modern consumption. *Environment and Planning A* 10, 423–443.

Goss, J. (1993) The 'magic of the mall': an analysis of form, function and meaning in the contemporary retail built environment. *Annals of the Association of American Geographers* 83(1), 18–47.

Guy, C. (1994) *The Retail Development Process: Location, property and planning.* London: Routledge.

Guy, C. (2007) Is 'demonstration of need' necessary in retail planning policy? *Regional Studies* 41(1), 131–137.

Haggett, P., Cliff, A. D. and Frey, A. E. (1977) *Locational Analysis in Human Geography.* London: Edward Arnold.

Hart, C., Farrell, A., Stachow, G., Reed, G., and Cadogan, J. W. (2007) Enjoyment of the shopping experience: impact on customers' re-patronage intentions and gender influence. *Service Industries Journal* 27(5), 583–604.

Haynes, J. and Talpade, S. (1996) Does entertainment draw shoppers? The effects of entertainment centres on shopping behaviour in malls. *Journal of Shopping Center Research* 3(2), 29–48.

Howard, E. (1997) The management of shopping centers: conflict or collaboration? *International Review of Retail, Distribution and Consumer Research* 7 (3), 263–285.

Howard, E. B. and Davies, R. L. (1987) *Retail Change on Tyneside: Third consumer survey in the MetroCentre*. OXIRM Research Paper D9. Oxford: Templeton College.

Howard, E. B. and Davies, R. L. (1992) *Meadowhall: The impact of one year's development.* OXIRM Research Paper A14. Oxford: Templeton College.

Kirklees Metropolitan Borough Council (1991) *Economic Development Strategy.* Huddersfield: Kirklees Metropolitan Borough Council.

Lackey, S. A. and Eckenstahler, C. (1995) The forgotten role of retail in economic development. *Economic Development Review* 13(2), 85–87.

Lowe, M. (2005) The regional shopping centre in the inner city: a study of retail-led urban regeneration. *Urban Studies* 42(3), 449–470.

Lowe, M. S. and Crewe, L. (1991) Lollipop jobs for pin money? Retail employment explored. *Area* 23, 344–347.

Miller, D., Jackson, P. and Thrift, N. (1998) *Shopping, Place and Identity.* London: Routledge.

Mintel (2008) *Retail Review, UK, March 2008: Market research report.* London: Mintel.

Ouseley, D. (2000) Speech to British Council for Out-of-Town Retail Conference. Online source: http://www.bcotr.co.ukbctor-business.htm

Partridge, T. (2001a) Easy ride now over for large format retailers. *Planning*, 13 April, p. 22.

Partridge, T. (2001b) Decision will not be led by store format. *Planning*, 13 July, p. 22.

Peck, J. and Tickell, A. (1991) *Regulation Theory and the Geographies of Flexible Accumulation: Transitions in capitalism, transitions in theory.* Spatial Policy Analysis Working Paper 12. Manchester: School of Geography, University of Manchester.

Persky, J. and Wiewel, W. (1994) The growing localness of the global city. *Economic Geography* 70(2), 129–143.

Reeve, A. (2004) Town centre management: developing a research agenda in an emerging field. *Urban Design International* 9(3), 133–150.

Reynolds, J. and Howard, E. B. (1993) *The UK Regional Shopping Centre: The challenge for public policy.* OXIRM Research Paper A28. Oxford: Templeton College.

Robertson, J. and Fennell, J. (2007) The economic effects of regional shopping centres. *Journal of Retail and Leisure Property* 6, 149–170.

Ruiz, F. (1999) Image of suburban shopping malls and two-stage versus uni-equational modelling of retail trade attraction: an empirical application. *European Journal of Marketing* 33(5/6), 512–530.

Sassen, S. (1991) *The Global City: New York, London, Tokyo.* Princeton, NJ: Princeton University Press.

Sit, J., Merrilees, B. and Birch, D. (2003) Entertainment-seeking shopping centre patrons: the missing segments. *International Journal of Retail and Distribution Management* 31(2), 80–94.

Sparks, L. (2004) *Retailing, Sustainability and Neighbourhood Regeneration*. York: Joseph Rowntree Foundation.

Spies, K., Hesse, F. and Loesch, K. (1997) Store atmosphere, mood and purchasing behaviour. *International Journal of Research in Marketing* 14, 1–17.

Taylor, I., Evans, K. and Fraser, P. (1996) *A Tale of Two Cities: Global change, local feeling and everyday life in the North of England. A study in Manchester and Sheffield*. London: Routledge.

Wakefield, K. and Baker, J. (1998) Excitement at the mall: determinants and effects on shopping response. *Journal of Retailing* 74(4), 515–539.

Walker, M. (1995) *Regional shopping centres: a critical evaluation of Princes Quay, Hull*. Unpublished MA dissertation in Town and Regional Planning. Leeds: Leeds Metropolitan University.

Warnaby, G. and Medway, D. (2004) The role of place marketing as a competitive response by town centres to out-of-town retail developments. *International Review of Retail, Distribution and Consumer Research* 14(4), 457–477.

Whitehead, A. (1993) Regional shopping centre development: a rejoinder. *Local Government Policy Making* 20(2), 50–59.

Williams, C. C. (1992a) The contribution of regional shopping centres to local economic development: threat or opportunity? *Area* 24(3), 283–288.

Williams, C. C. (1992b) Impacts of regional shopping centres: myths and realities. *The Planner* 78(22), 8–11.

Williams, C. C. (1993) The implications of regional shopping centre development. *Local Government Policy Making* 20 (1), 50–55.

Williams, C. C. (1994) A critical evaluation of the opposition to regional shopping centres. *Local Government Policy Making* 21(3), 47–54.

Williams, C. C. (1995) Opposition to regional shopping centres in Great Britain: a clash of cultures? *Journal of Retailing and Consumer Services* 2(4), 241–249.

Williams, C. C. (1996) Rethinking the role of retailing and consumer services in local economic development: a British perspective. *Journal of Retailing and Consumer Services* 3(1), 53–56.

Williams, C. C. (1997a) *Consumer Services & Economic Development*. London: Routledge.

Williams, C. C. (1997b) Rethinking the role of the retail sector in economic development. *Service Industries Journal* 17(2), 205–220.

Williams, C. C. (1999) Local economic development. In Allmendinger, P. and Chapman, M. (eds) *Planning Beyond 2000*. Chichester: Wiley, pp. 175–188.

2 Retailing within towns and city centres as a tourist retail attraction

Christine Harris

Introduction

This chapter explores retailing within town and city centres as a major tourist attraction, a magnet that can be used to draw tourists to other attractions of the area. The first part explores the tensions within town centres' historical and modern developments, and the second part offers a number of focused solutions to enhanced tourist retail viability, particularly in respect of perceived tendencies towards 'clone towns', in order to maintain vitality as tourist magnets. Town centres allow the visitor to combine cultural and leisure activities with retail. Retail can be seen as a leisure activity in itself but it is difficult for centres to compete on retailing alone, when there are many similar centres. The development of a vibrant shopping area with the town centre can lead to increased tourism and subsequently increased investment in other aspects of the town, ranging from ambient leisure, through decorative accoutrements such as hanging baskets, to major attractions. The historical development of the UK coastal port city of Southampton is used as a case study to further explore aspects of these issues as they have arisen over time to the present day.

Development of a viable town centre with tourist retail attractions

The four-forces town centre development model

Town centres are not exclusively tourist attractions; they have a multifunction role and must serve diverse groups of stakeholders, including residents, business and local government as well as the needs of tourists. They must also compete with other towns/cities and out-of-town developments that all want a slice of any tourist income, impacting on the viability of any town centre under study. The needs of these groups are not always compatible; they pull the centre in opposite directions as illustrated in the outline model shown in Figure 2.1.

For economic viability, it is important for town centres to become a regional centre, to draw custom from a wider area and hence increase the money coming into the town. In retail terms, if this can be achieved then not only will it attract more stores, but the stores themselves with be upgraded and receive the first pick

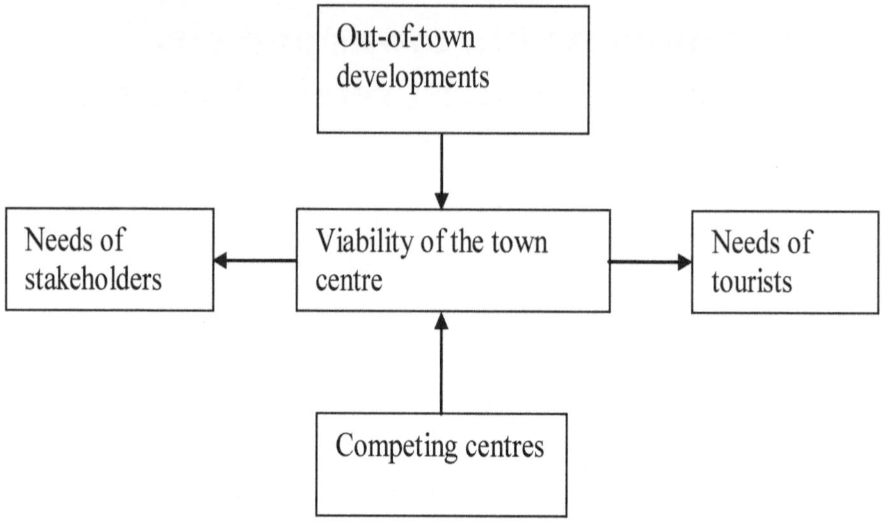

Figure 2.1 The four-forces model for town centre development (source: the author).

of the stock from suppliers and central warehouses. This creates an upward spiral, which attracts even more visitors and hence more retailers. With an influx of retailers come cafés, restaurants and hotels, followed by other tourist attractions and events, leading to a vibrant and sustainable town centre. It is not necessarily about size, although many centres are large; it is rather about providing something different that catches the public imagination.

The needs of local stakeholders – businesses, residents and local government – are not always compatible with tourists, or indeed sometimes with each other. Although large numbers of tourists can seem a bonus to a locality, there are downsides that can create tension. Residents complain about the lack of car parking space in the town centre, together with the traffic congestion and the crowds. Whereas tourists may be seen to support the retailers during the season, it is then the residents who must support them for the remainder of the year. In terms of shopping, however, the needs of tourists and residents are not always compatible. Tourist shoppers are likely to visit department stores and high-end fashion retailers, as evident in popular choices of locations such as New York and Paris. Residents, however, need to buy more mundane essential items, such as school wear, light bulbs and clothes pegs, so heading for the variety and discount stores.

Leisure facilities within cities can be shared by tourists and residents but there are conflicts here too. The residents are more likely to visit the free facilities such as parks, gardens, libraries and museums, whereas tourists are more likely to visit paid attractions and icon buildings such as the Empire State Building in New York, the Tower of London and the Eiffel Tower in Paris. For planners this is a dilemma: which types of facilities should be added to the city? Who will be the beneficiaries and on whom will the costs fall?

In order to examine this basic model, Southampton, located on the south coast of England, is used here as an example analysing the background of its growth as a viable town centre and to understand the current problems of city centres in general as visitor attractions.

Southampton's historical development: an example to emulate or avoid?

In examining the growth of multiple retailers in Southampton and implications for tourism, it is proposed to analyse the changing nature of the retail offer in the town from its early beginnings to the present day using local, historical trade directories as a major informational source. Early coinage (sceatta) has been found in the area (Southampton Archaeological Research Committee, 1975) and the Domesday Book records the presence of settlers (early 'visitor-tourists') of Norman French origins living in French Street of the city, which became a principal shopping area during the middle ages (Ruddock, 1951). Ruddock believes that it was the period after the Norman Conquest (1066) that heralded the first visitors who traded rather than raided, as opposed to the case with the earlier Danes. Many parts of the city that remain in evidence today, for example the Bargate area of the old city walls, now centrally placed in its high street, date from the medieval period.

By late medieval times there were not only Norman visitors but ships from all over Europe bringing merchants, crew and visitors. It was noted that that 'some of these vessels often lay up in the harbour for three or four months in the winter, with more than a thousand strangers from the Mediterranean ports sometimes crowding its narrow streets' (Ruddock, 1951: 149). Most noticeable among these traders were Italians bringing a large range of goods, from oriental silks to dried fruits. This gave the Southampton visitor access to one of the best Italianate ranges of merchandise outside London. By the middle of the eighteenth century, drinking mineral waters had become popular in Southampton, whereby it became a spa town offering invigorating waters and a bracing air. It has been suggested that the city 'offered varied and attractive views in all directions, not least the spa itself' (Patterson, 1966: 39). In recognition of the benefits of tourism to the town, the local council enhanced the facilities, with trees being planted along 'The Avenue', one of the major approaches into the city; these trees are still in evidence today. Even given such developments, the city still never reached the leisured popularity of the port town of Weymouth or beach town of Bournemouth, both further west along the coast, which attracted the royalty of the day, but three of the younger brothers of George III nevertheless became 'Southampton's social patrons' (Patterson, 1966: 44).

By 2009 Southampton had grown to 236,700 residents (Southampton City Council, 2009) and today it remains the home port to the Cunard and P&O cruise liners, but a declining merchant trade. There is no shortage of visitors passing through Southampton but the city centre's attractiveness is under threat.

Southampton is not dissimilar to many other major old ports and cities around the world, such as New York and Sydney, which continually seek to add new visitor attractions to counter the demise of shipping. Around the time of writing, Southampton was proposing to raise £15 million (Daily Telegraph, 2009) to develop a new visitor attraction based on the *Titanic*, whose fatal maiden voyage embarked from the port in 1912. It was anticipated that this would bring additional visitors into the city, and compete with the naval heritage exhibitions on offer at nearby Portsmouth. Many residents, however, were opposed to this scheme mainly because the finance was going to come from the sale of 3,500 works of art owned by the city. The residents' objection was that the exhibition would mainly be for the benefit of tourists, whereas the artworks would be of more benefit to the people of the city. Some businesses were also unhappy as, once opened, it would change the existing patterns of footfall in the city centre, which could disadvantage them. Concerns were also expressed about the upkeep of the attraction if it failed to attract sufficient visitors. Any shortfalls in income would then have to be met through increased taxation of residents and business or through the reduction of services to these groups.

Forces 1 and 2: Retail development and tourism – local versus tourist needs

Catering to the needs of tourists in a retail context is not a new phenomenon. During the eighteenth century, London-based businesses renting shops in Southampton for the summer visitor season helped to provide for expanded needs based upon tourist visitors. Two specific examples of this were Madame Graffard, the milliner, sited at 16 French Street in the town, and J. Mobbs, a retailer of hats and hosiery, at 23 High Street (Patterson, 1966). This can be seen as the start of national chains entering Southampton, albeit on a seasonal basis; the process effectively inhibited visitors from travelling to London to shop as well as dissuading the locals from visiting the capital. Coffee houses were also appearing in the principal streets, with some of these offering accommodation, thus demonstrating the linkage between tourism, retail and leisure. Since these links have developed and become stronger over the years, the size of the retail tourist offer has increased.

A historic day for Southampton city centre was 28 September 2000 with the opening of the West Quay shopping mall development in a prime central location. This was described as 'Europe's largest city centre shopping centre' (Travel. ciao.co.uk, 2008). The main entrance was from the existing main shopping street, Above Bar. It consisted of 75,000 square feet of shopping space. Its main 'anchor' stores were the variety retailer Marks & Spencer and the John Lewis department store but it also had several major, retail chain 'flagship' stores within an offer of over 70 retail outlets and a large food court (Lowe, 2005). Such a development was seen as a major turning point for Southampton; it once again become a magnet for shoppers and visitors across its county of Hampshire, as well as the neighbouring counties of Dorset, Wiltshire and beyond. Visitor numbers to West Quay initially exceeded expectations and, although there have been some changes to the retail mix, it continues to be successful today, with high footfall and occupancy rates; but this success has not been equally welcomed by all stakeholders within the city.

The centre has increasingly concentrated tourists in one area of the city, as a result, leaving other areas with significantly lower footfall. By the time tourists have explored all the shops within the centre they would seem to have little energy or desire to explore elsewhere (given also that their cars are more often parked within it). Residents, whilst appreciating the increased city retail offer, deplore the crowds and full parking at peak times together with seemingly endless road works to try and improve access to the centre.

The issue of local stakeholders versus tourists is unlikely to be resolved. Local councils will have to make difficult decisions in order to balance the needs of both groups. The vitality of the centre is also under threat from out-of-town shopping centres and competing town centres, a modern development that has been much decried by many since its explosion into the scene following increased car ownership since the 1950s.

Force 3: Retail development and tourism – out-of-town developments

Postwar out-of-town developments have been considered to have evolved in waves (Schiller, 1994). The first of these was seen as a force for good by most of the stakeholder groups, and was characterised by the general food store supermarkets moving out of town to gain more and cheaper space, which occurred from the mid 1960s onwards. In the UK, Asda (now part of the American Walmart 'family' of stores) was one of the leading exponents of this (Jones, 1981), with other retailers following suit. The increasing size of supermarkets' product ranges and the lack of suitable land in town for such expansion made this move largely inevitable, although tighter 'green' land use control in some areas has slowed the process. This removal of supermarkets to the edge of town allowed larger stores to better serve mobile residents of the suburbs in convenience terms, and left more room in the town centre for comparatively less functional goods, which attracted tourists and residents alike.

The second wave in the development of out-of-town (or edge-of-town) retail saw the arrival of warehouses, or 'big sheds' for do-it-yourself, garden centre and large homeware retailers, of which the UK furniture retailer MFI, which ceased trading in 2009, was one of the UK market leaders (Jones, 1984). Other sellers of bulky homeware retail brands such as Allied Carpets and DFS were soon to follow. These locations offered shoppers the opportunity to purchase large items out of town, either for delivery or to transport them in their own car from adjacent free and extensive parking areas. Other retailers and retail developments then located nearby, in a clustering effect, creating retail parks, which by the mid 1970s were commonplace in the UK and typically contained large goods retail warehouses, increasingly diversely ranged supermarkets and fast food outlets (Jones and Hillier, 2000).

The developing mix of these locations often indicated the idea of retail parks as day-out visitor attractions. Out-of-town location decisions such as these were generally welcomed by local councils, who saw it as useful to be able to retain the town centre for small shop formats and yet maintain retail variety in the surrounding area. It also reduced the number of cars in the town centre and allowed towns to expand outwards and apparently prosper. Concerns, however, were being raised about fewer residents visiting the town centre and the decrease in trade affecting occupancy levels in town.

The third wave of retail development in the UK was triggered largely by the decision of Marks & Spencer (M&S) in 1984 to start to locate out of town, thus giving fashion shoppers an alternative to the high street; M&S being primarily a fashion and clothing outlet. Although M&S also sells food, its out-of-town developments were generally in conjunction with a major food retailer such as with Tesco at Camberley, in the outer London commuter area, and with Sainsbury at Hedge End near Southampton. Some saw this as the start of the development of true 'regional' (as opposed to 'local') shopping centres, as other retailers congregated to an even greater extent than previous expansions to capture the consumer traffic that was generated by such developments (Schiller, 1994). By this stage in the process, the impact on the town centre was significant. Retail parks offering food, fashion and household goods gave people in many instances a viable alternative to the town centre for all their shopping needs.

Fashion retailers have grown out-of-town locations following the trend set by other sectors, with the arrival of the American out-of-town retailer, Matalan, near Preston in the UK in 1985. The 1990s saw the major in-town Dutch clothing retailer C&A 'closing up shop' regarding its UK division and leaving large empty sites in many British high streets, some of which are still not fully occupied. Not all fashion stores, though, have favoured out of town. Some have remained loyal to the high street location, but they are becoming fewer in number. There has also been a shift in population densities, moving from the town centre to the suburbs, and this has led to demand for goods outside the traditional high street (Guy and Lord, 1993). The out-of-town centres also had the ability to draw trade from more than one town centre. The opening of M&S at Hedge End between Southampton and Portsmouth caused existing stores within both towns to be downgraded, encouraging shoppers to look out of town, rather than in town.

Finally, in the wave theory, there was the development of out-of-town shopping malls. The economic 'boom years' of the 1980s heralded a number of new, extremely large-scale, out-of-town developments, similar to those already developed in the even more car-based society of America (Lowe, 2000). These included the MetroCentre in Gateshead and the Merry Hill Centre in the West Midlands, offering the consumer a major retailer choice that in many instances exceeds that of the adjacent towns and cities. These 'mega-malls' aimed to create a day-out destination for the whole family, providing not only retail but also leisure facilities as an alternative attraction to the traditional high street.

In the 1990s 'mega' Regional Shopping Centres (RSCs) such as Bluewater and Lakeside located east of London, south and north of the River Thames respectively, were said to have a major negative impact upon footfall in many surrounding high street areas. These developments are designed to be major visitor and tourist magnets with their offer of a comprehensive range of high street names in fully designed leisure surroundings, including restaurants, cinemas, sports centres and even lake and lakeside activities with easy road access and free parking. Consumers typically travel up to two hours to reach them but much longer journeys are not unknown. The MetroCentre, south of the river on the outskirts of the city of Newcastle in the north-east of England, attracts visitors from Scandinavia via the city's ferry links. In international comparison, West Edmonton Mall in Canada claims to attract visitors by air within a two-hour fly time. This mall also featured a trend in offering on-site hotel facilities, prolonging the length of stay and inhibiting shoppers from straying elsewhere in the locality.

The out-of-town developmental experience in the UK is not dissimilar to that of other parts of the world, although the rate and extent of change has varied. In France out-of-town retailing developed more slowly than in the UK, mainly because of the tighter planning regulations. In America it developed earlier and further owing to the higher proportion of car-borne shoppers and fewer restrictions on the use of land space. In Thailand out-of-town retailing is a relatively new phenomenon, driven by the large stand-alone overseas retailers, such as Decathlon from France and Tesco from the UK, entering the underdeveloped market. Visitors travelling long distances to these centres have generally very little retail exposure en route, and are unlikely to visit nearby towns, making their way directly to the centre to increase shopping and leisure time. This process has proven similar to the effect of leisure park developments, such as Legoland and Alton Towers in the south of England and Disneyland Paris in France, with day-out (and longer-stay) spend mainly taking place within the centre and with little spin-off for the adjacent area. The larger out-of-town centres have become internationally renowned and widely advertised to tourists across the world. Visitors may choose them in preference to established town or city centres, entering an enclosed bubble that they are discouraged from exiting by those managing it.

Southampton has sought to escape the worse effects of this latter stage of the wave trend, partly by building a large in-town, city-centre development as well as rigorously upholding planning regulations to stop further proposed, major out-of-town developments at an early stage.

Force 4: Retail development and tourism – competing centres

Adjacent out-of-town retail centres are not the only visitor 'leakage' problem; there are alternative city centres to be considered. Tourists' increased ability to travel both by car and by the use of discount airlines means that cities around the world compete against each other for trade. Despite this, many towns across the UK are becoming labelled as 'clone towns'. The term 'clone towns' has been used in a derogatory sense as an insult implying that the town or city has become a location not worth visiting, in that primarily the retail offer is poor, featuring only look-alike multiple retailers. Yet in some respects it would appear that this could not be further from the truth.

Giving a destination the label 'clone' implies that a reasonable selection of the major retailers must be present, so why is this a problem for the consumer? The answer would seem to be the resulting lack of differentiation for the general leisure visitor and tourist. If a consumer has shopped in Southampton on a Saturday, for instance, what is the incentive to explore the neighbouring towns or cities of Portsmouth and Bournemouth the next day, in terms of the retail offer? The New Economics Foundation (BBC News, 2004) has specifically warned against clone towns as reducing shopper variety and distinctiveness, seeing them as culpable in the squeezing out of independent stores and stating that 'between 1997 and 2002 specialist stores like butchers, bakers and fishmongers shut at the rate of 50 a week'. However, the growth of the clone town has been aided by a number of factors which are discussed hereafter, the first being the incremental (sometimes exponential) corporate growth of the national chains.

The introduction of national chains into cities is not new. By 1851 Southampton already had the National Savings and National Provincial banks (Post Office, 1851), and 12 retailers had more than one premises in the city (local multiples), examples being William Cawte, who sold boots and shoes, and D. Davis, who had premises on West Street and the High Street. There is some evidence of London shops locating an outlet in the area; for example Miller & Son, who had premises at 17 Middle East-Street selling tailored and woollen goods, which were advertised as 'also available' at their London shop. Nevertheless, the city's retail offer in the fairly distant past consisted mainly of small independent stores selling a narrow range of goods with no evidence of national 'chains' of stores.

By 1863 the trading documents (Post Office, 1863) list the first of today's recognisable retail multiples as having arrived. The modern-day bookseller and stationer W. H. Smith had by then located at the railway terminus and was listed as a 'book seller and bookbinder' in the city. It is still at its then location of the railway station today, in addition to its prime, high street, city-centre location. The store of E. Mayes had also opened at 174 High Street, selling clothes, furniture and linens, providing quite a wide product range for the times. This company was eventually to become a part of the Owen Owen group and traded in Southampton until the 1990s. Another major department store in the town was born soon after this, the 1871 directory (Cox's, 1871) listing Edwin Jones (a merchant venturer, originally from Romsey in Hampshire) trading in a single-fronted store at 32 East Street as a 'drapers, dressmaker and milliner'. This store later expanded into the Queens Buildings near to the High Street, control passing to Debenhams in the 1920s, although the name on the fascia did not change until 1973.

John Lewis, one of the present day's leading UK department store groups, had its origins in the city in 1897 when the department store of Tyrrell and Green opened at 21–24 Angelsea Place, moving only two years later to Above Bar, the principal high street sited above the city's Bargate. The company website (www.johnlewis.com, 2008) states that 'from the beginning Tyrrell & Green was a high class shop, renowned for its commissionaires, page boys and Italian chef'. Apart from during the Second World War, when heavy bombing on the night of 30 November 1940 (Brode, 1982) destroyed the premises and caused trading to cease for four months, it continuously traded under the Tyrrell and Green name until 2000 when it moved to the West Quay development under the John Lewis fascia, having belonged to the group since 1934 when the partnership wanted to expand beyond London (www.johnlewis.com, 2008).

The first half of the twentieth century saw the arrival of many more national chains in Southampton. By 1907 (Kelly's, 1907) the tailoring chain of Hepworths had arrived, later to be acquired by the Burtons tailors group. The Southampton retail Co-operative Society had been formed with its laudable ideals of providing fair prices across a wide range of products for the working classes and sharing the profits with its customers; although the reality was a chain of just eight stores across the Southampton area. They offered value but, by association, they possibly restricted choice and caused problems for independents.

By the 1920s the directories show a number of easily recognisable national chains in the city, for example a Halfords outlet, at that time listed already as a cycle specialist, which it remains today in addition to providing car parts; also Thomas Cook is listed as the first recognisable travel agent brand (Kelly's, 1920). Halfords has moved out of the city centre only in recent years, whilst Thomas Cook still has a high street presence, strengthened no doubt by Southampton's continued standing as one of the premier embarkation ports for cruise liners.

As with out-of-town developments, the UK since the 1950s has seen a sharp growth of the corporate multiple retailer, both organically (such as Marks & Spencer) and by acquisition (for instance the UK department store Debenhams). Common ownership of multiples would perhaps not be seen as much of a problem for a locality if, during this growth, management control had not also shifted markedly from store and regional level to national, corporate head offices, aided by developments in information technology. Local store management of multiples now has very little control over the interior of the store, the stock or the offers. Head offices, meanwhile, are concerned with a standard corporate image for the valid reason of offering customers the same experience in whichever individual outlet they are in. The downside of all of this is that there may be little or no perceived real incentive for a consumer to visit the same retailer in two different locations – hence the 'clone town' tag.

It is not, however, only the large multiples that are causing this sameness of leisure space in town centres. Even quite small chains, with less than 10 stores, can have stores in adjacent towns, thus providing local concentrations of sameness. For instance, there are very few independent department stores left in the UK. These were once a major tourist attraction – for the locality and beyond – and were thus pivotal in a town's overall visitor offer. The Beatties department store company, based in Wolverhampton, is now part of the House of Fraser Group and, likewise, Denners of Yeovil in Somerset is now owed by the larger Beales department store group (although it still, at present, operates under its original, localised name). Those few department stores that have remained independent mostly belong to the AIS (Associated Independent Stores) buying group, giving them access to the same stock as each other, and are increasingly stocking national brands, increasing the number of in-store branded concessions and loosing local distinctiveness.

The 'clone town' accusation of sameness is not just about the retailers' lack of distinctiveness, but also concerns their location policies – retailers having strong site preferences in terms of 'adjacencies'. For consumer comparison shopping purposes, jewellery shops like to locate near each other, as do shoe shops and so on. Also, the UK mother and baby chain Mothercare has traditionally located next to, or very near, Marks & Spencer, as they target the same broad demographic consumer but have little overlap on product range. It is not therefore only the appearance of the same retail outlets, in similar garb, which contributes towards a resulting clone town, but the appearance of the same mix of retailers in the same order on the high street that makes it difficult for the consumer to differentiate one location from another.

To combat this, there is a need for centres to be distinctive in order to attract tourist spend. Some cities have built towers to give an identifiable skyline to the town; examples of this are the Spinnaker Tower in Portsmouth and the Toronto Tower in Canada. These towers do increase the visitor numbers but to encourage repeat visits to the cities they need to be supported by a 'good' retail offer. The definition of a 'good' offer is open to interpretation, but would probably cover well-presented international, national and local stores, chain and independent, offering a wide range of goods. Independent retailers have found it increasingly difficult to break into the locational preserves of the multiples in the UK, including the traditional high streets, where perhaps tourists may be most likely to be found. They are often the last to hear about site availability; most landlords given a choice opt for the multiples because of their track record and perceived ability to be able to pay high long-term rents and maintenance rates. Clone towns therefore are a product of the modern age, in which economic Darwinian principles operate, and the multiples with their strong corporate brands flourish, resulting, though, in poor town differentiation for visitors and tourists.

So what has happened to any independent retailers in modern-day Southampton, as signifiers of retail diversity for visitors to the city? They have effectively been marginalised. The council has tried to retain the previous vibrancy of an off-high street secondary independents shopping strip in East Street, which was still a major trading street until the 1990s, but this has proved difficult to manage since the properties are owned by a variety of landlords looking for high short-term returns. The addition of the West Quay development has also lowered the footfall in that area of the town, even though it is only a short walk away. Some small independents remain in the street, but small multiple outlets are also there now, including the Game and Games Workshop chain outlets. What dominates the street, however, is a number of empty units and charity (thrift) shop outlets, which suggests that the economic retail health of the location is poor.

Two other city-centre retail 'clustered' locations where independents can be found are the relatively failed, smaller city-centre mini-malls of the Bargates, forming a link between East Street and Bargate itself, and another simply called 'The Mall' (originally 'The Marlands'), built in an old bus station location that links the main Above Bar high street with a large Asda store, retail park and extensive car parking. Both of these mini-mall centres were populated with national chains when they opened in the 1990s, prior to the West Quay mega-mall development. As footfall has moved elsewhere, however, they have seen a proliferation of units lying empty or changing hands and, whilst independents have been allowed to move into some of these, the overall feeling is of a distinctly secondary (or tertiary) shopping environment.

So, taking Southampton as an example, although customers may complain about 'clone towns' in the UK and they may indeed be reducing the locational distinctiveness of many locales for visitors, nevertheless any negative visitor effects are potentially masked by consumers 'voting with their feet' and giving new, chain store-dominated shopping centres economic success. Founding a town's principle retail offer on the basis of national names, though, may still not be the way forward in the long term, particularly for visitors and tourists to the city overall (although it is difficult to envisage a successful shopping centre without them). Hence, although some element of the 'clone town' is apparently required, city distinctiveness may be lost if the process goes too far. The danger is that 'clone towns' can be easily replicated in new developments elsewhere, with city-centre shoppers migrating towards them.

All the factors discussed so far highlight the problems for the town centre as it strives to enhance its tourist trade through its retail offer. It is now important to discuss what town centres can do to promote themselves. If town centres can capitalise on their inherent assets and meet such consumer needs then their future is more secure.

Future viability of town centre: potential solutions for tourist attraction

Five solutions to perceived town centre attractiveness

For assured viability in a tourist-centric age, it is important to understand what consumer (residents and tourists) want from a town centre. In this respect it has been proposed, in general, that:

> consumers, like wildlife, are likely to gravitate to a setting offering a favourable climate, a high potential for social interaction, a perceived freedom from safety concerns, and a large selection of consumable goods and experiences.
>
> (Bloch *et al.*, 1994: p. 23)

Although this statement was based on research in American shopping malls (Bloch *et al.*, 1991), it could be applied to consumers elsewhere. If the town centre can meet these conditions then their viability could be assured. It is, however, not only meeting these conditions but also excelling at them and communicating them to the visitor that will lead to success in an increasingly competitive environment. It is proposed here to examine five key retail visitor solutions for success in relation to existing town centre:

1 a favourable 'climate';
2 social interaction;
3 safety;
4 selection; and
5 experience.

Solution 1: a favourable 'climate'

If the word 'climate' is taken in its strictest sense, as relating to the weather, then some might see the temperate conditions in northern Europe as being on the side of out-of-town centres, which in many cases have covered malls. Inclement weather is outside the control of the town centre managers or retailers. However, its effects on the visitor's overall shopping experience can be managed. Transport links that bring consumers into the heart of the shopping area can reduce walking distances and hence exposure to the climate. The use of arcades, covered walkways and awnings can enable customers to move between shops without incurring too much discomfort from the bad weather.

There are, in fact, many days in the UK when the weather is surprisingly 'good' and visitors can take advantage of the sunshine in the town centre and soak up the outdoor atmosphere. When the weather is like this the town centre can thrive in contrast to the enclosed malls, which can seem lifeless and sterile in this aspect. At the Merry Hill Centre, for example, it is possible to access a large number of retailers via the attached enclosed car park and be oblivious to the outside world. Many UK inhabitants, as in other countries of the world, like to enjoy the 'good' weather when the opportunity is offered, particularly the tourist and visitor market, and may abhor the enclosed nature of the malls with their climatic controls. If consumers are going to enjoy the sunshine, however, then there needs to be places for them to sit that evoke images of summery days. Many long-standing city centres have fountains to aid this impression, noticeably in Rome, where tourists relax between bouts of shopping. The south coast UK tourist town of Bournemouth has a number of palm trees, gardens and seats within its town centre, as well as a beach within easy walking distance, and is proud of its beaches, as well as floral arrangements and hanging baskets, which have won awards. Even such simple improvements as this can make one centre more appealing than another.

Beyond the weather, I propose that we should consider the shopping 'climate' in its broadest sense, however, which is about the surrounding environment as a whole. The historical appeal of streets and buildings can have an effect here. Out-of-town centres are relatively modern in the UK and therefore have no history compared with town centres. Janet Street-Porter, a British socio-cultural columnist, writing in *The Independent* newspaper, praised town centres, suggesting that:

> towns have history, are places built up over centuries with good and bad bits, eyesores and beauty, peopled by local inhabitants, well known characters like newspaper sellers or fishmongers.
>
> (Street-Porter, 2005)

She then went on to describe the out-of-town MetroCentre, Gateshead, as 'a horror with zero appeal'. This is a view echoed by Schiller (1994: 46), who deplores town centre redevelopment and sees it as 'a loss of individuality, with historic street patterns often being destroyed' and goes on to say 'modern replacement tends to emphasize the similarity between towns with the same shop names appearing in each town'.

We have seen that the result of new developments, common in the UK, can be that out-of-town attractions and town centres become architecturally similar, offering the same retail outlets: the birth of the clone town. Southampton was a victim of heavy bombing in the southern UK during the Second World War, particularly on the night of 30 November 1940 (Brode, 1982), when the John Lewis store (bearing the fascia of Tyrrell and Green at the time) was destroyed together with much of the ancient town centre, including the medieval city wall. Southampton, instead of rebuilding as it had been, took this as an opportunity to build a new city. By contrast, on the European continent, ancient towns such as Ypres and Arras in France were rebuilt after the First World War to maintain their historic character to the extent of recreating medieval buildings and atmospheres. The trend in Britain since the war, at least up until the 1980s, was to build new, modernist, concrete buildings cumulating in many 1960/70s retail centres – some of which have now been revamped, as in the case of the Dolphin Centre in Poole town centre, Dorset, or even demolished, such as Tricorn Centre in the heart of Portsmouth. Only a few centres have bucked this trend, Worcester being an example in trying to maintain a Georgian façade on its main street, and new buildings having to conform to this 'old world' style.

Organically grown, historic town centres have many assets that built environments, including out-of-towns, do not and never will have. There is a history attached to many ancient shopping streets too, such in the Shambles of York, the Lanes of Brighton and the Rows at Chester, which are all tourist attractions. Aspects of these can be imitated in new builds but they can never match the original and provide the historic background that is built into the consumer's socio-cultural experience. As a major tourist city, Bath is an extremely attractive location and although many shoppers may head for the large in-town Marks & Spencer branch the fact that it is located in an historic town gives it some added cachet. In fact, the tourist visitor has tremendous potential for cities, as tourists tend to spend more than traditional shoppers (McIntyre, 2007).

Compared with cared-for, old-world environments, modern shopping centres can be 'often virtually identical' with each other (Burns and Warren, 1995: 5), although they may try to differentiate themselves by adding non-retail, visual attractions such as the large old clock situated in a primary location in the Victoria Centre, Nottingham. It would seem correct, therefore, that the 'historic environment provided by the urban fabric provides a wonderful backdrop for modern quality retailing, services and leisure-orientated operations' (Gransby, 1988: 15).

It is not only recognised historic towns on the tourist trail, however, that can promote themselves as having a distinctive attraction. It is also claimed that large metropolitan towns and cities, such as Nottingham and Birmingham in the UK, can 'make the town centre literally the centre of attraction again' (Falk *et al.*, 1995: 36). They can do this, it is claimed, by promoting existing natural features and local landmarks and with the introduction of historical notes to accompany town walks, featuring 'hidden' histories. Visitors are already familiar with such large place names but may be less certain of the overall visitor offer in terms of retail and leisure. It is a lack of communication or promotional focus upon the visiting consumer that can be the downfall of a town centre, unlike out-of-town centres, which have large centralised advertising budgets and focused activities.

A major promotional activity option open to town centres is the introduction of 'festival markets which can be seen as important way of revitalizing city centres' (Alzubaidi *et al.*, 1997: 80). This obviously works best when the venue is already a tourist destination; for example the uninformed might assume, on account of the historic ambience of the city, that the Christmas market in the cathedral town of Lincoln, in the UK's east midlands, had been there for several centuries rather than, as is actually the case, a few decades. The Bournemouth has recently introduced a 'German Christmas Market' in the town centre square that has increased the number of consumers in the town centre (although the town has no obvious links with Germany). Town centres often have open spaces that can be used for such events in contrast to their out-of-town rivals, who are forced to resort to using car parks and small spaces between malls for such events, which can hardly be a serious aesthetic challenge in terms of 'climate' of any kind.

Solution 2: social interaction

One assumes that tourists and visitors, as well as interacting with place characteristics, need also to interact with local people. In order to interact socially it is useful to have interaction spaces. Gaps between shops, rather than the unbroken line of the malls, can offer this space. Talking to friends and family enhances the shopping experience, and turns shopping from a chore into a leisure experience. It is creating this leisure experience that may provide an answer for the town centre (Schiller, 1999). In order to have social interaction it is useful to have space that is open and 'undemanding' – a slowing down of consumption – compared with the sensory, commercial overload of many areas within shopping malls, aiming for maximum consumption space utility.

Town centres have spaces and features that do not have to be 'filled' in terms of spatial cost-return, such as parks and paved areas. Within an out-of-town centre that is managed, each square metre has to be evaluated. Each water feature and plant display is balanced against attracting more customers and hence charged to retailers. Within town centres there are likely to be fountains and statues, paved areas and gardens, which are less likely to be removed and costs directly apportioned to the retailers, but instead are funded from council tax. These spaces and features can give the town distinctive atmospheres and individuality. Whereas retailers may wish to locate next to each other, it is these spaces that often define a town and as Falk suggest towns need to 'rediscover their open spaces' (Falk *et al.*, 1995: 37).

The town, like a built centre, can also create new features and meeting places to attract consumers but the challenge is 'to create new places that feel as convincing as those that have evolved over time' (Carr, 1990: 194) and this is where the established town centre has the advantage. Within an out-of-town development, the consumer is fully aware that the centre has been enhanced with non-retail features in order to attract them, but the sculptures and fountains need a context that a town centre can offer, such as in the case of the distinctive and place-defining statue of King Alfred in Winchester, the historical capital of England in the southern counties of the UK (Figure 2.2).

Solution 3: safety concerns

It has been stated that, for most consumers and visitors, providing a suitable shopping ambience is about 'creating places that feel special and safe' (Falk *et al.*, 1995: p. 38). In modern times, safety has also become a key concern in tourist terms. Town centres would seem to need to improve, or at least to alter some consumer perceptions in this respect. The out-of-town centre based on private property can exert some control over the people who enter the centre. For example, the Bluewater shopping centre, east of London in the UK, has banned young people wearing hooded tops or 'hoodies' because of the perceived threatening effect (BBC News, 2010).

Figure 2.2 The King Alfred statue, focal point upon entering the main shopping street by road, Winchester (source: the author).

Town centres do not generally have such control options available to them. They can, however, alleviate concerns about safety by increasing the levels of lighting and heightening the police presence and visibility. Consumers in the UK often see the police as less threatening than the security guards in the malls, representing a reassuring, historical presence rather than 'big brother'. Transport links direct into the town centres and reduced centre traffic can also help to alleviate safety concerns. Park-and-ride schemes, such as those offered in Cambridge, Oxford and Winchester in the south of the UK, also offer increased safety for consumers, taking the consumer to and from well-lit car parks on the outskirts to less traffic-dense central streets.

Safety is also about knowing where you are and avoiding that 'lost' feeling. The older generation are often confused by modern shopping centres. In this respect malls can be more confusing, with each of them having a similarity of design and commercial denseness that can make wayfinding difficult. Unlike in town centres, there are no distinctive features that aid the consumer to navigate, requiring most out-of-town centres to provide maps and information points. Finding the way back to the car park in a large malls can also be difficult. As one enters there is an immediate bombardment to the senses and many consumers forget to look back and check where their exit is, or in which lane and bay their car is parked. It is less easy to lose one's way in the town centre, where even the natural geography such as surrounding hills and rivers can be used as a guide, thus enhancing and reinforcing a secure and 'anchored' feeling in visitors.

Solution 4: selection

Many out-of-town centres are undoubtedly larger than the adjacent town and city centres and therefore can offer a larger range of retailers and products. The retail offer provided by town centres needs, in these cases, to be *different* from the out-of-town offer. The Bluewater Centre in Kent can be seen as 'a collection of fast food restaurants, chain stores and very few individual traders. It's not about one-off shops and unique design or special service' (Street-Porter, 2005). Each shop within these centres often offers similar products; they can be part of the same chain, for example the Arcadia Group, and although the fascias may be different, many aspects of the shops – layout, customer service, range – are similar. Thus they are in effect purpose-built clone towns!

Town centres, to compete, only need to offer a uniqueness that differentiates them. If the high street offer is a poor imitation of out-of-town centres, with lower-traffic, smaller multiple branches (and possibly more dated stock) then the customer's preference for shopping away from the town centre can be more easily understood.

There has been a tendency for retailers to locate their premier flagship stores out of town, due to additional space available, and lower the classification of their smaller town centre stores. To ensure their appeal in the high street as well, town centre branches need to review their offer to provide less breadth of product and more depth or distinctiveness within such (usually smaller) spaces. Many retailers have taken this on board in the UK, including Marks & Spencer's introduction of its 'Simply Food' sub-brand of food-only stores, Tesco's growing small format 'Metro' in-town stores and smaller Boots (The Chemists) stores focused on 'Health and Beauty'. Chain fashion clothing retailers appear to be lagging behind in this production of clearly defined and focused in-town stores to give consumers a feeling that the town centre has something special to offer; they tend towards mall branch similarity in the main.

As already stated, one advantage of town centres can be the presence of more independent traders than in the shopping centres. This appears to be particularly true in the restaurant sector, where fast-food outlets dominate mall food courts, but it can also apply to retailers of youth culture and distinctive fashions.

Independents, of course, are not necessarily averse to the trade available in shopping centres; but they have severe problems overcoming barriers to entry in trading there. First, they are often the last to hear about proposed new developments and vacancies, as they are low on any developer's contact list. The developers are more interested in well-known retailers that can attract customers, have a known record in achieving sales and are able to take on a long-term lease. Leases in the high street, by comparison, can be as short as three months in some instances, and there are many secondary sites that have lower rents. Groups of independent stores can thus be used to differentiate town centre attractiveness in a modern situation where 'consumers have become more retailer sensitive and less location sensitive in determining which center they patronize' (Eppli, 1998: 200).

A town centre's integration of independent food and retail outlets intermixed with other offers has generally arisen because of its natural development over time. To be able to continue to present such an 'organic' offer, town centres should perhaps resist excessive formal 'zoning' of their offers by organised planning, although the development of distinctive lifestyle town and city 'quarters' (Howard, 2007) would seem to be appealing for many visitors. In this spirit, Bennison, Warnaby and Medway (2007: 636), in a Manchester case study, examined the use of the city's 'cool' Northern Quarter as a marketing tool. They suggest that such quarter, although useful as a marketing tool, cannot be made or managed successfully and that they should be allowed to 'grow via their own endogenous creative spirit' and 'might therefore be seen as a critical element' in the development of a large heterogeneous city servicescape.

Shopping malls, in contrast, provide wall-to-wall shops, usually with full-sized windows, where even the size and shape of the windows are similar. Although this can be useful to display more merchandise, it can lead to consumer *overload*: the consumer not knowing where to look first, which side of the mall and which window – leading to shopper fatigue. Shops on the high street are interlaced with banks, offices and other features that give the consumer a rest. There is also the expectation of turning the corner or crossing the road to discover new outlets. There is a sense of discovery and each retailer can stand out from the competition, with the windows perhaps proving less stressful and more inviting in not displaying as much merchandise.

A study in Utrecht, a historic city in Holland, showed that the sectors represented within the old city had changed over the years with the growth of 'health foods, cooking supplies and telecom and home accessories'; the researchers interpreted this as the 'emergence of the recreational shopper' (Weltevreden *et al.*, 2005: 831). This recreational shopper needs an enjoyable experience rather than a clone town. High streets in town and city centres do need to change; but, if that change features the mimicking of out-of-town centres, it would seem not to be the answer for true visitor attractiveness.

Solution 5: experience

At the end of the 1990s Schiller (1998: 35) stated that the growth area of the future is 'leisure shopping, particularity eating out and drinking', and this is increasingly shown to be the case, not only in terms of eating but also in terms of the core shopping experience itself. Arentze and colleagues (2005) have proposed that people want other leisure attractions besides shopping so that they can combine the purpose of their visit. Shops are becoming more exciting, and locations need to follow this lead. An investigation in Dublin, Ireland, showed that city centres can be improved, using as an example:

> pedestrianisation of the primary streets, additional car parking, street furniture, improved lighting, flowers, additional litter bins and attractive murals and art work.
>
> (O'Callaghan and O'Riordan, 2003: 391)

This is not about improving the mix of retailers but about improving the features that add to the town centre shopping experience. Town centres have a degree of flexibility which allows them to develop some areas. In university towns, where there are young people, it is possible to create a continental café culture with street cafes and markets (Falk *et al.*, 1995), which would suggest a more leisurely consumer and the possibility of developing the early evening economy. This could be aided by the development of compact specialist in-town stores.

As I have said under selection, markets offer opportunities for town centres to create new interesting features that do not need to operate throughout the year, such as the French markets that are popular along the south coast of the UK in both large and smaller towns, such as Poole and Weymouth. Farmers' markets offering a variety of local products, usually at premium prices, are also popular with visitor consumers for adding local colour and interest to the town centre, for example in the UK village of Wimborne and the cathedral city of Lincoln. Covent Garden in London has a market that is attracting a variety of small traders, many of them independents, into the adjacent area, turning it into a major tourist shopping destination in the heart of the city. Street performers here as in many areas of towns and cities can give a heady carnival atmosphere. Bath also plays upon this mix in its cathedral square.

Besides the markets there is also the possibility of towns and cities featuring street traders, although these are not always popular! Cheltenham town council considers them acceptable in encouraging visitation provided they are 'selectively located where it can make a positive contribution to the vitality and viability of the town' (Jones *et al.*, 2003: 23). Although it is possible to offer these types of 'street entertainment' in out-of-town centres, this is often seen to be orchestrated and lacking the spontaneity of a town or high street. Crowds can cause problems in malls, such as fire risks, and they restrict access through the centre. If town centres can use all of these devices to create a memorable experience then the customers will be attracted, as has been already proved in locations such as Covent Garden and Bath. Outside the UK, the German tourist retail experience has also shown that the high spending leisure shopper can be attracted if:

> town centres are carefully and jointly managed and preserved to make them attractive to consumers and maintain a community atmosphere.
>
> (Alzubaidi *et al.*, 1997: 79)

A *community atmosphere* is difficult to create out of town, with the shops as well as the shoppers having come from geographical disperse locations, and having no joint history with the centre itself. Contrast this with a good town centre mix, a proportion of which will be related to the same history, schools, buildings, evening entertainments: then there is the beginnings of a community. Town centres can present a truly distinctive experience of local character that the visiting consumer wants, whereas out-of-town centres are often only a collection of retailers and very little else.

Chapter summary: the high street meeting the needs of the visitor consumer for future viability?

In agreement with the premise of Bloch and colleagues (1994), it can be seen that the town centre *can* meet many customer needs. It can provide an ideal location in terms for social interaction with plenty of open spaces. It already has the basis for a community, and can provide a meeting place for friends and acquaintances, many of whom are located within easy reach. The historical backdrop can help to provide a unique experience for the shopper. In some cities this has led to the development of 'quarters' which can be highly profitable for retailers and service providers, offering a unique selling proposition.

In considering the solutions to attractiveness viability presented here, the main outstanding problem areas would seem to be some continuing safety concerns of certain locations and the weather; but, even here, town centres can look to the positive aspects. Everyone is welcome in the town centre; the police are there to protect the public, as opposed to security guards in malls who are there primarily to protect the premises and the retailer. The weather is out of town centre control, but use of increased covered areas can alleviate such exposure.

It has been demonstrated that town centres have many strengths for tourist and visitor attraction, and these need to be emphasised and communicated. They must not try to be poor imitations of their out-of-town counterparts by trying to attract the same retailers. They need to provide an environment that meets the needs of the modern consumer – local, visitor and tourist. They have many advantages, none more so than the backdrop of an established town centre with space and distinctive features. Destroying existing architecture and replacing it with ultra-modern shopping centres may not be the answer, as has sometimes seemed to be the preference in town and city developments. This only gives high streets and town centres a sameness, which might cause shoppers to head for the largest centre, which may well be out of town, where safety, convenience and a greater multiple retail and fast-food product provision are the key factors. Such a potential situation may be envisaged to have been promoted, to some extent, by recent developments in the case of Southampton as featured in this chapter.

It is the individualistic uniqueness of a city, town and village centre with a diverse range of shops and facilities that can make it a success. It is not imitation of regional shopping centres, all with the same retail outlets, but a clearly defined tourist offer or 'product'. In particular, it would seem that the high street's assets, at least in the UK, need to be managed and promoted to the consumer to avoid an indistinct, clone town phenomenon.

References

Alzubaidi, H., Vignali, C., Davies, B. and Schmidt, R. (1997) Town centre versus out-of-town shopping: a consumer perspective. *International Journal of Retail & Distribution Management* 25(2), 78–89.

Arentze, T., Oppewal, H. and Timmermanns, H. (2005) A multi-purpose shopping trip model to assess retail agglomeration effects. *Journal of Marketing Research* 42(1), 109–129.

BBC News (2004) Think tank warns on 'clone towns'. Online source: http://news.bbc.co.uk/1/hi/business/3582704.stm (last accessed 20 July 2009).

BBC News (2010) Mall bans shoppers' hooded tops. Online source: http://news.bbc.co.uk/1/hi/england/kent/4534903.stm (last accessed 9 November 2010).

Bennison, D., Warnaby, G. and Medway, D. (2007) The role of quarters in large city centres: a Mancunian case study. *International Journal of Retail and Distribution Management* 35(8), 626–635.

Bloch, P. H., Ridgway, N. M. and Nelson, J. E. (1991) Leisure and the shopping mall. *Advances in Consumer Research* 18, 442–452.

Bloch, P. H., Ridgway, N. M. and Dawson, S. A. (1994) The shopping mall as a consumer habitat. *Journal of Retailing* 70(1), 23–42.

Brode, A. (1982) *The Southampton Blitz*. Newbury, Berkshire: Countryside Books.

Burns, D. and Warren, H. B. (1995) Need for uniqueness: shopping mall preference and choice activity. *International Journal of Retail & Distribution Management* 23(12), 4–12.

Carr, J. (1990) The social aspects of shopping pleasure or chore? The consumer perspective. *Royal Society of Arts Journal* 138, 189–197.

Cox's (1871) *Directory: Classified Professions and Trades Directory*. Online source: http://www.plimsoll.org/Southampton/streetdirectories/directory1871/directory1871 (last accessed 28 May 2008).

Daily Telegraph (2009) Public art sell-offs heading into troubled waters. Online source: www.Factiva.com (last accessed 28 October 2010).

Eppli, M. J. (1998) Value allocation in regional shopping centers. *Appraisal Journal* 66, April(2), 198–206.

Falk, N., Chase, M. and Hampson, S. (1995) Are our town centres sustainable? *RSA Journal* July, 35–55.

Gransby, D. M. (1988) The coexistence of high street and out-of town retailing from a retailing perspective. *Geographical Journal* 154(1), 13–16.

Guy, C. and Lord, J. D. (1993) Transformation and the city centre. In Bromley, R. D. F. and Thomas, C. J. (eds) *Retail Change, Contemporary Issues*. London: UCL Press, pp. 88–108.

Howard, E. (2007) New shopping centres: is leisure the answer? *International Journal of Retail and Distribution Management* 35(8), 661–672.

Jones, P. (1981) Retail innovation and diffusion: the spread of Asda stores. *Area* 13(4), 197–201.

Jones, P. (1984) Retail warehouse development in Britain. *Area* 16(1): 41–47.

Jones, P. and Hillier, D. (2000) Changing the balance: the 'ins and outs' of retail development. *Property Management* 18(2), 114–126.

Jones, P., Comfort, D. and Hillier, D. (2003) Managing the geography of street trading in the UK: a case study of local authority regulation. *Management Research News* 26(6), 21–30.

Kelly's (1907) *Directory: Classified Professions and Trades Directory*. Online source: http://www.plimsoll.org/Southampton/streetdirectories/directory1907/directory1907 (last accessed 28 May 2008).

Kelly's (1920) *Directory: Classified Professions and Trades Directory*. Online source: http://www.plimsoll.org/Southampton/streetdirectories/directory1920/directory1920 (last accessed 28 May 2008).

Lowe, M. (2000) Britain's regional shopping centres: new urban forms? *Urban Studies* 37, 261–274.

Lowe, M. (2005) The regional shopping centre in the inner city: a study of retail-led urban regeneration. *Urban Studies* 42(3), 449–470.

McIntyre, C. (2007) Survival theory: tourist consumption as a beneficial experiential process in a limited risk setting. *International Journal of Tourism Research* 9, 115–130.

O'Callaghan, E. and O'Riordan, D. (2003) Retailing at the periphery: an analysis of Dublin's tertiary city centre shopping streets (1972–2002). *International Journal of Retail & Distribution Management* 31(8), 389–400.

Patterson, A. T. (1966) *A History of Southampton 1700–1914, Vol. I: An oligarchy in decline*. Southampton: University of Southampton.

Post Office (1851) *Directory: Classified Professions and Trades Directory*. Online source: http://www.plimsoll.org/Southampton/streetdirectories/directory1851/directory1851.asp#10 (last accessed 28 May 2008).

Post Office (1863) *Directory: Classified Professions and Trades Directory*. Online source: http://www.plimsoll.org/Southampton/streetdirectories/directory1863/directory1863 (last accessed 28 May 2008).

Ruddock, A. (1951) *Italian Merchants and Shipping in Southampton*. Winchester: Wykeham Press.

Schiller, R. (1994) Vitality and viability: challenge to the town centre. *International Journal of Retail & Distribution Management* 22(6), 46–50.

Schiller, R. (1998) The future of the town centre. *Estates Gazette* 9844 (Special Insert), 35–39.

Schiller, R. (1999) Viewpoint: leisure shopping and the future of the high street. *International Journal of Retail and Distribution Management* 27(1), 5–7.

Southampton Archaeological Research Committee (1975) *Saxon Southampton: The archaeology and history of a port called Hamwih.* Southampton: Southampton Archaeological Research Committee.

Southampton City Council (2009) *Population.* Southampton: Southampton City Council.

Street-Porter, J. (2005) The snobbish delusions of a dreary mall: what Bluewater offers is as lacklustre and unrewarding as drunken sex or KFC from a bucket. *The Independent,* 25 May, p. 35.

Travel.ciao.co.uk (2008) Southampton in general review. Online source: http://travel.ciao.co.uk/Southampton_in_General__Review_5260252 (last accessed 10 January 2008).

Weltevreden, J., Atzema, O. and Frenken, K. (2005) Evolution in city retailing: the case of Utrecht (1974–2003). *International Journal of Retail & Distribution Management* 33(11), 824–841.

www.johnlewis.com (2008) The history of John Lewis Southampton. Online source: http://www.johnlewis.com/Shops/DSTemplate.aspx?Id=37(last accessed 10 January 2008).

3 Creating the sensual temporal marketplace experience and the role of planned events in tourist retail sustainable development

Joe Goldblatt

Introduction

During the last half century, retail design along with tourism marketing and distribution has grown dramatically in cultural importance. The economic and social changes that have triggered this are well documented, including increases in consumer spending and leisure time as well as, at least in part, being due to the introduction of the Internet. The latter development has resulted in an increased power of consumer in making choices based upon a new transparency in the marketplace. Furthermore, as competition has increased, owing to multichannel marketing and product distribution, consumers seek new roles to play in the changing retail and tourist landscape. This chapter presents a new conceptual framework for using the planned event to create temporary retail opportunities that may lead to greater sustainable tourist and visitor development. The chapter identifies the role of the emerging tourism festival retail marketplace in integrating the live planned event, serving as a catalyst for developing customer relationship marketing beyond the temporal, sensual experience of a one-off attraction. Finally, three mini-case studies are presented that demonstrate how many retail events are shifting from transactions to multisensory experiences that are often well integrated in festivals and other live events; and the chapter concludes with recommendations for building capacity in the tourist retail sector through the development of *sensual temporal marketplaces*.

Historical background

Since Marco Polo in the fourteenth century, merchant traders have sought greater opportunities to find new products to satisfy their customers' needs, wants and desires. To this effect, he successfully introduced Europeans to the wonders of Asia, just as modern traders search for products and services that will improve the lives of others, to enrich their businesses and attract visitors from afar.

The first shopping mall can be considered to be the Al Hamidyah Souk, created in Damascus, Syria, in the seventh century. By the eighteenth century, the cities of St Petersburg, Russia, and Oxford, England, had also erected purpose-built shopping 'arcades'. In North America, the term 'shopping centre' (or center) and 'shopping mall' are used interchangeably; in Europe and the United Kingdom, the term 'high street', 'shopping precinct' or 'town precinct' may also represent a concentrated shopping area. The principle, however, remains the same. Concentrations of retail outlets, whether described as medinas, markets or malls, offer the consumer access to stores in a constrained geographic area and offer businesses a concentration of consumers.

Many tourists have visited the Medina in Fez, Morocco. The term 'medina' means city or town in modern Arabic. The medina was originally conceived as a walled city and is found in many Arab conurbations. It is a veritable sensual pleasure house as hundreds of traders offer rich spices, tanning leather and other treats for the senses. The Medina was established in the ninth century and its narrow streets may have been designed to protect its inhabitants from potential invaders. When I personally, like many tourists before me, visited the Medina nearly two decades ago, I asked one of the ancient traders if they would accept a credit card. To my surprise at that time, he rolled back a Persian rug, quickly plugged in a credit card terminal and immediately swiped my card. I supposed that the new 'invaders' as customers had finally successfully entered the walled city, only to be welcomed by receptive modern-day traders.

In the United States, one of the earliest twentieth-century shopping centres is the Country Club Plaza, still operating in Kansas City, Missouri. During the 1950s, with the economic growth of the United States, shopping centres expanded their geographic footprint and therefore required more land area. This involved their relocation to the suburban area, a process that was simultaneously becoming popular with families, who sought larger homes on the outskirts of towns and cities. During this period the development of the modern shopping mall, an enclosed structure, became a staple iconic symbol of prosperity in post-Second World War America.

The modern shopping mall and later the mega-mall, as demonstrated by the creation of the Mall of America in Minneapolis, Minnesota, in 1992, sees the retail environment reaching its commercially concentrated apex, at least in America. From small outdoor strip malls to huge indoor mega-malls that include purpose-built amusement parks, the retail shopping environment both in America and throughout the world has dramatically changed.

Shopping is consistently rated in many studies of tourism as one of the key activities of all types of tourists while visiting destinations, including the growing attractiveness of shopping centres within tourist destinations. Tourists spend three to four times more than the average shopper at shopping centres and malls, according to the Travel Industry Association of America (Shopping Centre World, 2001).

According to Paige and Littrell (2003), shopping is a preferred tourism activity and is acknowledged as a primary means of generating tourism revenue. However, there are many complex factors that influence this activity. Using factor analysis from a survey of 290 persons, they identified a wide range of effects upon behaviours among different groups of tourists during their shopping activities. For example, it was more difficult to attract the outdoors, sports or adventure tourist to the shopping centre or mall. Even here, though, they recommend that by providing a wide range of shops – including a focus upon history, culture, and arts and crafts – shopping centres or malls may gain better traffic from this hard-to-reach group of tourists.

As the retail shopping experience continues to develop and evolve over time, the live events that could offer some of these cultural elements, including historical and arts and crafts performance, may provide a strong incentive for outdoor and sports tourists to visit, and perhaps later further engage with traders, either online or in a traditional brick and mortar location. As many live events within marketplaces in tourist areas often feature types of handmade or local products, they are already in many ways ahead of the game as compared, perhaps, with the traditional retail store location that is situated within a shopping centre or mall. Throughout the postmodern period of history, shopping centres and malls have endeavoured to provide a one-stop, convenient opportunity for shoppers to satiate all of their senses in a safe and secure surrounding.

My Big Town: a sensory shopping experience in development

As a safe outing event for a very young child in the USA, I often accompanied my mother to the local enclosed shopping centre in Dallas, Texas. According to historical record 'Big Town', as it was called, was the first purpose-built enclosed shopping mall in the south-western part of the United States. Big Town seems quaint by today's commercialised standards, but to a child of six it was a sensuous delight. Three key factors created a unique experience for shoppers in Big Town. First, major department stores were conveniently co-located with specialty boutique businesses in one geographic place. Second, Big Town used events and a purpose-built arcade featuring games and prizes for the lucky winners to entertain the children, whilst their mothers shopped around. Third, finally and perhaps most importantly, Big Town was air conditioned. In Texas, during the summer, when temperatures regularly climbed to over 100° Fahrenheit, air conditioning was a major advantage and had the additional benefit of extending the shoppers' visit. Longer visits resulted in increased sales. In fact, Big Town, may have been one of the first sensuous marketplace experiences. However, as of 2006, Big Town is largely disappearing and in its place the local authorities are planning to develop a sport and entertainment complex.

Throughout human history, the gender-based activities of hunting and gathering have been adopted and adapted by both men and women, as evidenced by the rapid development of the postmodern retail shopping experience. In the second half of the twentieth century, thanks in large part to the development of retail stores specialising in male products, the original 'hunters' were an increasing group in suburban malls. Nevertheless, the human experience of hunting and gathering has rapidly evolved in terms of consumer society satisfactions and motivations.

In the twenty-first century, the expression 'the consumer is king' has replaced the age-old adage of 'the customer is always right'. Through the use of weblogs and wikis, postmodern consumers may not only discuss their own shopping preferences but also influence others and so affect the future development of new retail experiences.

Motivations towards visiting the modern shopping environment

Perhaps through the application of Abraham Maslow's classic hierarchy of needs we may better understand the motivations for shopping. Maslow (1943) first argued in his paper 'A Theory of Human Motivation' that humans at the most basic level seek the satiation of their physiological needs. Next, he stated that personal and financial safety and security were highly desirable. He then progressed to identifying the importance of love and belonging, such as in familial relationships. Maslow identified a further two steps in human motivation theory as esteem and self-actualisation. He believed that when we have esteem it is more difficult to experience depression and when we are self-actualised we may achieve our highest ambitions and goals. This 'pyramid' of motivations is often depicted with the supposed 'higher' needs placed at the apex and most basic ones at the base. As basic retail functions are now available over the Internet, giving a new importance to heightened retail experience to tempt consumers out of their homes, this order may have to be inverted in terms of retail expectations of place: the previously considered most basic motivations can be taken as 'givens', whilst the need for personally self-enhancing experiences becomes a first-order motivation. Figure 3.1 attempts to depict this well-known theoretical structure for motivation within such an inverted context for motivations to visit in the postmodern shopping experience.

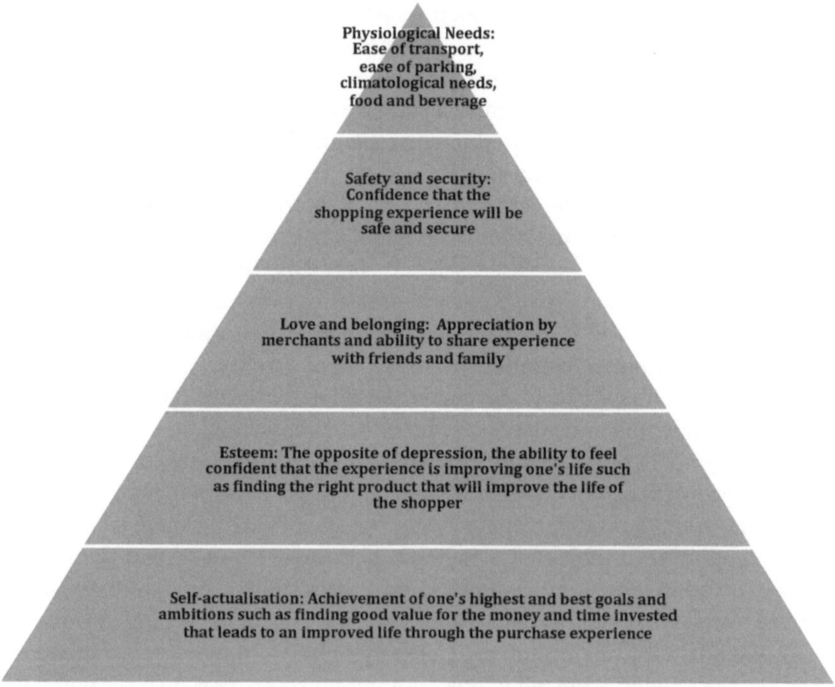

Figure 3.1 Inverted Maslow's 'Hierarchy of Needs' adapted for the retail shopping centre experience (source: the author).

In meeting rising motivations in the modern consumer society, with its increased leisure and tourism aspects, to derive visitor satisfactions, the cost of bringing new products and services to market has risen astronomically in the past half century. The risk in designing and opening a bricks-and-mortar retail business is significant and the time required to achieve a profit to pay investment back has simultaneously been reduced. The pressure is more intense than ever before for postmodern retailers to find new ways to market their good and services to achieve sustainable development, whilst meeting rising consumer expectations. Therefore, a new model may be needed required for attracting, informing, communication and persuading consumers to make purchases that lead to sustainable profits and business operations.

The 'black box' model (see Table 3.1) of consumer decision making has historically been used to identify the complex motivations that lead to the purchasing decision (Sanhusen, 2000). This model is introduced to begin the discussion of how a temporary event setting (such as a craft fair or pop-up store) may serve as a catalyst for innovation, development of sufficient retail attractions and even a revival of the shopping centre, mall, high street, shopping precinct or town precinct for enhanced visitor satisfactions in the modern age.

The future temporal sensual retail events model

We need to consider the complications and sophistications in designing continuously improving retail attractions to meet the needs of the black box consumer decision-making model, as shown in Table 3.1. The nature of the modern marketplace can be considered in the following quote:

> Products and services increasingly exist within a cloud of information, continuously and dynamically linked to virtual brochure sites maintained by sellers, journalist reviews, consumer ratings, social commentary, and aggregated

Table 3.1 The 'black box' model of consumer decision making

Environmental factors		*Buyer's black box*		
Marketing stimuli	*Environmental stimuli*	*Buyer characteristics*	*Decision process*	*Buyer's response*
Product Price Place Promotion	Economic Technological Political Cultural Demographic Natural	Attitudes Motivation Perceptions Personality Lifestyle Knowledge	Problem recognition Information search Alternative evaluation Purchase decision Post-purchase behaviour	Product choice Brand choice Dealer choice Purchase timing Purchase amount

Source: Sanhusen (2000).

> usage statistics. This cloud can be accessed any time in any place through multiple channels. While retailers traditionally see online and store marketing as competing businesses, customers ultimately care about convenience and perceived value – not the channel through which they are served.
>
> (Grünsteidl, 2010)

Grünsteidl and others within the twenty-first-century retail marketplace realise that the retail and distribution paradigm has rapidly shifted with the emergence of consumer-generated content that is distributed through the Internet. One tourist-related example of this in the services sector is the meteoric rise in importance of TripAdvisor (www.tripadvisor.com), upon which consumers can paste their own reviews and experiences of travel events. Between May 2007 and May 2008 the number of visitors to/users of Trip Advisor rose from 5 million to over 7 million. During the same period the number of individuals posting a review regarding their accommodation or other trip experience increased from 0.04 to 1.2 per cent (Trip Advisor Blog, 2003).

The combination of the growth of the Internet and the rising power of consumer through knowledge to make increasingly sophisticated buying decisions requires a new model for creating temporal sensual retail events that may serve as a customer relations management tool to cultivate new customers and long-term clients. Figure 3.2 depicts a proposed new future model to simplify and promote the movement of goods and services to market through the use of temporal retail

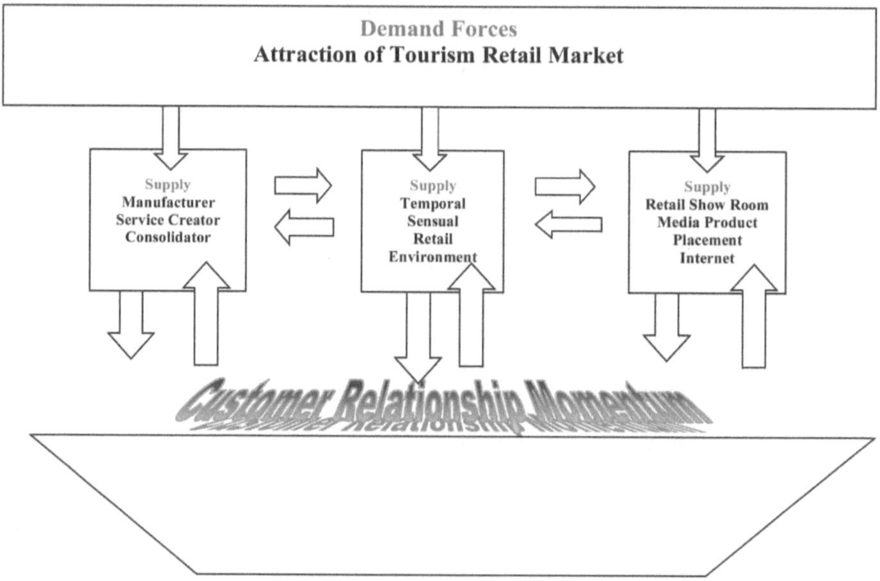

Figure 3.2 Future temporal sensual retail events model: adapted from Alexander Grünsteidl's Method's User Experience (Grünsteidl, 2010).

environments, whilst forging renewed and valued relationships along the distribution chain, including retail visitation.

A consideration of some aspects of this model's application are given in examination of three cases that help identify the present and future roles that live events may contribute to potential market growth in the retail visitation and tourist sector.

Case 1: static and dynamic experiences – Aunt Dot and The Rainforest Café™ versus Planet Hollywood™

The Rainforest Café restaurant chain is cited by Pine and Gilmore (2000) as a best experiential practice in retail restaurant design and management. A potential competitor for such commendation may be thought to be the chain Planet Hollywood, founded by the creator of the previously successful Hard Rock Café concept – their new formula perhaps also destined for success? However, I once escorted my wife's Aunt Dot to Planet Hollywood and, as soon as Aunt Dot entered the establishment and experienced the dark lighting, loud music and background noise, she quickly ran into the parking lot. I followed her to inquire what was wrong. She answered, 'This is what hell must be like!' – a deeply religious individual, Aunt Dot obviously did not have a positive experience during her one and only visit to Planet Hollywood. Regardless of the potential subjectivity of my Aunt Dot, many others appeared to feel the same way because, according to a report in the *New York Times*:

> Planet Hollywood went public in 1996 at $18 a share, representing an enormous multiple of earnings. It rose to $32, giving the company a paper value of $3.4 billion before the air went out of the soufflé. The stock was delisted just before its first bankruptcy in 1999. Most of its outlets were closed, and the founder, Mr. Robert Earl, his reputation took a pounding.
>
> (Siklos, 2007)

By contrast, The Rainforest Café has enjoyed consistent success by creating a dynamic, rather than static, retail environment that is filled with animation and, according to restaurant critics, consistently good food. Pine and Gilmore (2000) recognised the importance of getting the fundamentals right, such as consistently high-quality food and service, prior to focussing upon enhanced experiences leading to transformation. In the case of The Rainforest Café the patron arrives and is welcomed by a costumed host who gives them a vibrating beeper. The patron is then invited to explore the gift shop prior to the start of their dining experience. The exploration of the gift shop is similar to Act I in a play and allows the guest to become oriented, meet the characters and become comfortable with the surroundings. When the guest's table is ready, the guest is signalled using the vibrating beeper and, when they approach, the restaurant host announces 'Mr. and Mrs. Smith, your adventure is about to begin!' The guest then enters the rainforest where fish swim in enormous tanks and animatronic replicas of wild animals including lions and tigers roar every few minutes. However, most intriguing is that every few minutes a fine mist descends from the ceiling just as in a real rain forest in Brazil or other exotic destinations.

Unlike the Planet Hollywood atmosphere, The Rainforest Café delivers a dynamic experience underpinned by good food and high-quality service. Although some may argue that the target markets are different for these restaurant attractions, a more important consideration is the perception of basic quality and consistency of the offer. Both restaurants offer a total sensory experience. However, within The Rainforest Café there is greater variety within the dining experience to enable the guest to have multiple sensorial experiences throughout their visit. This may also stimulate multiple positive memories that may lead to reviews and referrals through consumer-generated content sites such as Trip Advisor.com.

Case 2: transformation: the Edinburgh Mela

A second case study that may be considered is that found in the Edinburgh Mela. The term 'mela' in Hindi means 'gathering' and for several years the event's organisers in Edinburgh have gathered together professional performers and traders to create a multicultural experience during the world-renowned Edinburgh Festival season in August. Because of the multicultural nature of this event the traders range from South Asian fabric sellers to African bead and clothing specialists. Historically its design and organisation around the stalls has been somewhat haphazard and uneven in quality. However, whilst conducting ethnographic research during this event in 2010 the author noted that the selection of the traders had dramatically improved in terms of overall quality, and the location and design of their stalls was also significantly better than the previous two years. As a result of these improvements, the number and upmarket nature of the customers seemed to improve as well. Some, not all, of the traders also operate traditional retail stores. Therefore, the Edinburgh Mela is an opportunity for them to meet new customers, greet current customers and continue to improve the customer relationship experience through their affiliation with this important local festival (Goldblatt, 2010).

Case 3: temporary city festival retail

The third and final case study is that of the growth of the temporary retail environment in Edinburgh during the festivals in August. It was noted that, in 2010, the growth in the number of traders, the wide geographic expansion throughout most of the historic city and the overall quality and variety of the merchandise significantly improved. This expansion and improvement was in contrast to the large number of retail storefronts in Edinburgh that posted 'To Let' signs prior to and during the festival season. It appeared that the temporal retail environment of the festival trading stalls had supplanted the traditional bricks and mortar environment of the past.

According to Richard Green (in an interview with the author), a 28-year veteran organizer of art and craft fairs at which the rule is that the artisans sell only what they have made themselves, 'I have definitely seen growth in this sector and

I have also noticed that many first time entrepreneurs now prefer to launch their new venture with a stall rather than a four wall retail store.' Green also states that he too has observed that, although many high streets are in decline, craft fairs and other temporary retail events appear to be growing exponentially throughout Great Britain. He started his career as a furniture maker who exhibited at local craft fairs, starting in the 1980s. However, he and some other stallholders did not believe these fairs were particularly well organised so he decided to organise his own fairs. His first fair was at the Edinburgh Assembly Rooms in the New Town district of Edinburgh. Green says that location is critically important for a craft market and that the Assembly Rooms is a well-known venue with good transport links. The venue has the virtue of attracting passing trade whilst also being a well-known destination. His business expanded over the years, with craft markets in Glasgow and other Scottish towns being added. He quickly found that it is also crucial to get the timing right; consumer interest is seasonal so it can be difficult to sustain a regular monthly event, for example. After some years Green found that one further way to grow his business was to organise 'special' marquee-based events – mostly on an annual basis at some of the stunning castles and country houses that Scotland is so well known for.

To monitor attendance and establish a perception of value, Green charges buyers a nominal entry fee. This revenue stream helps to keep down costs to the exhibitors, who have to pay a fee for their pitch. Marketing is approached in a traditional manner through newspaper advertisements, flyers and posters. In recent years he has delegated marketing to key individuals (not agencies), as this is not one of his strengths. In 1983 he approached Neville Chamberlain, the grandson of the famed British prime minister of the same name, who served as minister of St John's Church between 1982 and 1997. Chamberlain was a major influence in raising the visibility of the church community and one of his key ideas was the establishment of a market during the Edinburgh festivals each August. Richard Green accepted this challenge and the original market in 1983 consisted of approximately 40 exhibitors. However, over the past 27 years this has grown to 140 individual artists exhibiting their work. The fair has traditionally been an outdoor event with purpose-built wooden stalls. The church's grounds and part of a disused graveyard are transformed into a labyrinth of gigantic platforms and walkways. Green says 'clearly with this event, its continuing success is down to the unique experience the public have when they visit. I aim to give them a sense of discovery as they walk round. New treasures are to be found round every corner.'

Currently Richard Green hosts nine or ten shows per year, including the St John's Church West End Fair. Green believes the growth of the temporary markets and retail fairs in city-centre settings is being driven by local councils, which are nowadays continually looking for ways to animate the retail core of the city and are prepared therefore to help facilitate these programmes. He states that one of the challenges is the shortage of appropriate locations for these types of programmes to be successful. According to Green, an exhibitor does not require a business license to participate in one of his fairs and therefore the barrier to entry, as compared with a traditional retail location, is very low. Furthermore, Green believes that the emergence of the pop-up store model is related to the temporary retail exhibit such as he has pioneered in Edinburgh and throughout Scotland.

Coda: the temporary sensual retail environment and the pop-up shop/pop-up show phenomenon

The pop-up store is one where a retailer suddenly, and without major fanfare, opens a new retail location. These stores are usually located in a specific site for a limited duration. Major retailers such as Target in the United States have embraced this trend as a way to quickly bring their products to their customers. However, retailers such as hand-made arts and craft exhibitors, as showcased by Richard Green, are also an increasing trend in using pop-up shops to provide a temporary home for their customers to visit and make their purchase. The obvious question is: why would a small local entrepreneur, of the type often associated with the tourist market, choose to use a craft or other event to bring their goods and services to market rather than a retail store front? Perhaps a better way to ask this question is: what is the most efficient and profitable way for them to bring products and services to market in the twenty-first century? According to Alexander Grünsteidl, and our previous adaptation of his model, answering this requires a radical approach. In this respect, Grünsteidl asserts that:

> We have to radically rethink how retail businesses earn revenue when sales margins are declining. The challenge is to design user experiences across offline and online environments that focus on different types of transactional values. As sales margins may decrease due to competition and reduced consumer spending, business models must change. Retailers must embrace the fact that monetary transactions are moving elsewhere, and often at a different time. As a result, retailers are becoming places that manage customer relationships and form and maintain brand awareness. Designing for customer relationships opens exciting opportunities for up-sell, cross-sell, rediscovery, and consumer advocacy. These relationships can be built using insights from lifestyle editors, fashion, hospitality, and community to create continuous experiences across retail channels. In a saturated retail environment, one cannot compete on convenience, price, or relationship alone. To remain relevant, retailers must design experiences that merge the physical and online store.
>
> (Grünsteidl, 2010)

Perhaps the future intersection for this merger or convergence is the live event. The live event has the possible potential to create a temporal sensual retail experience with perhaps a lower threshold of financial risk and potentially a greater opportunity for future sales generation, both online as well as in the retail showroom. Through the live event the retailer may use the often highly sensual environment of the outdoor or multisensory marketplace to create a temporary experience for the customer that may result in a stronger long-term relationship in the future. As businesses compete for customers and the issue of sustainable business development becomes more complex and costly, perhaps the return to the original festival event marketplace may be the missing piece in the puzzle that solves the perpetual retail riddle of how to reach new customers and retain existing ones in the twenty-first-century world of retailing. The ultimate answer may be to deliver dynamic and high-touch experiences through live events that create memories and impressions that encourage customers to find additional touch points such as Internet commerce and even the traditional retail store.

References

Goldblatt, J. (2010) *The Edinburgh Mela Past, Present and Future*, professorial lecture, International Centre for the Study of Planned Events, Queen Margaret University, Edinburgh, Scotland, 24 March.

Grünsteidl, A. (2010) *Four Keys to Surviving the Future of Retail,* 10X10, Method. Online source: http://www.fastcodesign.com/1662269/changing-retail-currency (last accessed 9 November 2011).

Maslow, A. (1943) A theory of human motivation. *Psychological Review* 50, 370–396.

Paige, R. C. and Littrell, M. A. (2003) Tourism activities and shopping preferences. *Journal of Shopping Center Research* 10(2), 7–25.

Pine, J. and Gilmore, J. (2000) *The Experience Economy*. Cambridge, MA: Harvard Business Press.

Sanhusen, R. L. (2000) *International Marketing*. New York: Barrons.

Shopping Centre World (2001) The mall's next mission: trap those tourists. 30(7), 6–9.

Siklos, R. (2007) Savour those curly fries: Planet Hollywood is back again. *New York Times*. Online source: http://www.nytimes.com/2007/09/24/business/24planet.html?pagewanted=2&ref=richardsiklos (last accessed 9 November 2011).

Trip Advisor Blog (2003) Online source: http://blog.compete.com/2008/07/03/tripadvisor-reviews-travel/ (last accessed 3 July 2008).

4 Retail tourists as co-creators of tourist retail place and space

Charles McIntyre

Introduction

The primary objective of this chapter is to consider space and place in light of the formations and varieties of retail experience that could attract and/or result from tourist activity. The place and space content comes from the consideration of retail formation studies within three key areas: (1) macro-environmental, socio-geographical theories of retail spatial organisation, (2) meta-level studies into various retail environment characteristics and effects upon consumers' experience, including shopping street and mall studies, and (3) micro-environmental concepts concerning the consumer effects of intra-store atmospherics and design. As the orientation of Part I of this book concerns retail formations, this chapter will predominantly focus upon the first two of these areas, examining macro and meta aspects of tourist retail, although it touches from time to time on some relevant micro-environmental issues. The overall positive outlook on the individually beneficial, or 'healthy', aspects of tourist retail will hopefully add perspective to elements in other chapters, including helping to frame some of the questions and issues to arise in Part II, on 'formats'.

Tourist retail: form and function – beyond the souvenir!

Retail function as an increasing part of the tourist experience

There has been a conceptual shift in recent times away from thinking of shopping activity as only a functional purchase of tangible objects, and towards a significant human need of personal satisfaction and development (Baker, 2000; Clarke, 2003; Falk and Campbell, 1997; Miller, 1998; Miller *et al.*, 1998; Stobart, 2008; Wrigley and Lowe, 2002). This movement partly stems from the hedonistic characterisation of fantasies, fun, feelings and spatial play within modern consumption theory, including retail formations acting as festival marketplaces (Holbrook and Hirschman, 1982; Langman, 1992; Maclaran *et al.*, 1999). The orientation towards retail events as sensory and psychological experiences of 'being', rather than only concerning the procuring or 'having' of products (Fromm, 1978), would seem eminently applicable when considering tourist behaviours. For tourist shoppers, such a *cultural essentialist* standpoint of shopping activity involving looking for elements of meaning and self-identity, fun, sociality, display and spectacle would seem to make sense in a holiday environment – even although functional shopping motivations may be considered to contribute more as everyday, economically essentialist or pluralist shopping motives (Williams, 2002).

A review of past tourist retail literature shows a tendency towards a focus upon what may be considered as essentially functional souvenir products and their relative authenticity, particularly concerning the study of local arts and crafts as worthwhile socio-cultural artefacts or keepsakes to take back from, and represent or objectify, the holiday experience (Evans, 1999; Gordon, 1986; Hitchcock and Teague, 2000; Littrell, 1990; Littrell *et al.*, 1991, 1993, 1994). This would possibly concur with a tourist concept of 'authentic' cultural experiences, with gift shops and souvenirs providing only 'add-on' consumption opportunities. Concerning the role of souvenirs and their relation to visitor experiences, Weaver (2007) has focused upon Belk and colleagues' (1989) concept of sacred and profane purchases: the products being sacred or iconic relics. Thus their inherent value is linked to memory-embodied images, experiences or logos, linked to the pilgrimage treasures associated with the limited travels of past, pre-industrial times (Houlihan, 2000).

In an experiential study on museum visits and their shops (Falk and Dierking, 1992), Weaver placed tourist retail as the finale of a socio-cultural leisure visit. This agrees with ideas of tourist consumption processes being around the accrual and collection of mementos, symbols and memorabilia products to take back home, purchased towards the end of the experience that they represent (Baker *et al.*, 2006; Belk, 1997; Csikszentmihayli and Rochberg-Halton, 1981). A focus on holiday shopping as a process of tangible gift or personal souvenir collecting in a consumer culture (Belk *at al.*, 1991), however, limits tourist retail within a restricted form of consumption: namely the purchase of products that only reflect upon or remind of another (and meaningful) experience in the holiday space, as opposed to being part of a significant tourist experience as an activity in itself. The souvenir tourist retail perspective links to collecting behaviours, involving 'holiness transfer' of representative product attributes that embody emotions of place and experience that have also, at times, been related to more domestically located, yet highly experiential and non-everyday, leisure shop visits, such as Niketown purchases (Sherry, 1998).

This view of tourist retail as a secondary experience, relating to the primary holiday experience domain only through embodied, memory-jogging, product characteristics (the classic souvenir featuring place images and names), would seem to conflict with data that show that shopping is a major – if not *the* major – activity of people in holiday environments, implying that retail places, spaces and activities are in themselves important to the tourist experience and not subsidiary to it, and may even be the main motivation or attractive 'magnet' for travel to a location. The centrality of retail to the tourist experience has been particularly clearly demonstrated in studies within the American travel industry (see Table 4.1). Dealing with both domestic and foreign tourist holiday activities of choice,

Table 4.1 Activities undertaken by tourists, USA 2000, in % of person trips: showing shopping in the pole position

Domestic tourists	*%*	*International tourists*	*%*
Shopping	33	Shopping	87
Outdoor activities	17	Dining in restaurants	84
Historical/museums	14	Sightseeing in cities	43
Beach	10	Theme/amusement park	31
Cultural event/festival	10	Visiting historic sites	31
National/state park	10	Visiting small towns	28
Theme/amusement park	9	Water sports/sunbathing	23
Nightlife/dancing	7	Touring the countryside	21
Gambling	8	Art gallery or museum	20
Sports events	6	National parks	20
Golf/tennis/skiing	4		

Source: TIAA (2001, cited Timothy, 2005).

shopping generally appears at the top, or next to top, stated activity of choice, even in locations where one would not expect this to be so, such as the gambling hot-spot of Las Vegas or skiing resorts (Beck, 1998; Matheusik, 2001; TIAA, 2001: Timothy, 2005).

In recent years, the souvenir *product* (souvenir) emphasis has begun to switch towards the tourist retail *process* as being a cultural experience in itself, in line with mainstream retail theory upon leisure shopping, ascribing a heightened importance for tourists to the interpersonal and experiential elements of the exchange encounter (Kim and Littrell, 2001; Littrell, 1996; Yu and Littrell, 2003, 2005). This tends more towards psychogeographical and *flâneur* aspects of leisure retail activity (Benjamin, 1973, 1999: Debord, 1958) – this involving not just product selection and purchase, but also the looking at objects and promenading: 'consumers' (or more properly 'visitors') going 'out of their way (*se déplacer*) to look at displays of the marvels of modern industrial production' as noted historically at the birth of the great Parisian department store boom – in respect of which it was stated that there was 'nothing obviously functional in a tourist trip' (Bowlby, 1985: 1).

Modern shopping is a much more socially widespread leisure and entertainment activity than that of past privileged sectors of society. So from a middle-class and bourgeois *spectacle de la merchandise* within *La Société du spectacle* (Debord, 2009), retail spaces can now seen as being of importance to the increased leisure times available across much of society, including participation in (and possibly travel motivations for) the tourist experience. Thus retail can be seen as contributing widely to the experiential attractions of tourist place and space.

Tourist retail formations: cities, resorts and built environments

Within service experience design, one of the formative, building-block space staging frameworks is that of Langeard and colleagues' (1981) servuction model. A relatively recent application of this model to city space design can be seen in Figure 4.1 to include all the elements that could be assumed to be present and relevant in any tourist area, not only city-centre or city-break ones (Warnaby and Davies, 1997).

In the field of geo-economics, Williams (1997) has made the case for leisure shopping environments as effective economic magnets, not necessarily based upon city-centre magnitudes, as they are able to attract visitors over extremely wide areas, including across regional and country border divides. To illustrate this he used the examples of built 'mega-malls', such as Gateshead MetroCentre (which included the entertainment of an indoor fun fair) and cross-border shopping trips into France from the UK in the form of 'booze cruises' involving specially set-up border malls and mega-outlets (with a day-trip to reach them). Such examples showed the place-enhancing effects of retail developments as tourist attractions, with social as well as economic pulling power making the locality more attractive overall (both to visit and to live in). West Edmonton Mall in Calgary has also often been quoted as having this 'super-gravitational' pull for tourists, with a heightened socio-economic attractiveness and an ongoing place development effect (Butler, 1991; Shields, 1989). All these examples show retail spaces as attractive leisure spaces that inherently contribute to place attractiveness for tourists. They do not just feature shopping as a secondary activity or

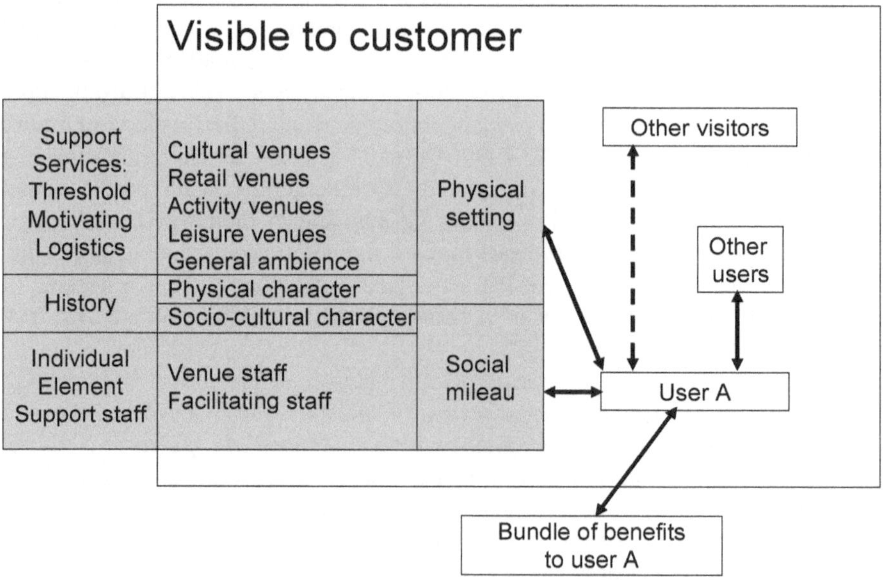

Figure 4.1 The city servuction model (source: Warnaby and Davies, 1997).

by-product of primary, non-retail tourism/leisure environments. The focus here is primarily upon retail attractions as large, concentrated retail agglomerations.

Looking at tourist retail within a small seaside resort, Charles Stansfield Jr (Stansfield, 1969), identified the spread of more dispersed and varied retail formations that appear, not just as a concentrated, central business district (CBD), but also in localised concentrations of luxury goods in both a recreational business district (RBD) at a prime tourist space, as well as scattered 'isolated nodes' of specialist retail individual outlets and clusters. These dispersed luxury-good retail outlets appear in almost a reversal of Christaller's (1966 [1933]) central place theory of retail, in that lower population areas seem to feature luxury or 'higher-order' goods. The non-central resort retail spaces can generally be seen from Stansfield's work (see Figure 4.2) to follow transport routes into and around various natural attractions of the resort.

The RBD is an interesting concept related to a seaside pedestrian boardwalk, assumed to have originated in the USA from initial seaside incursion by rail. This was as opposed to more widespread incursions of seaside roads in the UK, with road traffic necessitating the building of boardwalks over the sea as piers. The visitors in tourist locations from the earliest times of mass travel would be expected to promenade, and explore the environment by foot, in a form of continuous *dérive* (Debord, 1958).

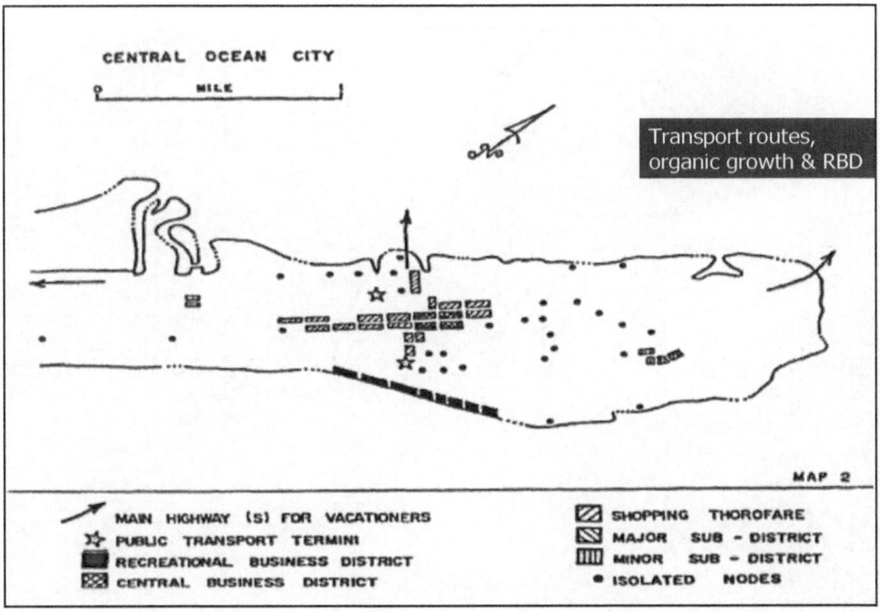

Figure 4.2 Excerpt from Stansfield (1969) showing the presence of a recreational business district (RBD) and isolated, luxury retailing nodes set apart from the local central business district (CBD), in relation to various transport routes and natural beauty/tourist activity spots.

In a small-scale study of a tourist street in a holiday town on the Mediterranean island of Crete in 2009 (Harris and McIntyre, 2011) an audit of the types of stores prevalent in the main shopping strip, as shown in both Table 4.2 and Figure 4.3, showed promenade areas of mainly luxury goods, rather than a predominance of downmarket souvenirs (although both feature in the overall selection available). The selection included an extremely high occurrence of upmarket jewellery outlets – high-value but small, personal 'treat' items that may require an extended choice process but can handily fit into return luggage! An interesting aside was that a number of shopkeepers were originally British in origin, taking up a new lifestyle in the form of a 'holiday extension' career – thus the social worlds of tourism and ongoing lifestyle development and choices can be seen to mesh.

Of course large resorts, as well as cities, can feature larger retail formations of a more 'built' than organically arising nature. An example of this is the Atlantis holiday centre in the Arab Emirates, which boasted, in 2008, of the opening of the Dubai Mall as the largest shopping centre in the world with over 600 outlets under one roof. The desire to shop is often a key attraction of many leisure destinations, alongside sporting activities, restaurants, bars, nightclubs, theatres, museums and galleries. In the case of the Dubai Mall the shopping centre included various integral leisure attractions, such as an aquarium/discovery centre, an ice rink, a 22-screen cinema, a fashion catwalk, a large hotel and service apartments – not to mention 160 food and beverage outlets (Medler, 2009). Like many city break

Figure 4.3 Main shopping street in Cretan resort: as audited in Table 4.2 (source: the author).

Table 4.2 Retailer mix audit in the main shopping street of a Mediterranean resort: on the holiday island of Crete, 2009

Retail frontage	*Window/display*	*Window/display*	*Retail frontage*
Café	Takeaway crêpes, snack and ice cream hatch	Jewellery glass displays	Jewellery shop
Female fashion	Dresses on manikins (3)	Sunglasses on spinners	Casual wear
Estate agent	See through to office with property pictures and details	Large menu board and poster pictures of meals	Restaurant to roof garden
Bank	Glass entrance and cash machine on wall	Bags, fridge magnets and sunglasses on spinners[a]	Kitchenware and ornament store
Mini-supermarket	Bottles of spirits, wines and ice cream board	T-shirts, dresses and tops – male and female	Casual wear
Bag/handbag store	Hanging bags, handbags and rucksacks	Glass display of goods and hanging kaftans	Homewares and fabrics
Jewellery store – 'Gold and Silver Workshop'	Deep window with gold and silver jewellery behind glass – bangles and beads on extending stands	Open door, open menu on stand and palm in large colourful earthenware pot	Restaurant
Casual fashion store	Shirts, shorts, T-shirts, tops, dresses and children's wear	Open store with hats, scarves, jewellery and belts hanging in entrance	Fashion accessories
Art gallery	Paintings on street and in window; open door	Hanging display of belts, bags and chains	Fashion accessories
Children's accessories	Belts, bags and other accessories	Bangles, hats and belts; door to high arch store	Upmarket accessories
Car and bike hire	Pictures and pamphlets of local attractions; see through to office; palm outside	Books and CDs in glass cases; door with stairs up; café tables	Upmarket book and CD shop – including café
Souvenir accessory and toy store	Bags, fridge magnets, scarves, toys, wall hangings and bangles[a]	T-shirts, tops and dresses	Casual clothing
Upmarket accessory store	Designer-type bags, scarves and bangles	Bags, hats, scarves, sunglasses, fridge magnets and sandals	Souvenir and accessory store
Jewellery store, titled as 'Workshop'	Deep window with gold and silver jewellery in glass display; display tables visible within	Flat window and glass entrance – all full height with expensive jewellery and watches	Jewellery store, titled as 'Workshop'
Jewellery store	Flat window and entrance – full height with expensive jewellery	Line of designer chairs and tables fronting and to side of entrance	Café/ restaurant

Table 4.2 (continued)

Retail frontage	*Window/display*	*Window/display*	*Retail frontage*
Souvenir and accessories store	Bags, scarves, sunglasses and soft toys – some local logos[a]	Wrought-iron entranceway and metal signage	Museum
Car rental and travel agency	Picture of local attractions, window to office: tree outside	Line of designer chairs and tables fronting windows and entrance	Café/ restaurant

a With 'tourist' style souvenirs apparent, as per local logos.

destinations, Dubai, which is otherwise a beach location and travel hub – the latter like Singapore – now features shopping as one of *the* major attractions of a stay there for many potential visitors.

The tourist shopper: escaping the everyday for healthy, co-creative consumption

Conceptually, Smith and Olsen (2001) have outlined a developmental process of increased 'sophistication' in the modernisation of tourist retail as having taken place in three stages. The first of these is a transition away from so-called 'cheap souvenirs', then moving through a secondary phase of purchasing 'more authentic art forms' related to place characteristics, and finally into a stage of the tourist participating in activities and purchasing behaviour that is more integrative with the destination in an attempt to deepen their knowledge of that destination through consumption. Tourist retail in this latter stage can therefore be considered as an activity serving as a form of educational or (co-)creative consumption (Payne *et al.*, 2008), or 'project of the self', mediated by differential supportive spatial types to encourage *Immersive, Interpretative, Investigative* and *In-the-world (4 'I')* tourist-based, creative retail behaviours (McIntyre, 2009a). The modern aim in tourist consumption can thus be considered to be one of deepening (or heightening), extending or aiding the personal tourist experience *in the place and space of its enactment* (the holiday domain itself) and not, as with souvenir products, to simply purchase place-denoting semiotic or symbolic product attributes and characteristics for display and recall at a later time, in everyday space sometime after return.

In another application of self-concept theory to tourism purchase, Todd (2001), whilst focussing largely on purchase of holiday 'package' elements in everyday environments, nevertheless also assumes a differential, affective, experiential and developmental nature to consumptions when individuals are in the tourist role – commonly assumed to involve a search for a state of 'happiness', as also illustrated in Table 4.3.

As opposed to more cognitively balanced, pluralistic everyday consumer

Table 4.3 The role of affect and experience related to purchasing when on holiday: stated agreement (multiple claims possible) of % individuals in a domestic holiday environment within the UK

Premise	*Agreement (%)*
I spend on holiday because I feel happy/relaxed	81
I feel freer to spend more when on holiday	79
I spend to take the memory of an experience home	68
I make more impulse purchases than at home	67
I spend on holiday to share an experience with others	60
I spend on holiday to add to an experience	49
I spend on holiday to make me feel happy/relaxed	45
I spend on holiday to replace a missed experience	13

Source: McIntyre (2007).

behaviours – a mixture between the economically essentialist and cultural essentialist views (Williams, 2002) – the tourist role can be assumed to be one of heightened affect-based, or mood enhancing purchasing whilst in an emotionally open and culturally experiential domain. Such a culturally essentialist, emotional effect has been well documented in general consumer behaviour theory, related to impulse buying (Holbrook, 1986; Peterson *et al.*, 1984; Rook and Gardner, 1993). The notion of spatial play and the seeking of utopian environments within which the consumer exercises aspirations towards a 'myself-that-could-be' is present in studies of generic shopping and malls, as well as specific escapist tourist locations (Belk, 1996; Goss, 1993), as well as in relation to festival marketplaces (Maclaran *et al.*, 1999). The dimensions of festival marketplaces – generally ascribed to regenerative projects in run-down city locations to make them more attractive to ludic or playful consumers – include spatial contradictions of *past versus present*, *local versus global*, *unique versus mass market retail*, *hedonic versus utilitarian* and *consumption versus production* characteristics for the consumer to play with/amongst. The novelty of such environments would seem to be key to their effectiveness, and indeed, in a study on consumption effects of repeat short-term tourists, Godbey and Graefe (1991) found that on each successive day-tripper revisit to the same non-home environments there was a partial reduction of an originally noted positive and playful, or ludic, effect of increased tourist consumption – as the space became more familiar.

A distinctive or altered tourist state of mind, with a similar dependence on a 'travel life-cycle' position and its diminution according to a process of adaptation to a repeat holiday environment has also been shown by Oppermann (1995). Whilst one would expect tourists to be largely in a positive (happy) affect state, being pleasure-seeking or hedonic in nature, the immersion of an individual within a non-everyday holiday setting has also been postulated to generate negative psychological and physical stress states similar in response to a 'culture shock' effect, although this is able to be overcome where personal tolerance of ambiguity is high (Cort and King, 1979; Furnham and Bochner, 1986; Oberg, 1960).

The idea of the tourist as a more open and emotionally charged, playful and learning consumer in an affect-driven and unfamiliar 'limited risk' space leads to the concept of 'risky consumerism', which is also linked to the more obviously motivated learning risks of adventure-type holidays (Ewert, 1985, 1989; McIntyre, 2007; Walle, 1997). In a relevant study of small retailers near outdoor crag-based attractions, a key finding was that the business's 'interpretation of their customers and their motives' was informed by people's escaping from their daily routine in a leisure pursuit mode, using shop environments as 'an oasis to relive their experiences' with the odd 'bewildered tourist' but most being considered within a broad assumption that 'in a place like this one has to imagine that they are on holiday' (Pioch and Byrom, 2004: 228). The tourist retail mindscape, by extension, can be considered to exist in a state of altered levels of cultural and social risk related to putting oneself 'out-in-the-world' in a similar way to psychological effects proposed by Adler (1975) and Mandel (2003), whereby behavioural moderation is achieved for developmental reasons of the individual through the seeking out of temporal culture shock or 'risk domains'.

Tourism consumer lifecycle modelling systems (McKercher, 2005; Plog, 1974, 2001) generally relate to various levels of risk tolerance or aversion in different consumers, with some being, no doubt, more open to seeking playful or exploratory personality states than others. The is relevant to a tourist mindscape, including perhaps Gabriel and Lang's (1995) *chooser*, *explorer* and *identity-seeker* types. Other segmentation criteria for differential travel consumers have included sociological, experiential and existential exploration, with evaluation of the self facilitated by social interaction and education, or a dualistic typology separating tourists into those who wish to escape and 'get away from it all' and those primarily concerned with *ego-enhancement* (Cohen, 1979; Crompton, 1979; Dann, 1977). All still assume a different tourist mindscape from that of their everyday environment while on holiday. This idea of self-construction (and self-exploration) as a motivator for immersion in a non-everyday holiday domain fits with postmodern theory of the emergence of identity through situational choices involving a pluralisation of lifeworlds in which the individual negotiates multiple and contradictory identities as they traverse different public and private spheres, placing mediated experience at the centre of social life (Giddens, 1991; Slater, 1997).

In the consideration of recreational or hedonic retail as opposed to the simple acquisition of goods, a common assumption is that shopping is mainly a female activity. The profusion of female fashions and jewellery retail outlets in small resorts, as previously noted, would seem to back this up. However, if we are assuming the tourist role to involve both genders, then we can perhaps consider classic retail literature about the existence, or non-existence, of the *flâneur* or *flâneuse*: the detached, pleasure-seeking strollers hypothesised on the nineteenth-century streets and onwards as loiterers, frittering away time; either as a dandyesque male or females who were 'just looking' or 'shopping around' rather than 'shopping for things' (Benjamin, 1973; Bowlby, 1985; Clarke, 2003; Falk and Campbell, 1997; Shields, 1994; Tester, 1994; Vidler, 1993; Wilson, 1995). As examples of potential male *flâneur* behaviours, consideration could be given either to the regency male dandy or their modern metrosexual alternative in Table 4.4, and one may wonder whether the male in a tourist role may not also display more of these archetypal features, given the extended leisure time and opportunities for 'promenading', personal development and display available on holidays.

It remains debatable whether such solely diversionary creatures as *flâneurs* or *flâneuses* exist in generic modern retail spheres, as most everyday shoppers would surely at least claim some level of economic and acquisitive purpose for their shopping trips; but tourist retail – where people act as tourists in 'bathing in' or 'soaking up' the environment – is surely the one role in which people could truly act out such 'risky' roles? A personal instance illustrating a different tourist role

Table 4.4 Comparison of the features of the classic male 'dandy' at the turn of the nineteenth century and modern 'metrosexual' characteristics: demonstrating possible continuing male proclivities for promenading that could be as relevant to male tourist retail behaviours as to female shopping proclivities whilst on holiday

Dandy	*Metrosexual*
'Don Juan' characteristics	Caring, female characteristics
Sequential womanisers	Largely monogamous
Mixture of high-life/low-life 'manly' activities (racing, gambling, etc.)	Settled home-lover, comfortable in female company
Clothing and actions not to openly revolt against the established order, but rather to play with conventionalities: fashion as a means to an end	Can be comfortable in female leisurewear and accessories (the wrap, jewellery, perfume); change in gender conventions: fashion as end in itself
Not a feminine 'fop' – favours dark colours and understatement: 'any element of arrogance confined to the perfection of cut' (D'Aurevilly, cited in Burnett, 1983)	Female characteristics: result of the levelling of gender activities and blurring of roles in the workplace and the home – more feminine in display
Springs from the unending struggle between propriety and boredom – a male 'club' with affectations of the intellectual aesthetes	Springs from economic re-organisation away from hunter-gatherer, lo-tech manufacturer/worker and towards hi-tech services/manager
A construct of the leisured classes, pre-Veblen?	A construct of female emancipation
Maintaining different shopping motivations and attraction/avoidance factors from those of females (the predatory male?)	Enacted by young males integrating fashion and music shopping: clothes shopping motivations and attractions related to shopping as a pleasurable activity

Sources: Burnett (1983) and the author.

view of a shopping strip was a recent trip I made into the centre of Bournemouth. I was accompanying some relations who were on holiday in the area and by the end of our walk was firmly in a tourist role alongside them. At one point, in the main shopping street, I looked up above the shop fronts and noticed some very 1930s art deco effects above the common glass-and-plastic store fronts and identified where a cinema had obviously been in the past. Yet after 14 years of living in the locality I looked up in the 'vertical' fashion of a casual observer, tourist or *flâneur*, only when I was placed in a tourist role. This substitution of the horizontal for the vertical gaze is a proposed variance of view when in a tourist role, along with an increased 'dandyesque' propensity to be voyeuristically looked at as well as to look for in a 'hunters gaze' scopic regime (Falk, 1997: 182–3). This extended tourist gaze (Urry, 1995) can be taken as a result of moving from the normal, everyday screening of diverse sensory inputs in a defence reaction, to avoid neurasthenia/nervous exhaustion by the development of a blasé attitude (Beard, 1869; Simmel, 1950). Personally, I was not aware of such precise tourist gaze distinctions at the time of my 'tourist role' shopping trip, so it was later interesting to me, upon reflection, that it was only when I was in that role that I appreciated distinct, vertical, culturally diverse elements of my normal everyday shopping environment, resting my gaze in a hitherto unknown fashion.

As opposed to the traditional approach of souvenir product value inherent in *hunting and having* things, be they for status, self-extension or memory purposes, should the tourist therefore not be more beneficially considered as a postmodern, playful or risky consumer? The focus is then shifted from holiday purchase products as obvious, rather kitsch keepsakes for display as proof of having visited a place towards a more meaningful concept of tourist retail process allowing a more broadly categorised meaningful socio-cultural contact with a locality – a cultural immersion or 'bathe' in a type of restful and leisured scopic regime, as has been associated with museums and galleries as well as in tourist shopping streets (Falk, 1997; McIntyre, 2007, 2009b). This leads us to consider how the spatial service characteristics of the tourist retail domain may be supported, represented or conceptualised as co-creative environments.

Retail space and tourist place: forms and formations

Frameworks for retail public realm organisation: historical development

Both Shields (1989, 1992) and Zukin (1991) have noted that an accelerated development of a lifestyle shopping orientation in the post-1980s western world (featuring consumption of time as well as services and products) has taken place in new, socially controlling spatial forms which synergise leisure and consumption activity. Using Zukin's term, such spatially constructed landscapes of power are often typified by purpose-built mega-malls and theme parks. Developments in international mass tourism design, such as the Dubai Mall, increasingly incorporate shopping as a major visible part of the holiday domain and thus raise the question of how socially controlling (or socially controlled) retail spatial forms are within tourist locations. This question, however, seems to stem from a 'top-down', non-authentic (and unhealthy), commercial culture approximation of tourist retail activity. If we are aiming at not restricting our idea of tourist retail only to the imposition of souvenir outlets and commercial exploitation at tourist, traveller and visitor locations (including duty-free and airport retailing), but instead examining it from a consumer, 'bottom-up' experiential view being a more central part of the holiday experience, what then is the nature of tourist retail in terms of its key characteristics of place and space to support the desired tourist motivations, experience and outcomes?

At a micro level, within company-controlled retail environmental spaces, spatial effects upon individual consumers have been based upon established, operational facets of ambient factor atmospherics (Kotler, 1973; McGoldrick, 2002), service measurement structures, such as SERVQUAL (Parasuraman *et al.*, 1985, 1988), and place-marketing features involved in a servicescape (Bitner, 1992). These frameworks consist largely of functional lists of contributing processes and attributes to consider in designing a retail unit (or units). In attempting to study retail public space and place holistically from a consumer-led, leisure-setting attractiveness orientation, as we are drawn to with holiday environments, we need to consider broader meta- and macro-organisational frameworks, as cited in town/city centre and shopping mall studies (either built or organically derived) and socio-economic place development study. This is in order to determine how retail can contribute to a sense of a distinct place-based experience and place identity development.

Macro-level tourist place development

In geographical, socio-economic place development theory, Christaller's (1966 [1933]) 'central place' model of retailing spatial organisation proposed that 'higher-order' retail (of non-essentials) would essentially form only within high-density population locations, such as large regional towns and cities. Smaller population areas, therefore, should have only 'lower-order' (essential) retail outlets. Subsequently there was a general acceptance of a hierarchy of retail space developments – from functional essentials to luxurious non-essentials – based upon the 'threshold of a good' theory (Berry and Garrison, 1958a,b), the 'law of retail gravitation' theory/ 'point of indifference' theory (Reilly, 1929, 1931) or the 'law of shopper attraction' (Huff, 1965). These traditional retail organisational forces, including those of Losch (1954), are all based largely on geographical population density and spread affecting a local economies' abilities to be able to support a mix of retail varieties, which can be broadly divided into regular 'essentials' and irregular 'non-essentials', or luxury/leisure products and services.

Large-scale tourism upsets this classic theory, with an influx of non-residents to a place, being intent upon having non-everyday, leisure experiences and interactions, even although the holiday location may still not be of city dimensions overall. Changes in transport infrastructures as well as increased consumerism and leisure time patterns thus at least partially displace central place theory, as we have seen in small-resort studies such as that of Stansfield (1969). These effects in the postmodern world do not just concern what is generally accepted as 'tourism', if we accept that term as relating only to stays of over three days. In fact steadily increasing mobility and 'day tourism' over the last 50 years can be seen to also have upset the first-order/second-order assumptions as people have become more willing to travel for essential products in attractively leisured environments such as in shopping malls. This development has contributed, many say, to the 'death' of many small-town – or even city – high streets and the creation of disadvantaged ghettos for those with poorer mobility. In the UK, these factors have resulted in government policy-makers at times switching their planning regulation positions relating to an on-going in-town/out-of-town debate (Jones and Hillier, 2000).

Tourists have come, over the years, to feature in such debates in as much as they concern town and city-centre locations becoming less attractive to the visitor; this has promoted a resurgence of mixed shopping and leisure developments in town and city centres and planned renewal of attractive urban spaces, often specifically with tourists in mind, although it must be remembered that out-of-town developments also promote regional tourism (Williams, 1997).

Nevertheless, although city centres can still exert a pull effect on travellers from other regions and countries, as a concentrated magnet of retail activity serving a 'threshold' indigenous population, a tourism retail experience implies a varied socio-cultural form of structure to sufficiently enhance a place's 'magnetic' power, effectively 'putting on a show' in terms of the experiential and 'experience economy' literature (Fisk *et al.*, 2007; Grove and Fisk, 1997; Pine and Gilmore, 1999). The same leisure retail considerations need to be assimilated into variously populated tourist resort areas, if retail is seen to be a desired element in the tourist place experience in general.

Meta level tourist space effects: leisure and healthy biophilic response

> . . . a piece of nature in the most intimate sense . . . this profusion of eccentricities, this dream in masonry and living rock, is not a drop-scene in a theatre, but a city in the world of every-day reality.
>
> Robert Louis Stevenson (1879) on Edinburgh

The organic development of leisure retail alongside, and in view of (or giving view to) naturally pleasing features, as sought by tourists, follows strongly upon environmental psychology findings concerning human tendencies towards certain natural and otherwise biologically appealing, or *biophilic*, forms. This has led to schools of biomorphic and zoomorphic architecture, in both natural and built public realm environments, aiming to develop pleasing and preferential spatial forms and environmental qualities of biologically pleasing natural mimicry, allusion and illusion to create 'healthy' and socially beneficial public spaces (Ulrich, 1981, 1983, 1993; Ulrich *et al.*, 1991; O. E. Wilson, 1984; Yannick, 2007).

The concept of a biophilic affective, stress-reducing response and preference towards natural forms and landscape elements is used in the design of modern shopping malls, but can be assumed to have historically been a large influence upon creating many other organically derived tourist space and place identities. It would seem obvious that we would tend towards biologically (and subconsciously psychologically) pleasing environments. Thus the grand city design and reconstruction projects of previous ages, such as those of Paris and Barcelona or Princes Street in Edinburgh, where retail streets blend into natural and architecturally pleasing features – tree-lined avenues, monuments, pleasing buildings, gardens, even castles or crags – can be seen to have a biophilic affinity in common with less urban locations, such as the seaside town boulevard.

Not only large-scale, retail-related city development over time can be seen to be biologically pleasing, but so may be the appeal of the small-scale 'lane' retail environments of Covent Garden in London, Bath, Brighton and any number of partly preserved old-world town and cityscapes. Thus, biophilic landscape characteristics of a specific location can help to define the spatial characteristics and spread of retail concentrations, 'clusters' and niche dispersions of outlets for tourists and, vice versa, biophilic retail agglomerations can enhance the place characteristics in a pleasing fashion to enhance tourist place attractiveness. They can also be considered to be, in themselves, festival marketplaces, with many of the spatially playful, postmodern contradictions and characteristics inherent within that concept (Maclaran *et al.*, 1999).

In analysis of optimal tourist place attractiveness, place branding has grown as a concept to help classify key attributes for attractive tourist resorts, cities, regions and even countries as in 'Brand America' (Anholt and Hildreth, 2004). Hankinson (2004, 2005) has attempted to establish such destination-branding concept characteristics for both general and business tourists, using repertory grid analysis of various location factors, including market towns, historic centres, new towns, seaside resorts, ports and commercial centres. These give various clusters of key desirable attributes divided into 'organic' and 'induced' place image factors, the former including the highly rated ones of history, heritage and culture. In this work, the induced image factor cluster of 'activities and facilities' gave the greatest perceived ratings, being described as encompassing 'good shopping'; these were followed by the two organic clusters of 'history, heritage and culture' and 'ambience/character of the environment'. This again denotes tourist retail spaces as a mixture of social, cultural and economic opportunities to give attractiveness of place, with the so-called 'induced' factor of retail attractions rating potentially higher than the more 'organic' place history and ambience characteristics.

A long list of preferred space characteristics in urban environments for more general social-space attractiveness, akin to biophilic health studies, has been built up by some specific retail geographical work. Here, findings about consumer preferences when visiting shopping environments include such consciously and subconsciously pleasing aspects as *spaciousness* as well as others of *refuge*, *coherence*, *legibility*, *complexity*, *mystery*, *typicality*, *nature* and *age* (Herzog, 1989). In this work the factor of *coherence* (how well a scene 'hangs together') along with those of *mystery* (the promise of more to be seen if one immerses oneself further) and *nature* (elements of wild or tended natural environment present) were the most significant preferences for urban spaces, including retail elements. In a later study by Uzzell (1995) in Guildford in southern England, sensory-physical *comfort* and *proxemic environment* (sufficient non-invaded personal spaciousness) were more preferred by shoppers than a defined *retail environment* (meaning, in this case, the actual provision of *shop variety*). So the most pleasing aspects of the retail place is seen to be defined not by the functional aspect of the variety of shop provision, but rather by space characteristics surrounding whatever retail was provided, and this in public spaces that would probably be only tentatively considered as tourist retail spaces by many. A summary of these urban spatial science preferences is given in Table 4.5.

Considering the effects of tourist retail and the future of shopping

The benefits of still going out in-the-world: 'active' retail and going shopping

Where does all this consideration of the attractiveness and characteristics of public and retail spaces leave us in considering the form and function of tourist shopping? For a start, we have conceded that a leisure-time 'day out', short break or even just 'going out' into public spaces often involves retail opportunities; sometimes apparently these are central and motivational to an outing (retail

Table 4.5 Various attributes preferred in urban spaces by the visiting public

Comfort[a]	Thermal, acoustic, luminary
Spaciousness[a]	Non-invaded personal space; feeling of depth: long way to reach furthest point
Refuge	Space provides opportunity for being hidden
Coherence[b]	How well the scene 'hangs together'
Legibility	Ease of navigation within the depicted environment
Complexity	How many elements of different kinds: going-on and to look at
Mystery[b]	Promises more to be seen if immerse further
Typicality	Extent scene representative example of its class
Nature[b]	Elements of 'natural' environment present – wild or tended
Age	Familiarity and dependability characteristics of having been part of a long-term environment or aspects of accepted modernism
Retail provision	Retail offers or 'retail environment'

Sources: Herzog (1989) and Uzzell (1995).

Notes

a Most significant according to Uzzell.

b Most significant according to Herzog.

tourism) and on other occasions they may just be part of a socio-cultural and economic event when in the role, and state of mind, of a tourist (tourist retail). Economic exchange, as well as socio-cultural exchange, would seem to be within the postmodern 'going out' event, whether the prime aim of the trip is shopping or not, and is further related to general leisure trips. Of course in the Internet age, even stay-at-home leisure involves shopping, albeit of a more passive, virtual nature; but tourist retail, by its very nature, involves going out. A hypothetical mix of tangible and intangible consumptions related to a continuum of various 'going out' events away from 'stay-at-home' virtual or passive leisure is illustrated in Figure 4.4 as a progression of physical, socio-cultural consumption forms that decrease when replaced by virtual media consumption. Tourist retail is a physical socio-cultural event which fulfils more needs than are associated with basic purchasing when not being restricted to souvenir shopping.

We could, of course, insert the word 'experience' in any of the spaces in Figure 4.4, rather than consumption. People are perhaps more comfortable using this word in some of these realms. Therefore, in moving from the purely home dimension towards the holiday one, we are potentially increasing *active experience* at the expense of *passive consumption.*

This positive view of tourist retail is possibly contrary to Urry's (1995) tourism concept that we 'consume' places (and spaces) and effectively use them up or wear them out in a consumption process. It is also contrary to many people's assumptions that retail (or any commercialisation aspect) of socio-cultural events, places, spaces or destinations adds anything other than a negative dimension. It may, however, be more correct to say that we 'consume' holidays when we consider them on the web and buy the travel package? There is definitely an environmentally damaging process in buying air travel and hotel space. That

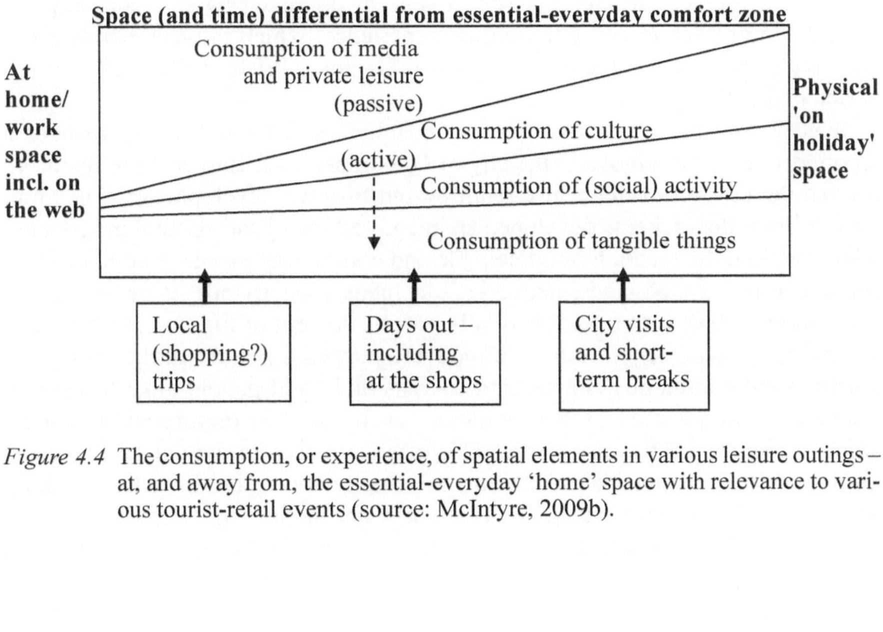

Figure 4.4 The consumption, or experience, of spatial elements in various leisure outings – at, and away from, the essential-everyday 'home' space with relevance to various tourist-retail events (source: McIntyre, 2009b).

said, physical spaces can no doubt be spoilt by too much of a retail hard-sell orientation, overdevelopment or inappropriate forms of commercialisation. Still, a positive orientation to tourism retail maintains that the transformation processes of a holiday for most people, involving consumption processes as part of the experience package, are not necessarily damaging to the visit's socio-cultural elements if planned better to immerse the self in a locality, varied spaces and places and their points of difference, peoples, objects and surrounding environments.

On the contrary, if there is a curative process in taking a holiday derived from escaping our rationally irrational 'iron prison' of increasing generalised consumption in our everyday world, this must involve immersing ourselves in the sought-after pleasing spatial dimensions of a suitable holiday space, extending socio-cultural benefits to all. It is up to the location's planners, local people and businessmen, including retailers, to make sure that the local offer is not degraded through chasing pure consumption but is appended to pleasing and sustaining events and attractions. So museums, art galleries, local festivals and crafts, for instance, do not have to be self-financed by either entrance fees or retail/souvenir takings, as they attract and 'bleed' consumption and local economy benefits to the surrounding locality, in both the short and long term. Furthermore, people seem to like and want buying opportunities – not just in tourist events, but whenever they 'go out'.

There is potentially a curative and stress-relieving purpose, as well as economic benefit, to 'day-out' shopping in affectively pleasing spaces related to increases in active versus passive behaviours, involving increased physical, social and cultural consumption along with that of exchanged tangible goods and services. This is opposed to passive consumption in the home which in our technologically driven modern consumer society is heavily dominated by electronic media and 'staying in'. If we accept that cultural and social activity is inherently more 'experiential' by being active in spaces beyond the individual's personal, passive 'comfort zone', then tourists are moving from a state of dominant passive consumption towards one of active consumption, or experience, which is theoretically more affectively pleasing, curative and stress-relieving (Ulrich, 1981, 1983, 1993; Ulrich *et al.*, 1991).

It is interesting, as an example of 'healthy' tourist retail space, to note a reportedly successful move in the city of Granollers (near Barcelona in Spain) to reverse the erosion of the centre retail by out-of-town developments. The Gran Centre Granollers scheme developed an integrated social and cultural programme related around the creation of humanistic and community events, entertainments, and social-hub zoned areas, networks and 'pedestrian islands' (Coca-Stefaniak and Parker, 2005). Conceptually, relating to the content of Figure 4.4, they have managed, it would seem, to have effectively pushed a pointer further along the tourist–retail continuum to appeal to tourists and local people alike to prevent economic 'leakage' out of town for either novelty or other reasons and provide a human 'magnet' for the city centre. This offers a reason to get out of the house, away from the computer terminal, and be socially and culturally active, making the space and place more attractive as a tourist destination. In the same way, who has not been to an attractive holiday location without having to admit afterwards that the main meaningful personal contacts they had with the local people during their visit, and possibly their main contribution towards those people's economic betterment, was through visiting local shops and bazaars?

Final thoughts: tourist retail as an escape from the everyday in respect of third place and flow theory

In considering human recreational needs, retail spaces, as with other leisure-time places such as public houses, cafés or health clubs, have been theorised as potentially serving as a required social 'third place' – neither work nor home – deemed necessary and supporting for ongoing personal human development, satisfaction and the pursuit of happiness (Kent, 2007; Mikunda, 2004; Oldenburg and Brissett, 1982). For these spaces to be effective, one assumes that they must serve as a supportive, long-term bridges to the achievement of a sought-after personal long-term balanced health or happiness state. In the western, developed world, holidays too have been thought as being required to ensure ongoing health and happiness, by de-stressing and helping the individual to cope better with the everyday pressures of home and work, having come back from a 'break' refreshed and revitalised. In this way, holidays continue to be advised for those in ill health (Hunter-Jones, 2003).

'Retail therapy' is a phrase that has seen increasing general usage by the general public in recent times, although few health specialists would claim, for retail activity, a discernible associated beneficial healthy psychological effect as they have for holiday taking. In fact retail activities are more likely, in the health literature, to be considered for their potentially harmful psychological effects such as compulsive or addictive consumer behaviours (Baker, 2000). Yet there has been an acceptance of retail as a major pleasurable leisure activity for many, as seen in the generally developing integrated leisure and retail mix in most social gathering places. This trend has been particularly obvious in destination shopping malls and 'supermalls' since the late 1980s with their cinema complexes, food courts and sports activities. We have noted that retail attractions within holiday attractions can be of great importance to visitors – to the point where they may outstrip other cultural attractions for some in major cities (such as can be seen in the practice of December shopping tourism, for instance to New York or in German Christmas markets). By these developments, we can see increasing evidence of integration of the retail and tourist domains of study, particularly relevant to theories of experience spaces within a leisure economy, with consumers in their everyday life space seeking a form of personal interactional value.

Tourism value is obviously largely about immersion in socio-cultural place, and many past retail studies have been about space from a socio-economic viewpoint. It would seem now that we are seeking a combination of orientations in tourist retail spatial study – towards more of a visitor-sought socio-cultural economic immersion process in space and place. The holiday consumption state is readily associated with the concept of seeking to attain happiness through the holiday situational in a transitional process away from the everyday. In terms of growing needs for leisure and entertainment within a heavily mediated society, there has been a developing literature strand concerned with the pursuit of 'flow' in experiences as a source of personal meaning and happiness (Csikszentmihayli, 1975, 1999; Nettle, 2005; Seligman, 2002). The basic flow model hypothesises a seeking after increasing experiential challenge (or risk) realms throughout learning life processes, balanced by a corresponding increase in life-skills and ability to cope. In everyday domains it may be that the increased risk becomes very predictive and therefore could lead to boredom, affecting ongoing positive development, as illustrated in Figure 4.5.

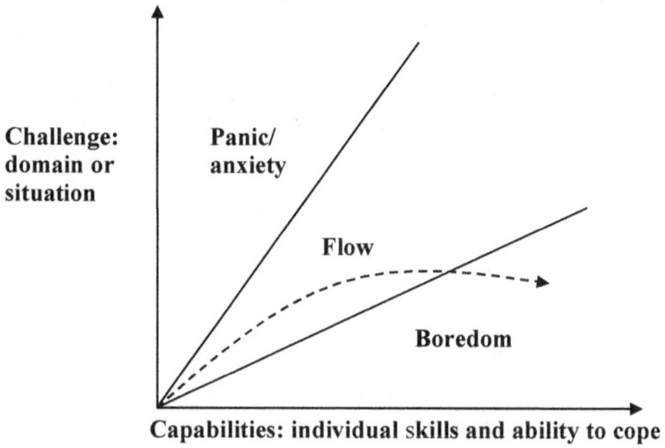

Figure 4.5 Potential life-flow outcome of constant everyday situation: adapted from Csikszentmihayli (1975, 1999); flow as an optimum satisfaction model.

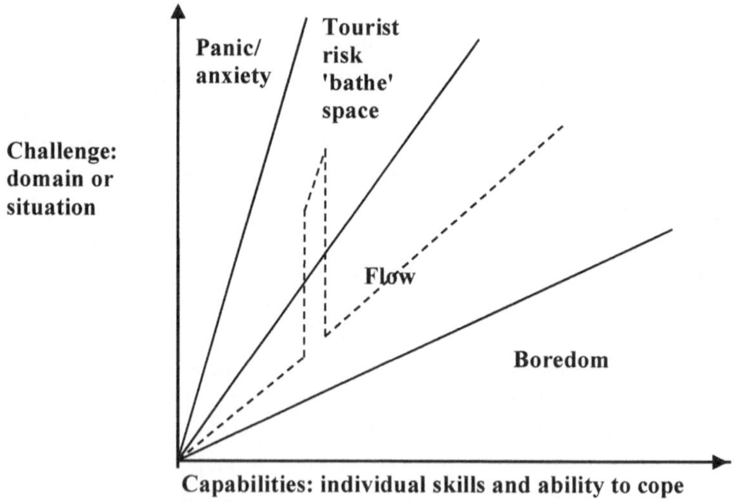

Figure 4.6 Potential life-flow outcome of temporal 'bathe' in tourist-space relative to constant everyday situation.

Taking a holiday could have a beneficial 'bathe' affect if the visitor deliberately entering a spatially higher realm of risk than normal, giving a temporarily higher risk domain to stimulate the tourist and allay boredom in the ongoing everyday, as illustrated in Figure 4.6. In the author's own tourist and leisure retail studies (McIntyre, 2007, 2008, 2009a, 2009b) the notion of 'risky consumerism' has been put forward as a main tourist retail orientation, also falling in with ideas of kinds of 'creative' consumption and socio-cultural 'bathing spaces' for various consumer activities that are deemed important to personal education, development and well-being. Tourist retail has been proposed as involving a high proclivity to spend experientially on many services and products in a 'risky' or 'playful' consumption' manner; this occurs outside normal restrictions relative to a generally positive affective state and developmental and educational satisfactions.

In contrast to a positivist, learning orientation towards holiday consumption, some conceptual frameworks such as Pearce's (1982) non-involvement tourist model and Urry's (1995) 'tourist gaze' appear to offer a more negative view of the tourism experience, as can also be seen in views on overcommercialised retail and socio-cultural interactions, such as are evident in exploitative tourist destinations with 'tacky' souvenir shops and inauthentic, constructed experiences. The alternative, positive developmental learning and orientation, as evident in Fennell and Butler's (2003) human ecological approach to tourism interactions, can help envisage tourists as healthily 'bathing in them' as part of an overall human learning process similar to a process that can be imagined in other leisure time pursuits that involve cultural-learning organisations such as museums and art galleries (McIntyre, 2008, 2009b) – a favoured activity when on holiday, planning days out or escorting visitors holidaying in the home environment. Such an apparently obvious connection becomes intriguing when it is considered that many large retail institutions such as Galleries Lafayette in Paris and major malls such as West Edmonton Mall, Mall of America and Dubai Mall also hold art and cultural exhibitions. In physical retail environments that are rapidly changing due to the incursion of alternative virtual purchasing channels, the question becomes how much all physical retail *spaces* need to become tourist retail *place*, in order to effectively encourage people to still 'go out' and interact with their physical environment and the others that they share it with? Will all active and immersive retail become tourist retail?

References

Adler, P. (1975) The transitional experience: an alternative view of culture shock. *Journal of Humanistic Psychology* 15, 13–23.

Anholt, S. and Hildreth, J. (2004) *Brand America: The mother of all brands*. London: Cyan Books.

Baker, A. (2000) *Serious Shopping*. London: Free Association Books.

Baker, S. M., Kleine, S. C. and Bowen, H. E. (2006) On the symbolic meanings of souvenirs for children. In Belk, R. W. (ed.) *Research in Consumer Behaviour, Volume 10*. Oxford: JAI Press, Elsevier, pp. 209–248.

Beard, G. M. (1869) Neurasthenia or nervous exhaustion. *Boston Medical and Surgical Journal* 80, 245–259.

Beck, R. (1998) Forget the beach, travellers opt for the mall on vacations. *Sentinel Tribune* (Bowling Green), 30 July.

Belk, R. W. (1996) On aura, illusion, escape and hope in Apocalyptic consumption: the apotheosis of Las Vegas. In Brown, S., Bell, J. and Carson, D. J. (eds) *Marketing Apocalypse: Eschatology, escapology and the illusion of the end.* London: Routledge, pp. 87–110.

Belk, R. W. (1997) Been there, done that, bought the souvenirs: of journeys and boundary crossing. In Brown, S. and Turley, D. (eds) *Consumer Research: Postcards from the edge*. London: Routledge, pp. 22–45.

Belk, R. W., Wallendorf, M. and Sherry, J. F. Jr (1989) The sacred and the profane in consumer behaviour: theodicy and odyssey. *Journal of Consumer Research* 16, 1, 1–38.

Belk, R. W., Wallendorf, M., Sherry, J. F. Jr and Holbrook, M. B. (1991) Collecting in a consumer culture. In Belk, R. W. (ed.) *Highways and Byways: Naturalistic research form the consumer behaviour odyssey*. Provo, UT: Association for Consumer Research.

Benjamin, W. (1973) *Charles Baudelaire: A lyric poet in the era of high capitalism.* London: New Left Books.

Benjamin, W. (1999) *The Arcades Project* (trans. H. Eiland and K. McGlaughlin). Cambridge, MA: Belknap Press, Harvard University Press.

Berry, B. and Garrison, W. (1958a) A note on central place theory and the range of a good. *Economic Geography* 34, 304–311.

Berry, B. and Garrison, W. (1958b) Recent developments in central place theory. *Proceedings of the Regional Science Association* 4, 107–121.

Bitner, M. J. (1992) Servicescape: the impact of physical surroundings on customers and employees. *Journal of Marketing* 56(2), 57–71.

Bowlby, R. (1985) *Just Looking: Consumer culture in Dreiser, Gissing and Zola*. London: Methuen.

Burnett, T. A. J. (1983) *The Rise and Fall of a Regency Dandy: The life and times of Scrope Berdmore Davies*. Oxford: Oxford University Press.

Butler, R. W. (1991) West Edmonton Mall as a tourist attraction. *Canadian Geographer* 35(3), 287–295.

Christaller, W. (1966 [1933]) *Central Places in Southern Germany* (trans. Baskin, C. W.). Englewood Cliffs, NJ: Prentice-Hall.

Clarke, D. B. (2003) *The Consumer Society and the Postmodern City*. London: Routledge.

Coca-Stefaniak, J. A. and Parker, C. (2005) Gran Centre Granollers: city, culture and commerce. *International Journal of Retail and Distribution Management* 33(9), 685–696.

Cohen, E. (1979) Rethinking the sociology of tourism. *Annals of Tourism Research* 6, 18–35.

Cort, D. A. and King, M. (1979) Some correlates of culture shock among American tourists in Africa. *International Journal of Intercultural Relations* 3, 211–225.

Crompton, J. (1979) Motivations for pleasure vacation. *Annals of Tourism Research* 6, 408–424.

Csikszentmihayli, M. (1975) *Beyond Boredom and Anxiety*. San Francisco: Jossey-Bass.

Csikszentmihayli, M. (1999) If we are so rich, why aren't we happy? *American Psychologist* 54(10), 821–827.

Csikszentmihayli, M. and Rochberg-Halton, E. (1981) *The Meaning of Things: Domestic symbols and the self.* Cambridge: Cambridge University Press.

Dann, G. (1977) Anomie, ego-enhancement and tourism. *Annals of Tourism Research* 4, 184–94.

Debord, G. (1958) Situationist International #1. In Knabb, K. (ed. and trans) *Situationalist International Anthology* (revised and expanded edition, 2006), Berkeley: Bureau of Public Secrets, pp. 47–61.

Debord, G. (2009) *Society of the Spectacle* (trans. Knabb, K.). Eastbourne: Soul Bay Press.

Evans, G. (1999) *Souvenirs: From Roman times to the present day*. Edinburgh: NMS Publishing.

Ewert, A. W. (1985) Risk recreation: trends and issues. *Trends* 2(3), 4–9.

Ewert, A. W. (1989) *Outdoor Adventure Pursuits: Foundations, models and theories*. Columbus, OH: Publishing Horizons.

Falk, P. (1997) The scopic regimes of shopping. In Falk, P. and Campbell, C. (eds) *The Shopping Experience*. London: Sage, pp. 177–185.

Falk, P. and Campbell, C. (1997) *The Shopping Experience*. London: Sage.

Falk, J. H. and Dierking, L. D. (1992) *The Museum Experience*. Washington, DC: Whalesback Books.

Fennell, D. A. and Butler, R. W. (2003) A human ecological approach to tourism interactions. *International Journal of Tourism Research* 5, 197–210.

Fisk, R. P., Grove, S. J. & John, J. (2007) *Interactive Services Marketing*, third revised edition. London: Houghton Mifflin.

Fromm, E. (1978) *To Have or To Be*. London: Jonathan Cape.

Furnham, A. and Bochner, S. (1986) *Culture Shock: Psychological reactions to unfamiliar environments*. London: Methuen.

Gabriel, Y. and Lang, T. (1995) *The Unmanageable Consumer: Contemporary consumption and its fragmentations*. London: Sage.

Giddens, A. (1991) *Modernity and Self-Identity: Self and society in the late modern age*. Cambridge: Polity Press.

Godbey, G. and Graefe, A. (1991) Repeat tourism, play and monetary spending. *Annals of Tourism Research* 18, 213–225.

Gordon, B. (1986) Souvenir: messenger of the extraordinary. *Journal of Popular Culture* 20(3), 135–146.

Goss, J. (1993) The magic of the mall: an analysis of form, function and meaning in the contemporary retail built environment. *Annals of the Association of American Geographers* 83(1), 18–47.

Grove, S. J. and Fisk, R. P. (1997) The impact of other customers on service experiences: a critical incident examination of 'getting along'. *Journal of Retailing* 73(1), 63–85.

Hankinson, G. (2004) The brand images of tourism destinations: a study of the saliency of organic images. *Journal of Product and Brand Management* 13 (1), 6–14.

Hankinson, G. (2005) Destination brand images: a business tourism perspective. *Journal of Services Marketing* 19(1), 24–32.

Harris, C. and McIntyre, C. (2011) The role of local retail and need for its focused investment within a tourist destination economy. Working paper delivered at the International Association of Tourism Economics (IATE) Conference, Bournemouth, 4–7 July.

Herzog, T. (1989) A cognitive analysis of preference for urban nature. *Journal of Environmental Psychology* 9, 27–43.

Hitchcock, M. and Teague, K. (eds) (2000) *Souvenirs: The material culture of tourism*. Aldershot: Ashgate Publishing.

Holbrook, M. B. (1986) Emotion in the consumption experience: toward a new model of the human consumer. In Peterson, R. A., Hoyer, W. D. and Wilson, W. R. (eds) *The Role of Affect in Consumer Behavior*. Lexington MA: Heath & Company, pp. 17–52.

Holbrook, M. B. and Hirschman, E. C. (1982) The experiential aspects of consumption: consumer fantasies, feelings and fun, *Journal of Consumer Research* 9, 132–140.

Houlihan, M. (2000) Souvenirs with soul: 800 years of pilgrimage to Santiago de Compostela. In Hitchcock, M. and Teague, K. (eds) *Souvenirs: The material culture of tourism*. Aldershot: Ashgate Publishing, pp. 18–24.

Huff, D. L. (1965) A probabilistic analysis of shopping centre trade areas. *Land Economics* 39, 89–90.

Hunter-Jones, P. (2003) The perceived effects of holiday-taking upon the health and wellbeing of patients treated for cancer. *International Journal of Tourism Research* 5, 183–196.

Jones, P. and Hillier, D. (2000) Changing the balance: the 'ins and outs' of retail development. *Property Management* 18(2), 114–126.

Kent, T. (2007) Creative space: design and the retail environment. *International Journal of Retail and Distribution Management* 35(9), 734–745.

Kim, S. and Littrell, M. A. (2001) Souvenir buying intentions for self versus others. *Annals of Tourism Research* 28(3), 638–657.

Kotler, P. (1973) Atmospherics as a marketing tool. *Journal of Retailing* 49(4), 48–64.

Langman, L. (1992) Neon cages: shopping for subjectivity. In Shields, R. (ed.) *Lifestyle Shopping: The subject of consumption*. London: Routledge, pp. 40–82.

Langeard, E., Bateson, J. E. G., Lovelock, C. H. and Eigler, P. (1981) *Services Marketing: New insights from consumers and managers*. Cambridge, MA: Marketing Science Institute.

Littrell, M. A. (1990) Symbolic significance of textile crafts for tourists. *Annals of Tourism Research* 17, 228–224.

Littrell, M. A. (1996) Shopping experiences and marketing of culture to tourists. In Robinson, M., Evans, N. and Callaghan, P. (eds) *Tourism and Culture: Image, identity and marketing*. Newcastle: University of Northumbria, pp. 107–120.

Littrell, M. A., Riley, R. and Stout, J. A. (1991) In-home businesses: profiles of successful and struggling craft producers. *Home Economics Research Journal* 20(1), 26–39.

Littrell, M. A., Anderson, L. and Brown, L. (1993) What makes a souvenir authentic? *Annals of Tourism Research* 20(1), 197–215.

Littrell, M. A., Baizerman, S., Kean, R., Stout, J. A., Niemeyer, S. and Gahring, S. (1994) Souvenirs and tourism styles. *Journal of Travel Research* 33, 1, 3–11.

Losch, A. (1954) *The Economics of Location*. New Haven, CT: Yale University Press.

Mandel, N. (2003) Shifting selves and decision making: the effects of self-construal priming on consumer risk-taking. *Journal of Consumer Research* 30, 30–40.

Matheusik, M. (2001) When in doubt, shop. *Ski Area Management* 40(1), 66–7.

Maclaran, P., Brown, S. and Stevens, L. (1999) The utopian imagination: spatial play in a festival marketplace. *European Advances in Consumer Research* 4, 304–309.

McGoldrick, P. (2002) *Retail Marketing*, second edition. London; McGraw-Hill.

McIntyre, C. (2007) Survival theory: tourist consumption as a beneficial process in a limited risk setting. *International Journal of Tourism Research* 9(2), 115–130.

McIntyre, C. (2008) Museum food service offers: experience design dimensions. *Journal of Food Service* 19(3), 177–188.

McIntyre, C. (2009a) Diminishing varieties of active and creative retail experience: the end of the music shop? *Journal of Retailing and Consumer Services* 16(2), 466–476.

McIntyre, C. (2009b) Museum and art gallery space characteristics: an entertaining show or a contemplative bathe? *International Journal of Tourism Research* 11(2), 155–170.

McKercher, B. (2005) Are psychographics predictors of destination life cycles? *Journal of Travel and Tourism Marketing* 19(1), 49–55.

Medler, J. (2009) Dubai Mall. Online source: www.thedubaimall.com/en

Mikunda, C. (2004) *Brand Lands, Hot Spots and Cool Spaces*. London: Kogan Page.

Miller, D. (1998) *A Theory of Shopping.* Cambridge: Polity Press.

Miller, D., Jackson, P., Thrift, N., Holbrook, B., Rowlands, M. (1998) *Shopping, Place and Identity.* Abingdon: Routledge.

Nettle, D. (2005) *Happiness: The science behind your smile*. Oxford: Oxford University Press.

Oberg, K. (1960) Cultural shock: adjustment to new cultural environments. *Practical Anthropology* 7, 177–182.

Oldenburg, R. and Brissett, D. (1982) The third place. *Qualitative Sociology* 5(4), 265–284.

Oppermann, M. (1995) Travel life cycle. *Annals of Tourism Research* 22(3), 535–552.

Parasuraman, A., Zeithaml, V. A. and Berry, L. L. (1985) A conceptual model of service quality and its implications for future research. *Journal of Marketing* 49(4), 41–50.

Parasuraman, A., Zeithaml, V. A. and Berry, L. L. (1988) SERVQUAL: a multi-item scale for measuring consumer perceptions of service quality. *Journal of Retailing* 64(1), 12–40.

Payne, A., Storbacka, K. and Frow, P. (2008) Managing the co-creation of value. *Journal of the Academy of Marketing Science* 36(1), 83–96.

Pearce, P. L. (1982) *The Social Psychology of Tourist Behaviour*. Oxford: Pergamon.

Peterson, R. A., Hoyer, W. D. and Wilson, W. R. (eds) (1984) *The Role of Affect in Consumer Behavior*. Lexington, MA: Heath & Company.

Pine, J. and Gilmore, J. (1999) *The Experience Economy: Work is theatre and every business is a stage.* Boston, MA: Harvard Business School Press.

Pioch, E. and Byrom, J. (2004) Small independent retail firms and locational decision-making: outdoor leisure retailing by the crags. *Journal of Small Business and Enterprise Development* 11(2), 222–232.

Plog, S. (1974) Why destination areas rise and fall in popularity. *Cornell HRA Quarterly,* 14(4), 55–58.

Plog, S. (2001) Why destination areas rise and fall in popularity: an update of a Cornell Quarterly Classic. *Cornell Hotel and Restaurant Quarterly* 42(3), 13–24.

Reilly, W. J. (1929) Methods for the study of retail relationships. *University of Texas Bulletin* 2944 (Bureau of Business Research, Research Monograph No. 4), 22 November.

Reilly, W. J. (1931) *The Law of Retail Gravitation.* New York: William J. Reilly.

Rook, D. W. and Gardner, P. A. (1993) In the mood: impulse buying's effective antecedents. *Research in Consumer Behavior* 6, 1–28.

Seligman, M. E. P. (2002) *Authentic Happiness*. New York: Free Press.

Sherry J. F. Jr (1998) The soul of the company store: Niketown Chicago and the emplaced brandscape. In Sherry, J. F. Jr. (ed.) *Servicescapes: The concept of place in contemporary markets*. Chicago: NTC Business Books.

Shields, R. (1989) Social spatialization and the built environment: the case of the West Edmonton Mall. *Environment and Planning* 7(2), 147–164.

Shields, R. (ed.) (1992) *Lifestyle Shopping: The Subject of Consumption*. London: Routledge.

Shields, R. (1994) Fancy footwork: Walter Benjamin's notes on *flâneurie.* In Tester, K. (ed.) *The Flâneur*. London: Routledge, pp. 61–80.

Simmel, G. (1950) The metropolis and mental life. In Wolff, K. (ed.), *The Sociology of George Simmel*. New York: Free Press, pp. 409–424.

Slater. D. (1997) *Consumer Culture and Modernity*. Cambridge: Polity Press.

Smith, R. K. and Olsen, L. S. (2001) Tourist shopping activities and development of travel sophistication. *Visions in Leisure and Business* 20(1), 23–33.

Stansfield, C. A. Jr (1969) Recreational land use patterns within an American seaside resort. *Tourist Review* 24(4), 128–136.

Stevenson, R. L. (1879) Edinburgh: Picturesque Notes. Chapter one, Introductory. Originally published London: Seeley. Online source, Ogmios Press, 2000: http://www.cyberstudia.com/ogmios/texts/stevenson/edinburgh/edinburgh-picturesque-1.html

Stobart, J. (2008) *Spend, Spend, Spend! A history of shopping*. Stroud: History Press.

TIAA (2001) *The Shopping Traveler*. Washington, DC: Travel Industry Association of America.

Tester, K. (ed.) (1994) *The Flâneur*. London: Routledge.

Timothy, D. J. (2005) *Shopping Tourism, Retailing and Leisure*. Clevedon, UK: Channel View Publications.

Todd, S. (2001) Self concept: a tourism application. *Journal of Consumer Behaviour* 1(2), 184–196.

Ulrich, R. S. (1981) Natural versus urban scenes: some psychophysiological effects. *Environment and Behaviour* 13, 523–556.

Ulrich, R. S. (1983) Aesthetic and affective response to natural environment. In Altman, I. and Wohlwill, F. (eds) *Human Behaviour and the Environment, Vol. 6: Behavior and the Natural Environment*. New York: Plenum Press, pp. 85–125.

Ulrich, R. S. (1993) Biophilia, biophobia and natural landscapes. In Kellert, S. R. and Wilson, O. E. (eds) *The Biophilia Hypothesis*. Washington, DC: Island Press, pp. 73–137.

Ulrich. R. S., Simons, R. F., Losito, B. D., Florito, E., Miles, M. A. and Zelson, M. (1991) Stress recovery during exposure to natural and urban environments. *Journal of Environmental Psychology* 11, 211–230.

Urry, J. (1995) *Consuming Places*. London: Routledge.

Uzzell, D. L. (1995) The myth of the indoor city. *Journal of Environmental Psychology* 152, 299–310.

Vidler, A. (1993) The explosion of space: architecture and the filmic imaginary. *Assemblage* 21, 44–59.

Walle, A. H. (1997) Pursuing risk or insight: marketing adventures. *Annals of Tourism Research* 24(2), 265–282.

Warnaby, G. and Davies, B. J. (1997) Commentary: cities as service factories? Using the servuction system for marketing cities as shopping destinations. *International Journal of Retail and Distribution Management* 25(6), 204–210.

Weaver, S. (2007) *Creating Great Visitor Experiences: A guide for museums, parks, zoos, gardens and libraries*. Walnut Creek CA: Left Coast Press.

Williams, C. C. (1997) Retailing and economic development. In Williams, C. C., *Consumer Services and Economic Development*. London: Routledge, pp. 108–125.

Williams, C. C. (2002) Why do people use alternative retail channels? Some case-study evidence from two English cities. *Urban Studies* 39(10), 1897–1910.

Wilson, E. (1995) The invisible *flâneur*. In Watson, S. and Gibson, K. (eds) *Postmodern Cities and Spaces*. Oxford: Blackwell, pp. 59–79.

Wilson, O. E. (1984) *Biophilia*. Cambridge, MA: Harvard University Press.

Wrigley, N., Lowe, M. (2002) *Reading Retail: A geographical perspective on retailing and consumption spaces*. London: Arnold.

Yannik, J. (2007) Architectural lessons from environmental psychology: the case of biophilic architecture. *Review of General Psychology* 11(4), 305–328.

Yu, H. and Littrell, M. A. (2003) Product and process orientations to tourism shopping. *Journal of Travel Research* 42(2), 140–150.

Yu, H. and Littrell, M. A. (2005) Tourists' shopping orientations for handcrafts: what are key influences? *Journal of Travel and Tourism Marketing* 18(4), 1–19.

Zukin, S. (1991) *Landscapes of Power: From Detroit to Disney World.* Berkeley: University of California Press.

Part II
Tourist retail formats

5 Tourist and retail relationship in departure points and travel hub consumption

The start of the tourist retail relationship

Ruth Marciniak

Introduction

This chapter explores the relationship between travelling process locations, or travel hubs, and retail. Adopting an historical perspective, it begins by examining the advent of travel for the elite and then moves on to its ensuing widespread development for the masses. In doing so, an emerging theoretical perspective is offered wherein recent retailing developments have drawn upon the principles of Disney theme parks in the integration of a leisure-based tourist retail experience. This perspective is evident in the case offered of the St Pancras International Railway Station (SPIRS). St Pancras is shown to be rising to a challenge in providing a combined national and international railway passenger service, a retail destination and a site of cultural tourism in itself. The overall objective of the case is to capture the process of building the St Pancras International brand and enhancing its presence as a national and international departure point where retail, travel and cultural tourism are all interlinked. By this process, the chapter supports emerging academic interest in retail-led regeneration, as reflected in government policy, which, since the early 1990s, has focussed on regeneration of urban locations. This study complements other, similarly focused academic studies such as Lowe's (2007) examination of retail provision at Portsmouth's city centre as an example of retail regeneration linked to cultural tourism. The chapter also draws upon the work of Ritzer and Liska (1997) and Bryman (2004) in order to examine the extent to which SPIRS could be identified as having organisational processes similar to those found at theme parks.

The beginnings of travel for leisure and tourism

The development of leisure travel and tourism in the United Kingdom has been associated with the country's historical period of the industrial revolution. However, its roots go further back than this. There was a custom, which began at least before 1660, for England's male elite to undertake 'The Grand Tour'. This was seen as a rite of passage wherein young men, often travelling with a guide or a tutor, would follow an itinerary that would take them to specific cultural sites within Europe. The aim was educational, that is, to expose these young men to classical antiquity and the viewing of culturally determined important works of art, which they otherwise would not have had access to. In addition, there was a perceived need to introduce them to the fashionable societies in Europe to prepare them for diplomatic and professional careers for which acquaintance with European people and sites was important (Rojek and Urry, 1997). Accompanying this process, retail opportunities were plentiful for the well-to-do traveller in the form of the purchase of art, books and other items of cultural interest, all bought in order to increase the individual's prestige and standing (Craik, 1997). This custom continued after rail and steamship travel made the grand tour easier in the nineteenth century. Growing rail networks within the UK, as well as in the industrialising USA, also facilitated increased general domestic travel and tourism, initially for the burgeoning industrial middle classes and later for the factory workers.

Britain can be credited with having the world's first intercity railway, which ran from Liverpool to Manchester and was opened in 1830, carrying both passengers and freight. The industrial revolution at that time was creating an increasingly affluent middle class, whose wealth contributed to the growth of the railways thanks to their enthusiasm for railway shares in a form of economic investment 'bubble' during the 1840s. These investments have been described as the Railway Mania, implying irrational investor behaviour. As the price of railway shares increased, more and more money was attracted to inwards investment until an unavoidable collapse, due to unachievable growth expectations, that resulted in financially unviable companies selling off failed lines to larger companies such as Great Western in a rationalising consolidation process (Wolmar, 2007). Although many middle-class families lost their savings during the investment mania, Britain nevertheless benefited from a vast expansion of its railway system during the period. It was not just heavy industrial towns such as Manchester that benefited from the expansion, but also the seaside resorts and spa towns that grew to serve them, such as Skegness and Buxton, attracting increasing numbers of leisure visitors. However, although tourism is dependent upon travel and its history is strongly identified with transport innovation, the increasing availability of rail transport did not immediately bring overnight transformations in leisure behaviours to all. For example, according to Walton (2009), it took a generation after the arrival of the railway for England's northern town of Blackpool to develop its identity as one of the world's first major working-class seaside resorts.

Retailing at travel hubs and departure points

Rail travel and railway station retailing

Mass travelling locations and retailing have had a long association. With regard to railway stations, the 1911 Shops Act, for instance, stated that 'every shop, save as otherwise provided by this act, be closed for the serving of customers not later than one o'clock on one work day every week'. The trades and businesses exempted were: 'the sale of refreshment including the business carried on in a railway refreshment room (and) the business carried on at a railway bookstall or adjoining a railway platform' (Railwaysarchive.co.uk, 2009). Even prior to this act, retailing was evident at railway stations, at least as far back as W. H. Smith, the famous UK stationer and bookseller, having its first retail store in London's Euston Station by 1848 (Cooper, 2008).

Over time various public realm commercial institutions have developed into the provision of specialist settings for consumption as well as leisure. For example, cinemas, museums, theme parks and sports stadiums are all typically accompanied by a variety of retail opportunities. This places the process of shopping as a leisure activity or pastime, no longer primarily involving the functional haggling with a seller over pure necessities of exchange, but rather being part of an enjoyable, time-filling leisure experience in itself. A shift has taken place wherein shopping places are hybrid spaces mixing transactional goods and services with leisure-time activity (Sassatelli, 2007).

Whereas airports led the way in the decades after the 1960s in terms of exploiting the provision of retail services to the traveller, even attracting non-travelling consumers to come and shop at an airport, the idea of railway stations as distinctly developing retail destinations is now experiencing innovative treatment too. One leading example of this is Grand Central Station in New York, which commenced a restoration project in 1996 and has now become an international example of a successful urban project that restored an historic building as a cultural and leisure setting. Similarly, Washington's Union Station in the USA has been transformed from a working train station into a lucrative retail destination, whilst Canada's Toronto Union Station is another revered heritage landmark that has similarly been overhauled from a down-at-heel dingy transport location towards integrated retail nirvana. This trend is also happening within the UK, the most recent example being St Pancras International in London, which has over the years attracted much cultural interest, mainly because it reflects the prevailing Victorian architectural style of the day.

Retailing at railway stations can contribute to the revenues accrued by the owners, despite various challenges associated with shops at busy transitional railway hubs. It is estimated that over a 12-month period 66 per cent of UK adults will have used a railway station (Mintel, 2005), presenting an attractive footfall and potential customer market for retailers located at stations. To put this footfall into a retail context, it is estimated that London Victoria railway station has three times the footfall of Bluewater shopping centre in the nearby county of Kent and that London's Liverpool Street station's Accessorize retail store is estimated to be the retailer's most profitable of all its UK outlets (Cooper, 2008). It has also been indicated that, although travel for work continues to be a major source of revenue for the railways, leisure travellers are the fastest-growing category of travel consumers and in recent years up to 27 per cent of adults have shopped at a railway station without using the station for travelling purposes (Mintel, 2005). Factors stated as stimulating the growth in leisure shoppers at stations also include the introduction of high-speed rail services, for example Eurostar High Speed 1, as well as environmental concerns motivating some consumers to identify forms of low-impact travel such as rail as an eco-friendly alternative to flight. Further factors that present railway stations as attractive commercial opportunities for retailers include the presence of the cash-rich commuters, typically falling into the ABC1 social grouping.

However, a key challenge for retailers is the fact that railway stations' prime function is to serve rail services, and issues of safety, congestion and avoidance of delays takes precedence over any heightened retail functionality. An additional challenge for retailers at stations is that, although commuters may be cash-rich, typically, they may also be time-poor, rushing for trains or connections. In contrast, it is estimated that leisure travellers will spend between 23 and 37 minutes at a station before boarding the train, although on average only seven minutes of this is used as shopping time; one explanation offered for this is that the travellers are busy looking at the departure boards (Abbott, 2007). Thus railway stations may still not be seen as spaces of ideal leisured consumption by many, beyond the traditional picking up of reading matter for a journey.

Li and colleagues (2005) undertook a study that examined the overall impressions that users have of Tokyo's large railway terminals. The results suggest that, depending upon why the user is visiting the terminal, various impressions are accrued. For instance, the impression of *convenience* is when a station is mainly considered a transport facility, a *pleasure* impression is when a station is mainly considered a place of communication or leisure, and a *crowded* impression derives from social hub aspects of the station's layout and atmosphere. In addition, they found that different types of station-based stores also produced varied impressions. For example, the presence of clothing stores enhanced the impression of *pleasure*, whereas food and beverage stores enhanced the impression of *convenience*. These results indicate that the various aspects of a station's use and design affect potential consumers' impressions, including the terminal user's choice of a railway station as an integrated shopping venue or destination.

Air travel and airport retailing

Whereas the railways laid the foundation for modern tourism at the outset of mass leisure tourism, and the private motor car further transformed lifestyles and travel, it has been the aeroplane, the third part of the increased transport revolution, that has had the greatest impact on travel and associated retail development (Chew, 1987). Because of this, much in the way of retail academic research upon travellers in recent decades surrounds the airline traveller. Economic growth has historically been a key determinant of leisure travel demand but research indicates that airline demand is now becoming less sensitive to changes in consumer earnings, rather becoming driven by price reductions (Graham, 2006). With the demand for air transport dramatically increasing over the past three decades, increasing travel pricing competitiveness, airport authorities have been compelled to look at alternative ways of generating revenue, and airport (and on-board) retailing has contributed to increasing such revenue. Related research has shown that travellers, unlike high street shoppers, suffer from a degree of anxiety or anticipation about their journey (Newman and Lloyd-Jones, 1999), and, once they arrive at the airport and have checked in, they are then a captive audience in that they have nowhere else they can go to as they wait for their flight. They have little to do for diversion except shop where airport shopping can be provided, in a retail experience that has been described as reaching for timelessness and placelessness (Rowley and Slack, 1999). Being restricted within the airport environment, travellers may be in a unique frame of mind as they have just experienced the heightened pressures of getting to the airport on time and now may be in a state of limbo, travelling by air continues to provide excitement and a degree of uncertainty over the correct procedures and operating schedules (Lamacraft, 1998). Bingman (1996) identifies a number of natural stress points involved in going through an airport process, including the stages of ticketing, check-in, security and confirmation of departure. Each stage has the potential to place the traveller under greater or lesser degrees of pressure. Time often becomes an important factor in this process as the primary purpose of being in an airport for the overwhelming majority of persons is to catch an aircraft at an allotted time.

In Thomas's (1997) study of airport consumer behaviour, two emotional shifts that affect the potential buying habit were identified. One was an increase in stress levels due to consumers' being out of their daily routine, and the other was an increase in levels of anticipation and excitement. Freathy and O'Connell (2000) have also pointed out that the uncertainty that surrounds many travellers when using an airport can have a negative impact upon spending. Some may suffer from 'gate lock', that is, moving to the departure gate earlier than required, thereby avoiding retail offers available to them. Some passengers will assemble at departure gates even when the aircraft has been delayed. Such behaviour illustrates the angst that many passengers feel when travelling. To compensate, many passengers allow more than the recommended time in order to ensure that they make their flight and to avoid the congestion that has become characteristic of many airports. This, combined with the increased security measures present in airports world-wide, has ensured an increase in passenger 'dwell time', that is, the time passengers spend within the terminal building prior to departure.

'Dwell time' or the period between checking in and waiting to board the aeroplane is identified by Thomas (1997) as being 'happy hour'. He suggests that shopping at the airport is all about manipulating this happy hour, adopting a range of retail strategies to increase venue, primarily by reducing anxiety and boredom. One way to reduce anxiety and boredom is to engage in impulse shopping and according to Thomas (1997), in an airport environment, highly impulsive shoppers are more likely to be receptive to sudden, unexpected buying ideas. This aspect of airport shopping has been further explored by Kent and Omar (2001), who examined to what extent it was normal to engage in impulse purchasing behaviour at airports. Although their findings supported Thomas's work, they also identified that sources of influence on purchasing behaviour included the extent to which the shopper was *socially visible*. For example, if shopping by themselves, they may feel less socially visible, and inhibitions about acting on impulse will be lower. Alternatively, if shopping was with a husband or wife, they may be more inhibited and therefore less likely to make a purchase. Their findings have implications for spending when a traveller is flying solo or accompanied by friends or family. Largely such research has shown that, if the airport environment is marketed carefully, 'dwell time' can be converted into shopping time.

Kent and Omar (2001) also looked at the market segmentation of retail consumers using airports. In all, they identify three main groups: *the shopping traveller* (the most important and lucrative group), *the browser* (includes impulse shoppers) and *the fast-track traveller* (least likely to shop). Alternatively, in an earlier study, Ryans (1969) identified airport user segments as *the international sophisticate*, *the sophisticate* and *the provincial* – international sophisticates interestingly being classed as 'world citizens', representing a small, select group of individuals who were sensitive to brand image and receptive to cultural difference, similar to the elite young men who engaged in the Grand Tour. Further work on segmentation has been undertaken by Freathy and O'Connell (2000), who segment airport customers by the type of travel they undertake: domestic versus international; short haul versus long haul; and business versus pleasure. Table 5.1 identifies each of these segments and examines their propensity, amount and nature of retail purchase.

Table 5.1 Segmentation of airport customers

Customer segment	*Propensity, amount and nature of purchase*
Domestic v. international v. transit	International travellers tend to spend longer in the airport and therefore there is a higher opportunity that they will make a purchase
Short haul v. long haul and scheduled v. non-scheduled	The types of product bought and the amount spent within an airport will depend upon the type of journey passengers are embarking upon. For example, long-haul passengers spend proportionally more than those on short haul. Scheduled passengers have a higher propensity to purchase duty- and tax-free branded products than charter passengers
Business v. pleasure	Business passengers represent a wealthier cohort than the average population. This is primarily because of the disproportionate number of professional and managerial persons in the category. These travellers have higher levels of disposable income and have identifiable spending patterns. Furthermore, business passengers are considered to have only a limited time to shop in the country in which they are visiting. Airports may therefore represent one of the primary opportunities for them to purchase products. However, as a segment, business travellers represent a challenge for the commercial operator. They are less likely to browse, may regard shopping as unnecessary and often spend less on any single journey because of their high frequency of travel

Source: Freathy and O'Connell (2000).

Case study: St Pancras International Railway Station (SPIRS)

St Pancras International Railway Station is a major London station, opened in 1868 by the Midland Railway as the southern terminus of the company's midland main line. The station is a Grade I listed building, particularly celebrated for its Victorian architecture. It has been referred to as the 'cathedral of the railways' as it includes two celebrated Victorian structures. The first of these is the main train shed, built by the engineer William Henry Barlow in 1868, which boasted the largest single-span structure at that time. Second, there is the frontage of the station: St Pancras Chambers, formerly the Midland Grand Hotel, built between 1868 and 1877 is an impressive example of Victorian gothic architecture. In all, the railway station is an example of Victorian industrial and cultural heritage and, as such, is an important landmark in London for cultural tourism, which *Time Out*, the London listings magazine, described as 'one of the seven wonders of London' (McKie, 2007).

During the first decade of the twenty-first century, it was reconstructed with the help of English Heritage and is currently expanded to include a terminal area for Eurostar trains to continental Europe, and the Olympic Javelin, which will take passengers to the Olympic Park for the 2012 games. It was estimated that, in 2009, 50 million passengers passed through St Pancras International – certainly an attractive footfall for retailers! Table 5.2 presents both the current and planned future rail services offered by St Pancras International. As can be seen, in addition to offering an international rail service, the station also serves domestic visitors and commuters in and out of London.

Table 5.2 Service patterns at St Pancras International

National Rail
East Midlands Trains Midland Main Line
First Capital Connect Thameslink
Southeastern Luton–Sevenoaks (commencing December 2008)
Southeastern CTRL-DS (commencing December 2009)
Special Service (2012) Olympic-Javelin CRTL-=DS
International Rail
Eurostar High Speed 1

Who visits St Pancras and why?

In attempting to define the population visiting St Pancras in retail terms, Howard's (2007) conceptual leisure segmentation model can been applied, as originally designed to identify characteristics of visitors going to shopping centres and illustrated in Figure 5.1. Categories of visitors in this model include, on one side, commuters who can be identified as using the station for utilitarian/time poor/ product purposes, primarily to travel to and from work. On the other side of the model are those who are time-rich and potentially looking for a heritage experience along with a social experience, such as tourists. Finally, there is a possible, hybrid third category that can be identified as those who are using the station both as a commuter and also as for a social experience, for example in using a bar or café at the station for a drink with work colleagues before embarking upon their homeward journey, or spending pre-travel free time in leisured shopping activity. It can be understood that personal, trip and place characteristics, as identified in Howard's model, can be used to identify different kinds of experiences for visitors to the station. In turn, awareness and understanding of these reasons can

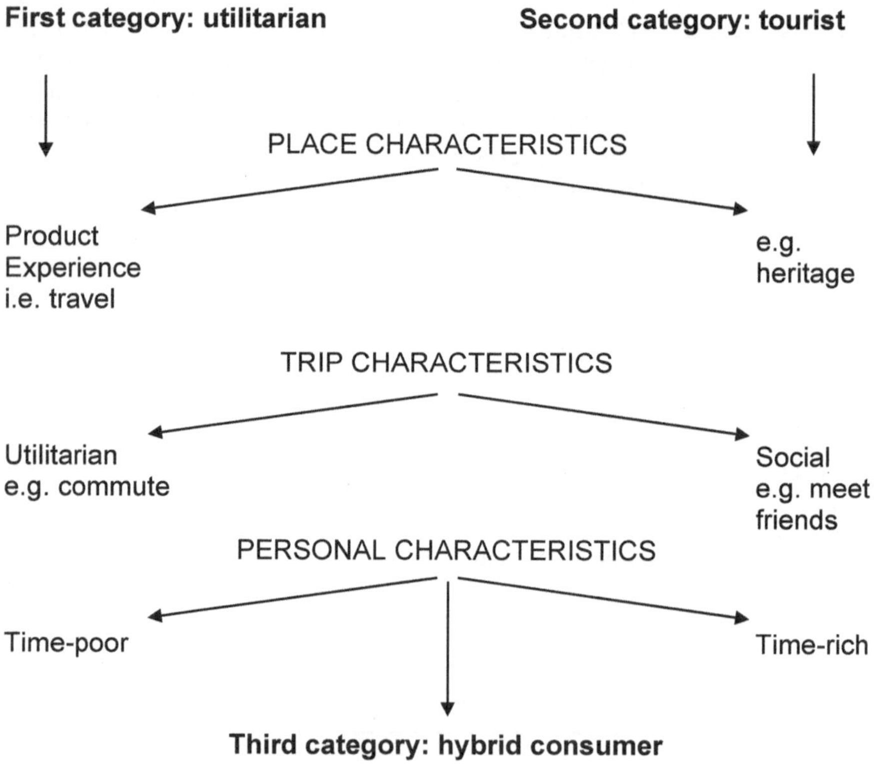

Figure 5.1 Categorised visitors to St Pancras and purpose of visit (source: adapted from Howard, 2007).

contribute to both the railway and retailer traders providing a better service experience for consumers coming into the station and inform the development of an integrated marketing communications strategy.

Identification of the retailers at St Pancras

In total, in July 2009 there were 45 retail units at SPIRS. Of these approaching 50 per cent (20 outlets) were involved in catering, that is, pubs, bars, restaurants and cafes, one of which boasts of being the largest champagne bar in Europe. In addition, there were eight fashion units, four retail units that sold newspapers, books and/or stationery, three beauty and three food shops. Further to this, one retailer was a florist, one a mobile phone specialist and one retail unit offered a hotel reservation service. No unit vacancies were identified. Figure 5.2 presents a review of the breakdown of retailers by number of outlets within categories of product/service offering. Retailers in this review were also identified by name, as per Table 5.3, which identifies all retailers as being branded chain outlets with no independents represented. Retailers identified as having experience of retailing at transport hubs included WHSmith, Hamleys, M&S, Thomas Pink, Accessorise, Monsoon, Starbucks and Caffè Nero, whilst retailers new to retailing at transport hubs included Foyles and Rituals, a Dutch beauty retailer.

Identification and critical assessment of integrated marketing communications at St Pancras

Ultimately the desire of St Pancras International in recent years was to move away from the grab-and-go mentality of previous rail travel consumerism (Cooper,

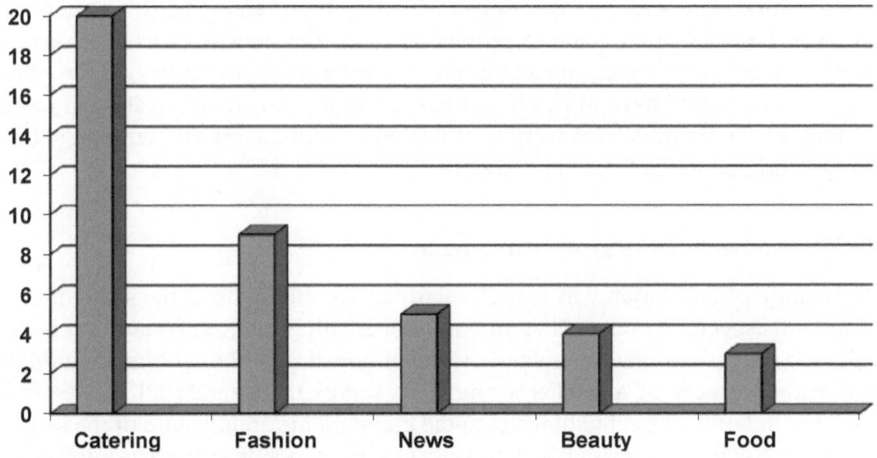

Figure 5.2 Review of retailers at St Pancras, 2009, by number of outlets within categories of product/service offering.

Table 5.3 Review identification of specific SPIRS retailers, 2009, by brand name

Retail type	*Retail brand*
Food/grocery seller (3)	M&S Simply, Neuhaus, Wilton & Noble
Newsagent (1)	WHSmith
Stationery/books (2)	Paperchase, Foyles
Department /variety store – food & fashion (1)	M&S
Restaurant/fast food/café (17)	Starbucks, Caffè Nero, AMT, Costa Coffee, Pret a Manger, Paul, Peyton & Byrne, Crepaffaire, Benugo, Fine Burger Co, Chopd, Camden Food, West Cornwall Pasty Company, Yo Sushi, Le Pain Quotidien, St Pancras Brasserie, Carluccios
Bar (3)	Betjeman Arms, des Vins Café & Wine Bar, The Champagne Bar
Pharmacy/cosmetics (1)	Boots
Clothing/fashion (8)	Fashion, La Senza, LK Bennett, Monsoon, Oliver Bonas, Thomas Pink, Accessorize, Fossil
Electronic (1)	Vodaphone
Beauty/cosmetics (3)	Rituals, Body Shop, Neals Yard
Toys (1)	Hamleys
Florist (1)	Isle of Flowers
Travel (1)	Hotel Reservations

Note: numbers in brackets are the sum of retailers within that retail type.

2008) and instead target it as a retail destination and a place to dwell for both tourists and travellers in a similar manner to well-developed airport retailing. To achieve this, there were a number of initiatives undertaken by the station in order to meet the need to continue to provide an effective railway passenger service whilst, at the same time, enhancing the commercial opportunities of the retail traders, who would have to pay high rents for their prime retail location in terms of footfall. These initiatives were coordinated into an integrated marketing strategy as outlined in the following sections.

SPIRS Marketing Strategy A: retail fascias

The policy of the station was that all retail fascias should be of the same dimensions and aspect. The result is retail units that are all glass-fronted uniform boxes with their signs confined to a single location and size. Although this may dilute the distinctiveness of a retailer's brand, its serves to integrate all the retailers together in terms of paying homage to the grand gothic architecture of the station itself. In essence, the retailer is subservient to the station in that it has allowed its brand to be diluted. In this way, as the photographer James Stroud, who has had an exhibition of his work at the station stated, 'While the area is regenerating, it is definitely not being sterilised or cleansed of its soul, character, attitude or heritage' (Stroud, 2008).

SPIRS Marketing Strategy B: strap line for St Pancras

The marketing strap line for the station, 'Meet me at St Pancras International', attempts to combine all the functions of the station, that is, the returning traveller together with the idea of meeting there to go shopping or a drink or to a restaurant. The strap line is reinforced by Paul Day's statue of two lovers embracing, called 'Meeting Place' (Figure 5.3).

Figure 5.3 Paul Day's statue of two lovers (source: the author).

The SPIRS Marketing Strategy C: use of technology

In order to alleviate stress, increase shopping time and deflect the traveller from focussing on the departure screens in the station hall, LCD departure screens were installed within most of the retail units. Further synergy between the rail and retail services have been created through the use of split-screen technology throughout, wherein one half carries an advert for a retailer and the other half travel information (see Figure 5.4).

Further, common to other retail destination locations, SPIRS has a dedicated website informing visitors of all the amenities, retail units and events that are taking place at the station. One feature included on the site is a community blog. This helps visitors to the station plan their time spent there and encourages social place bonding.

SPIRS Marketing Strategy D: layout of retail services

SPIRS retailers have been grouped together in order to complement each other's services. For example, boutique-style shops are grouped together in one area whereas retail stores focussed on convenience are grouped together in another area, closer to the platforms. Table 5.4 illustrates the different retail areas of the station and their specific associated functionality.

In order not to 'lose' shoppers who are travellers via Eurostar, the departure lounge for this train has a limited number of shops, that is, one café, a book shop and a tax-free offering. Those travellers wishing to browse and make further

Figure 5.4 The use of split-screen technology (source: the author).

Table 5.4 Retail areas of St Pancras International and their defined retail specific differentiation or 'clustering'

The Arcade	Boutique-style shops (fashion and beauty/cosmetics)
The Circle	Focus on convenience (travel, books and newsagent)
St Pancras Market	Food and a farmers' market
Departures	Eurostar departure lounge (tourist and gift/toy-related)
Rendezvous	Venues that facilitate meetings (cafes, bars etc.)

purchases need to do so beyond the departure area and therefore are reliant on the LCDs as identified above. The intention is that they will be more confident about their travel if departure information is close at hand and therefore the technology frees them to explore further than the boundaries of the departure lounge.

SPIRS Marketing Strategy E: St Pancras as a place to dwell

Since its retail-remodelled reopening in November 2007, St Pancras as a destination has marketed itself as a place to dwell and engage in culture, the arts or sport events. For instance, there is a sports-viewing space wherein visitors to the station have been able to view current major sporting events such as Wimbledon and the Grand Prix. In addition, a number of music events are frequently held in the Rendezvous area of the station, where most of the bars and restaurants are housed. Art exhibitions are also held there, together with events that attempt to attract families such as 'The Big Draw – Drawing Event' held in October 2008.

SPIRS as a theme park?

As established above, SPIRS operates as a functioning railway station serving both national and international destinations as well as a retail destination and a cultural tourism site. In this way, the station represents a trend whereby within its space the de-differentiation of consumption takes place; that is, where forms of consumption associated with different institutional spheres become interlocked with each other (Bryman, 2004). SPIRS, therefore, acts as a disguised marketplace as it provides a context where travel visitors are forced to pass through these shops to get to the tickets and the platforms. Ritzer and Liska (1997) have argued that increasingly tourist sites have become 'McDonaldized' by providing tourist experiences that are as predictable, efficient, calculable and controlled as a fast-food chain process. A similar term also used in tourism has been Disneyisation, a process by which the principles of the Disney theme parks dominate areas of society. To what extent can this be applied to SPIRS? In order to explore this, factors identified as being key to Disneyisation need to be considered. These have been identified by Bryman (2004) as primarily being those of *de-differentiation, theming, merchandising* and *emotional labour.* The first of these has already been discussed as an actuality in the SPIRS case above. The second factor, *theming,* applies to a restaurant or retail outlet drawing upon well-known accessible cultural themes, for example, Irish bars or American-style diners. Liverpool, home of the Beatles, has a number of commercial ventures which drawn upon these musicians, for example, such as 'The Beatles Hotel'. Theming can be found to be evident in the remodelled SPIRS concept, for instance in its drawing upon Sir John Betjeman, the English poet who took up the cause of protecting the station, resulting in the government's listing both it and the hotel as Grade I in 1967. In addition to a statue of the man on the upper concourse (Figure 5.5), there is a bar called 'The Betjeman Arms' (Figure 5.6).

Bryman (2004) describes the third factor, *merchandising*, as a key process identified with Disneyisation: the extensive promotion of goods bearing copyright images and logos. Although SPIRS does not sell any own-brand merchandise in any of the retail outlets, nevertheless aspects of merchandising have arisen. For

Figure 5.5 John Betjeman's statue on the upper concourse (source: the author).

Figure 5.6 Further theme development around 'The Betjeman Arms' (source: the author).

instance, the aforesaid Betjeman Arms pub has commissioned its own house brew from a brewery, naming it Betjeman Ale, and serves 'The Betjeman breakfast'. Other elements of experiential theming have been tied to integration with the nature of the classical Victorian station structure, as suggested in the design of the retail concourse itself (Figure 5.7).

Finally, the Disneyisation factor of *emotional labour* draws on ideas from scientific management and Fordism wherein work tends to be dehumanising and alienating, the equivalent of 'Mcjobs' in Ritzer and Liska's (1997) McDonaldisation process, which involves aspects of scripting in the interacting of service work (Bryman, 2004). Given that the retail and service workers, together with railway staff, are employed by a variety of different organisations, it is difficult to make any assessment with regards to this at present. However, with the omnipresent branded retail chain outlets in evidence throughout, it can be assumed that there are processes evident at St Pancras that are similar to those of theme parks and/or fast food outlets. The question remains whether this is a good or bad thing.

St Pancras International Railway Station, including its integrated retail offer, can be seen to be associated with special-interest tourism, which reflects the increasing diversity of leisure interests and taps into the experience industry, in this case Victorian industrial heritage and culture. Increasingly tourists are looking for experiences and emotional stimuli, in which regard they seek ambience, aesthetics and atmosphere with a desire to buy feelings or experience and not just products (Pine and Gilmore, 1999; Traver, 2006). Tourist visitors to SPIRS, it seems, can get all of this. Therefore it may represent the recent growth in cultural

Figure 5.7 Integration of the retail concourse with 'Victorian' structural station elements (source: the author).

tourism and associated non-everyday experiences, which Craik (1997: 121) defines as 'excursions into other cultures and places to learn their people, lifestyle, heritage and the arts in an informed way that genuinely represents those cultures and their historical contexts.'

Rojek and Urry (1997) indicate that such excursions embody a convergence between leisure and cultural consumption. This is evidenced by the leisure opportunities to be found at St Pancras including the restaurants, bars, cafés and shops in addition to the musical and cultural events that now take place there.

Conclusion

This chapter, which aimed to explore the relationship between travelling venues and retail, chose to examine these processes particularly through a focus upon the new developments in SPIRS. In all, building the St Pancras brand can be seen to have enhanced the station as a destination retailer, a site for cultural tourism and an effective provider of retail passenger services.

The chapter aims to make a number of contributions towards the literature on the subject area. First, it explores a neglected area in retail literature, which is retailing at transport hubs. Second, it applies models of place, trip and personal characteristics, previously applied only to shopping centres, to a transport location with retail facilities in order to explore purpose of the visit and who visits. Finally, the chapter identifies how tourism and retailing can apparently be successfully integrated; despite the challenges of retailers operating at a busy railway station, it is evident that SPIRS appears to be a successful integrated venue. By this project, the high rents accrued from retailer activities at St Pancras have furnished London Continental Railways (the owners) with the finances that have been required to undertake the estimated £800 million regeneration project (Cooper, 2008). It is anticipated that more such developments will be undertaken, with opportunities for further and longer-term study.

References

Abbott, J. (2007) Creating Europe's destination station. *Modern Railways*, March, 34–35.

Bingman, C. (1996) Airports as retail malls? What are the criteria for a successful airport retail mall? Presentation at the 5th Airports Council International Conference, Marseille, October.

Bryman, A. (2004) *The Disneyisation of Society*. London: Sage Publications.

Chew, J. (1987) Transport and tourism in the year 2000. *Tourism Management* 8(2), 83–85.

Cooper, G. (2008) The right side of the tracks. *Retail Week*, 22 February.

Craik, J. (1997) The culture of tourism. In Rojek, C. and Urry, J. (eds) *Touring Cultures: Transformations of travel and theory.* London: Routledge, pp. 113–136.

Freathy, P. and O'Connell, F. (2000) Market segmentation in the European airport sector. *Marketing Intelligence & Planning* 18(3), 102–111.

Graham, A. (2006) Have the major forces driving leisure airline traffic changed? *Journal of Air Transport Management* 12(1), 14–20.

Howard, E. (2007) New shopping centres: is leisure the answer? *International Journal of Retail and Distribution Management* 35(8), 661–672.

Kent, T. and Omar O. (2001) International airport influences on impulsive shopping: trait and normative approach. *International Journal of Retail & Distribution Management* 29(5), 226–235.

Lamacraft J. (1998) Retail design: new store experiences. *Financial Times* (London), 44–45.

Li, C., Yamamoto, T. and Morikawa, T. (2005) Analysis of user impressions of railway stations, focusing on the effects of adjunct retail facilities. In Brebbia, C. A. and Wadhwa, L. C. (eds) *Urban Transport XI: Urban transport and the environment in the 21st century*. Southampton: WIT Press, pp. 849–860.

Lowe, M. (2007) Rethinking Southampton and town centre futures. *International Journal of Retail & Distribution Management* 35(8), 639–646.

McKie, R. (2007) Seven wonders of London: St Pancras Station. *Time Out*, October. Online source: http://www.timeout.com/london/big smoke/features/3762/Seven_wonders_of_London-St_Pancras_Station.html (last accessed 20 July 2009).

Mintel (2005) *Railway & Motorway Retailing*. Online source: http:// academic.mintel.com/.../id=114747&type=RCItem (last accessed 27 June 2009).

Newman, S. and Lloyd-Jones, T. (1999) Airport and travel termini retailing: strategies, trends and market dynamics. *Financial Times* (London), 24.

Pine, J. and Gilmore, J. (1999) *The Experience Economy: Work is theatre and every business is a stage.* Boston, MA: Harvard Business School Press.

Railwaysarchive.co.uk (2009) Shops 1911. Online source: http://www.railwaysarchive.co.uk/documents/HMG_Shops1911.pdf (last accessed 9 November 2011).

Ritzer, G. and Liska, A. (1997) 'McDonaldization' and 'post-tourism': complementary perspectives on contemporary tourism. In Rojek, C. and Urry, J. (eds) *Touring Cultures: Transformations of travel and theory*. London: Routledge, pp. 96–109.

Rojek, C. and Urry, J. (eds) (1997) *Touring Cultures: Transformations of travel and theory*. London: Routledge.

Rowley, J. and Slack, F. (1999) The retail experience in airport departure lounges: reaching for timelessness and placelessness. *International Marketing Review* 16(4/5), 363–376.

Ryans, J. (1969) Is it too soon to put a tiger in every tank? *Columbia Journal of World Business* 2, 69–75.

Sassatelli R. (2007) *Consumer Culture: History, theory, politics*. London: Sage.

Stroud, J. (2008) 'Stare if you dare', destination: St Pancras International. Online source: http://www.desvins.co.uk/textanddata/destination_04.pdf (last accessed 9 November 2011).

Thomas, D. (1997) Retail and leisure developments at London Gatwick. *Commercial Airport*, 38–41.

Traver, B. (2006) Conceptualising special interest tourism: framework for analysis. *Tourism Management* 27(7), 183–200.

Walton, J. (2009) Prospects in tourism history: evolution, state of play and future developments. *Tourism Management* 30(6), 783–793.

Wolmar, C. (2007) *Fire & Steam: A history of the railways in Britain*. London: Atlantic Books.

6 Food and farmers' markets

Sean Beer, Andrew Murphy and Robin Shepherd

Introduction: forward to the past?

Historically consumers' relationship with the production of food has varied in terms of distance from, and intimacy with, the actual processes and people that produce it. Food markets, selling farmers' produce and home-processed goods, have been a regional presence for centuries, drawing visitors into villages, towns and cities (Wallgren, 2006). Food market spaces have often become a key part of the urban fabric, such as Covent Garden in London, now converted into tourist stores, bars and cafés. In their early twentieth-century incarnation, food markets tended to mix with craft and/or second-hand markets, or be dominated by retail and wholesale traders. This prompted the creation of more specialised and 'authentic' provider-driven food-only markets, now branded as 'farmers' markets' in the United Kingdom and elsewhere. The first of these in the UK, in the closing years of the twentieth century, is credited to Bath, one of England's top tourist place attractions (Kirwan, 2006).

A variety of explanations have been proposed for the increased global interest in farmers' markets by providers and consumers. A popular argument among sociologists and geographers is that they act as political sites of resistance to the large, corporate, cookie-cutter retail chains seen in Europe (Guthman *et al.*, 2006; Holloway and Kneafsey, 2000; Kirwan, 2004; Kneafsey *et al.*, 2008). As occasional sites of retailing and consumption, farmers' markets are thus a departure from (and sometimes conceived as a threat to) what is now considered 'conventional' retail, with its fixed spatial design and more predictable hours of operation. An alternative, but somewhat complementary, argument is that the markets are important in reconnecting consumers to small, local, often organic, and necessarily temporary and occasional suppliers of food (Szmigin *et al.*, 2003), and play an important role in fostering small business and community development (Guthrie *et al.*, 2006; Lawson *et al.*, 2008). They are frequently promoted as tourist drawcards as a way of establishing the 'old world' localness and uniqueness of particular places, therefore harking back to evocations of smaller-scale interactive retail spaces. This chapter explores these issues, from the perspective of farmers' markets in the UK and New Zealand.

Farmers' market attraction: questions about food, society, space and place

Food is far more than simple sustenance. Human beings have developed a relationship with food that is far more complex and brings in to play social, political, economic, technological and environmental dimensions as indicated in Figure 6.1.

The social dimension of food is complex and core to the nature of society. It might be considered that ethnicity is in many ways defined, in part, by the food that we consume (Beer, 2009). Certainly the type of food we eat, where it comes from and the relationships that we have with the people that produce it have a direct impact on the nature of society. There have been various extensive treatises and reviews on the sociological relationships surrounding food, including those by Harris (1985), Schwartz (1986), Mennell (1992), McIntosh (1996), Ritzer (1996), Warde (1999), Germov and Williams (1999), Atkins and Bowler (2001), Bryant and colleagues (2004), Kneafsey and colleagues (2008) and Goyan Kittler and Sucher (2008). In all of these, food consumption is seen to have distinct and overlapping areas of political and economic context.

The 'new world', industrialised food industry is very large, with attempts to add value to the basic commodity along the supply chain, although we will debate whether some of this 'value' is justified. It is a global industry with foodstuffs being shipped round the world to satisfy demand for specific products. Thus consumers in the UK can purchase strawberries from local supermarkets every day of the year, even though strawberries grown naturally in the UK are available locally only in the early summer months. Similarly, a kilogram of meat can be shipped anywhere in the world for just a little over £0.10 (Beer, 2001). The large global food industry is important to government politics in terms of commerce, security and the environment, and is featured in continual negotiations by the

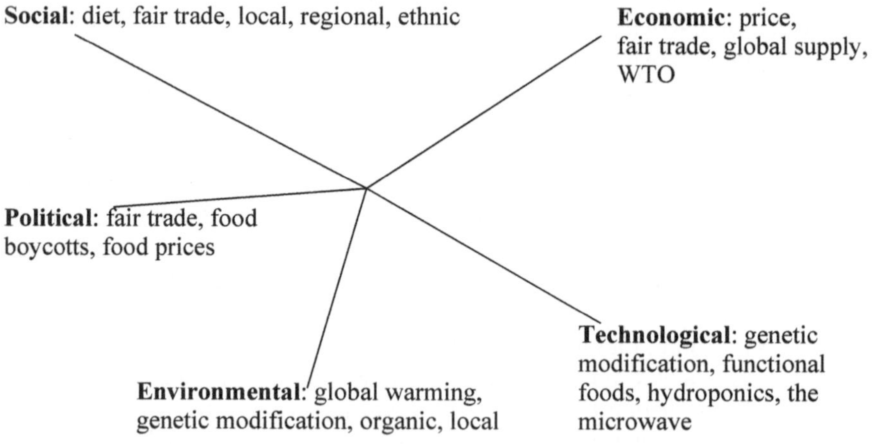

Figure 6.1 Model to illustrate the varying conceptual dimensions of food consumption (source: Beer, 2008).

World Trade Organization (WTO), upon regulations of production and supply; the politics of plenty and hunger is central to the existing North–South geopolitical divide (Blythman, 2005; Clapp and Fouchs, 2009; Lang *et al.*, 2009; Millstone and Lang, 2003; Nestle, 2004; Patel, 2007; Weis, 2007).

The environmental dimension of technological advances has been a cause for humanistic concern for a long time. In the eighteenth century, the economist Malthus is noted as warning of the dangers of an expansion of agriculture creating shortages of food for the poor (Cable, 2009). Many, more recent arguments are widely published, giving additional insight into the downside of modern food production systems (Bellamy, 2005; Body, 1982, 1984, 1987; Clunies-Ross and Hildyard, 1992; Harvey, 1998; Nellemann, 2009; Roberts, 2008; Schlosser, 2002). In the 1960s, Rachel Carson's *Silent Spring* (Carson, 2002) warned of the dangers of the use of DDT (dichlorodiphenyltrichloroethane), a synthetic pesticide, in modern mass food production systems. For many this was the 'wake-up call' that heralded increased concern about the human impact on the environment with regard to food systems and sustainability – a topic also of increased concern due to the advent of mass tourism and its effects upon nature's balance.

We are what (and where) we eat: the tourist authenticity dimension

Given that food is such an important part of our existence, it is not really surprising that food and drink should be a key component of the tourist experience. Historically we have definitely seen the 'going out', and indeed roaming about, to seek new food experiences as a necessity. Richards (2002) argues that food is central to defining individual and tourist identity or *who* we are: we are *what* we eat, we are *where* we eat (to this could be added we are *how*, *why* and *when* we eat; see Marshall, 2005). The consumption of food not only helps to define us but helps to link us to places. It links us to the place where we live; it happens when we as tourists consume, and also when we return home; consumption of food acts as a link to our travels and prompts our memories of and feelings for place. Hughes (1995a: 114) points out the self-evident truth that there is a notion of a natural relationship between a region's land, its climatic conditions and the character of the food that it produces. It is this geographical diversity which provides for the regional distinctiveness in culinary traditions and the evolution of a characteristic heritage. Added to this must be the flow and migration of cultures, their gastronomies and goods. Some take this further such that:

> Culinary tourists are eating the Other (as something distinct from their own culture), but they are also eating the differences between various Others; differences that are often produced and consumed through mobility.
>
> (Molz, 2007: 79)

In more prosaic terms, Richards (2002) maintains that food structures the tourist's day. Much time is spent on eating, drinking and deciding when, where and what to eat and drink. This is all part of everyday life, but holidays are not part of the everyday; they are different. Thus there is also an appreciation that food may have a special role for the tourist above and beyond the mundane. It may be special. It may be the specific focus of the trip. Food and drink may, in fact, be the peak touristic experiences (Quan and Wang, 2003), or something that simply supports the experience; however, if that support is removed the total experience may disintegrate rapidly. It is not the intention here to produce a comprehensive overview of the relationship between food and the tourist. This has been undertaken in texts by the like of Hall and colleagues (2008) and Long (2004). What is sought here is an understanding of the centrality of food to the tourist experience and how it surrounds a particular debate upon the nature of a tourist retail search for authenticity, and thus reflects upon the nature of food marketplaces.

The treatment of authenticity by authors writing in the tourism literature is extensive. Many commentators (Chhabra, 2008; Cole, 2007; Wang, 2007) trace the initial genesis of this discussion to MacCannell (1973, 1976), who seemed to establish a basis for an objective truth upon which authenticity is based. In this, authenticity is taken to be a self-explaining concept that is fully genuine and trustworthy within a tourist experience that may still in some way be staged; as in a tourist experience as a performance of authenticity that is put on by a host. This harks back to Smith's (1977) discussions of the relationship between the self (the tourist) and the other (the host) that was developed further by Cohen (1988, 1989, 2001, 2007) in looking at the way that authenticity might emerge as a result of this interaction, or might actually become *negotiated* and agreed (Bruner, 1994; Hughes, 1995b). Wang (2007) considers that the constructivist arguments are expanded upon by a series of post-structuralist interpretations of authenticity by authors such as Boynton (1986), Daniel (1996), Millinger (1994) and Silver (1993). These are characterised by pessimism with regard to any notion of authenticity and a focus on the experience of the toured object. The state of pessimism with regard to the idea of authenticity has been developed further by others, who maintain that:

> authenticity is too unstable to claim the paradigmatic status of a concept. As a result, the concept-free term authenticity should be replaced by more explicit, less pretentious terms like genuine, actual, accurate, real, and true when referring to judgments that tourists and scholars make about the nature and origins of artefacts [sic] and tourism activities.
>
> (Reisinger and Steiner 2006: 67)

Building on a longstanding body of theory as outlined by individuals such as Berger and Luckmann (1966), Burr (1995) and Gergen (2009), the nature of authenticity can be considered to be a social construct: a dynamic between individuals, others (society) and things, in this case food. Thus authenticity, with reference to food as a form of defined reality, could be based on interplay between the individual (self), the food (thing) and society (others), as illustrated in the diagram Figure 6.2.

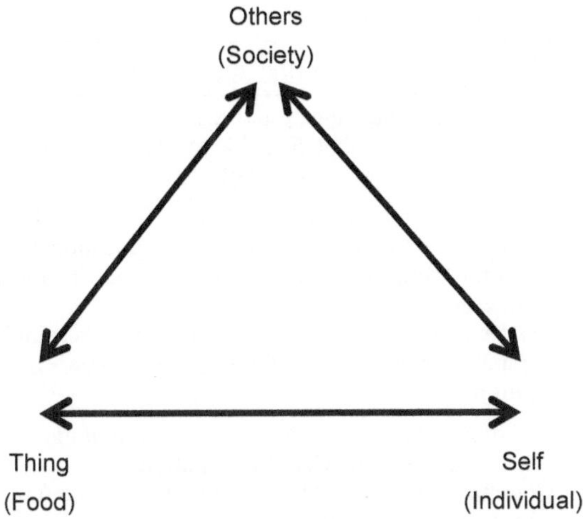

Figure 6.2 The relationships that define food authenticity (source: Beer, 2008).

With regard to how individuals arrive at their definitions of authentic reality that they may be seeking in their travels, it is possible that they may have multiple definitions of the authentic, although society may offer a consensus, accepted view. This is apparent when we consider place-related food branding and designations of product–place food authenticity covered in law such as Appellation d'origine contrôlée (AC), Protected Designation of Origin (PDO), Protected Geographical Indication (PGI) and Traditional Speciality Guaranteed (TSG) (Defra, 2010; O'Connor, 2010.)

Another key component of the concept of authenticity is the time dimension, with changes in the broader context of the consumer's relationship with food and how that food is produced, processed and distributed, giving rise to a series of food eras or cultures, and therefore differing perspectives on what might be considered worthy of a tourist search for 'authentic' experience. We can, for instance, outline a process of *cultural shift* with regard to patterns of food consumption, characterising the twentieth century after the Second World War in the UK into a series of socio-cultural eras: those of *Dig for Victory*, *Food Rationing*, *Techno-Farming* and *New Environmentalism*, as indicated in Table 6.1.

The concept of New Environmentalism within this schema is characterised by a renewed interest in food, with regard to its origin or provenance and the characteristics of its distribution. We see a growth of interest in alternative food supply systems as people become more open to ideas that link their food consumption and food transport to the natural environment, as well as to ideas and concerns of global (and local) social justice. Thus it is in the 1990s and early 2000s that we see a growth in local farmers' markets and their 'pull' factor for day-out trippers and tourists, akin to 'old world' food markets in the village squares of traditional European resort locations.

Table 6.1 Characteristics of different eras of food culture in the UK since 1939

Era	*Characteristics of principal relationships*
Dig for Victory c. 1939–1945	Farmers as combatants, Land Army Consumers as combatants, able to share in the war effort Farmers as heroes and icons of popular culture
Food Rationing c. 1945–1958	Demand for good-quality, consistent food at a cheap price 'Education and purse period'. Better education and increased income were supposed to give rise to new healthier purchasing patterns Farmers still seen as popular heroes but increasingly taken for granted especially with 'new' imported foods and continued rationing
Techno-Farming c. 1958 – 1990	Use of new technology viewed as a good thing, with science as a social saviour (the Green Revolution) Common acceptance of science is shaping the future, e.g. new food horizons in terms of choice of cuisine Further distancing of consumer from primary producer leads to an increasing lack of understanding about agriculture amongst the public
New Environmentalism c. 1990–	Farmers under pressure as producers of food of dubious quality (welfare, disease, chemicals, hormones); to spoilers of the countryside, and recipients of large amounts of taxpayers' money Growth in consumer awareness; conscience with regard to the environment, animal welfare and other 'green' issues and a desire for new food products which enhance lifestyle Increasing interest in the origin of food, demands for new products from home and abroad, growing awareness of the concept of quality and demand for an immediate response to consumer pressure

Source: Beer and Redman (1996).

Local food authenticity and the 'new', tourist-appeal supply chain – journey into the past!

There is a certain irony with regard to the recent development of alternative food supply systems. The food supply chain has evolved over centuries from an initial period when human beings consumed the food that they could hunt and gather within their individual day's travels. After a period of time it is envisaged that individuals within the various social groups became more specialist with regard to hunting and gathering and that this further developed with the practice of agriculture, when through the practice of animal and plant husbandry food was produced under more controlled conditions. The producer, as opposed to the collector or hunter, of the food then passed it on to other consumers, through a developed process of food distribution and exchange via local markets and individual food vendors. Gradually this process developed until we reached the position that we are in today with supply chains dominated by a few large retailers and larger processors moving foodstuffs around to convenient locations for consumers to be drawn to (usually in their cars) for all their needs in the form of large supermarkets, as summarised in Figure 6.3.

The irony of the recent ethical, authentic and sustainable food developments, including the rise of farmers' markets, is that they are, in effect, the reinvention of supply chains that were predominantly used in the past. Thus their description in some quarters as a relative novelty (Spiller, 2007) is a little curious. Some of these supply chains have remained intact for hundreds of years. In the market town of Barnstaple in north Devon there has been a record of a 'farmer's market' since the tenth century, the latest manifestation of which is 'The Pannier Market' held on a Friday in the centre of town and named after the pannier baskets in which the local farmers used to bring their produce to market on the back of donkeys (see BPM, 2010). This particular market serves the local community in a form of retailing that has been maintained for hundreds of years, and is also is an important tourist attraction in its own right. Although under pressure over the years, many stallholders can trace their lineage back through generations, and still come to the markets on Fridays to sell their own local produce, at the tables where their grandparents sat.

However, these tourist-appeal, historically based food supply systems are certainly not the prevalent forms of today's food supply chain, as they were in the 'attractive' past of rustic 'market towns' and individual, mobile food vendors. Negative, industrialised impressions of the 'everyday' corporate subjugation of small food producers and traditional food cultures have been a factor in the revival of alternative supply chains, of a nature similar to those prevalent in the past. There is also a postmodern demand for varieties of seasonal food and food that is local to the place of consumption, particularly of interest to tourists seeking place authenticity and sustainability. Such increasingly varying demands form a rich 'demand mosaic' of consumption and a complex picture of consumer preferences as indicated in Figure 6.4.

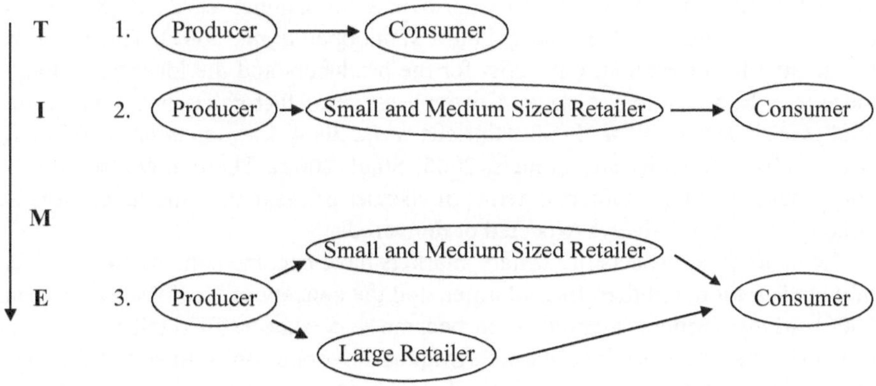

Figure 6.3 Stages in 'distanciation' of the food supply chain (source: Beer, 2001).

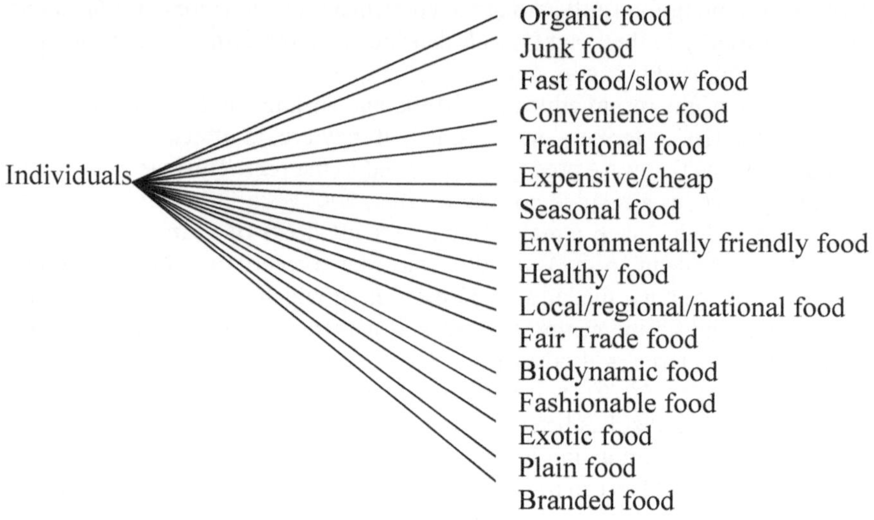

Figure 6.4 The post-modern 'demand mosaic' for food (source: Beer, 2008).

The food marketplace as a tourist event and local social hub: a brave new world of food?

What is a farmers' market?

The modern idea of the farmers' market is that, as an alternative to modern industrial food retailing systems, it is a place where local farmers sell their products directly to local consumers, as in days gone by. This brings together two connected but isolated groups, farmers and consumers, in a commercial and social setting (Ãseb *et al.*, 2007; Kirwan, 2004, 2006). It thus satisfies values relating to the appeals of the environment, better health, increased social justice and a love of 'real' food as it relates to locality (Brown, 2003; Connell *et al.*, 2008; Guthrie *et al.*, 2006; King, 2008; Seyfang, 2003; Vannoppen *et al.*, 2001). This can give rise to significant economic benefits for the producers and the locality, although these may be variable and dependent on a range of factors (Brown and Miller, 2008; Govindasamy *et al.*, 2003; Hinrichs *et al.*, 2004; Lawson *et al.*, 2008; Saili *et al.*, 2007; Schneider and Francis, 2005; Stagl, 2002). There may also be economic benefits for consumers in terms of cheaper prices than in the supermarkets, although this is not always expected or delivered.

Two particular aspects of farmers' markets have become contentious: the idea of what is a farm and therefore a farmer, and the concept of localness (Belliveau, 2005). Many farmers' markets soon became very successful retail venues and providers that were not local farmers wanted the opportunity to sell at the markets. This led to a wide variety of local food 'producers' trying to gain access to farmers' markets to sell under their banner. This, and the second concern with regard to localness, led to the development of 'rules' for the conduct of markets, as defined according to their core criteria by the National Farmers Retail and Markets Association (FARMA, 2009) in the UK, and similar efforts by Farmers' Markets New Zealand (FMNZ). Specifically, with regard to localness, FARMA defines local in terms of proximity to the market – '30 miles is ideal, up to 50 miles is acceptable for larger cities and coastal or remote towns and villages' – or by county boundaries or other geographic boundaries, such as a National Park, that is similar in size to the radius option, although a dispensation may be given to go further afield, up to 100 miles.

Growth of the postmodern farmers' market attraction

What might be called the postmodern farmers' market movement originally developed in the late 1980s and early 1990s in the United States, as indicated by A. Brown (2001, 2002). These markets seem to have flourished, though experience has been variable (Stephenson *et al.*, 2008). Several individuals were working along similar lines in the UK, possibly as a result of experience of the successful food markets in France, Spain, Portugal and Italy, for example. In the early 1990s, in an important focal point for modern farmers' market development, Harriet Festing undertook a Winston Churchill Fellowship looking at farmers' markets and published *Should Farmers Market Direct to Consumers?: America Says Yes* (Festing, 1994). In the UK over the next four or five years a number of different organisations – including district councils, local food charities, private collectives and business organisations – formed markets and these 'families' of markets aggregated and divided according to local political machinations. As an example, the Women's Institute, with 20,500 members forming the largest voluntary organisation for women in the UK (WI, 2010), has been developing its own local produce markets. The Bath Farmers' Market in southern England has provoked much local and tourist interest, and it was around this that the National Farmers' Retail and Markets Association developed, distinguishing between what they term 'authentic markets' and others.

Local farmers' markets were originally designed to link producers of food to local consumers, with strong evidence of positive, local economic effects of farmers' markets (Bentley *et al.*, 2003), but it is also apparent to any visitor that many of the producers are in fact not primary producers but individuals who have spotted opportunities in the food supply chain at other stages. Thus visitors are able to buy olives and coffee, as well as pies and cakes, in English farmers' markets. UK farmers' markets, in fact, feature a range of consumers with varying aspirations (Govindasamy *et al.*, 2002), although often there is a marked contrast between different counties and different areas within the country. The markets often take place in more affluent (and scenic) areas or conurbations and, as is common in Mediterranean countries, are appealing to tourists and day visitors wishing to partake in local or rural colour and willing to spend more. In contrast to this, the original ethos in the United States seemed to focus on disadvantaged farmers taking their produce to disadvantaged urban areas for the purpose of mutual benefit, although there is still considerable variation within the United States, as indicated by Alkon (2008a,b), who highlights a clash of economics and ethics in farmers' markets.

The economic and social benefits of farmers' markets are not clear cut (Hinrichs and Allen, 2008; Jarosz, 2008). In economic terms, there is much more to the markets than an efficient, functional exchange of the necessities of life. One of the ideas behind the farmers' market is supply by local producers to local people. However, consumers often travel considerable distances to buy the food (Ãseb *et al.*, 2007). Can it really be considered that a UK producer who travels 100 miles to a market, or 124 miles as noted in parts of Canada, is a local producer (Higgins, 2006)? How does this fit in with the concept of place and localness that theoretically should characterise the markets (Belliveau, 2005)? Also simply being local does not necessarily result in environmental or health (food safety) benefits given the complexity and inefficiency of many local supply chains (Wallgren, 2006; Worsfold *et al.*, 2004).

Another aspect of farmers' markets to consider is the social nature of the interaction which producers and consumers seem to enjoy (Baber and Frongillo, 2003). This contributes to the atmosphere and theatre of this cultural space (Hunt 2007), and draws strong parallels with the concepts of staged authenticity as discussed generically in tourist attraction formation by MacCannell (1973) and developed by Knudsen and Waarde (2010), who consider that authenticity represents a surplus of experiential meaning and feeling, deriving from what we do at and in places. These interactions are far from simple (Smithers *et al.*, 2008) and have been seen to represent an opportunity to develop a critical cultural mass around an area of academic consideration (Zukin, 2008). The social interaction can also develop between producers and producers, as well as between consumers and producers, thus facilitating business networking and cooperation (Chiffoleau, 2009) in a co-created experience (Payne *et al.*, 2008).

Farmers' markets and tourist retail

A useful perspective upon the tourist experience is to consider it fundamentally as a retail process, containing a whole series of purchases/exchanges that contribute to the tourist consumption. As part of this, purchasing food and goods is something that tourists do in general and in some cases may even be the specific object of travel, related to local traditional food and/or craft marketplaces. Markets have always represented spaces for financial transactions to take place, along with a wide range of social interactions and transactions. Andreatta and Wickliffe (2002) consider that they represent a specific form of cultural space. Having said this only limited research has been undertaken specifically with regard to farmers' markets and tourism (Smith and Honggen, 2008). There is, however, considerable interest in food and drink tourism in general (Boniface, 2003; Hall *et al.*, 2008; Long, 2004).

Local markets, farmers' markets and other unbranded marketplace events represent major tourist attractions within a town and region, as has been noted in some examples already. During the winter months they may still be well attended, but it is during the summer months that they are often swamped with locals and tourists browsing an eclectic mix of market traders, local food producers and what might be called the genuinely authentic local producers. The juxtaposition of such a market to local shops, such as the Panniers Market in Barnstable in proximity to Butchers Row, a street occupied by butchers' shops and other small, speciality food shops, can make this a very special place for a day-out experience – although this is not a farmers' market by strict definition. A similar situation is the Dorchester town market, in the southern UK, which again attracts visitors from all over the region, with tour companies organising specific bus trips to take groups of tourists to market days. Similarly Matakana market, located 120 km north of Auckland, draws many Auckland day-trippers to experience the fine locally sourced foods and wines, swamping the town's car parking capacity.

For many in the postmodern age local food, including grow-your-own and pick-your-own, has now become the leisure activity for 'townies' wishing to 'get back to the country'. The net effect of modernist, industrialised consolidation of the food-retailing sector to a small number of national supermarket retailers can be to reduce the choice of local foods while increasing exposure to non-indigenous and unseasonal foods. The farmers' market is the antithesis of this process, offering limited choice and limited convenience combined with much potentially uncomfortable social intercourse. The increasing sophistication of consumers with touristic experience, searching for difference and authenticity of place, offers the local food producer market a distinct opportunity. Local food, as well as being of nutritive value, can be recognised as a fundamental part of an area and therefore part of its (developing) heritage – thus an attraction for a high-spending tourist customer base. It can serve to identify visitors with the local environment, endowing the daily meal experience with greater meaning and pleasure, as it ideally should be doing with local purchasers, but without local purchasers where is the authenticity? How can the culinary tourist 'eat the Other', if the Other is absent?

In the longer term, for the relationship between the tourist and the local supplier that they meet while visiting a farmers' market, this may involve the development of a long-distance love affair facilitated by technology, which allows a deeper relationship to develop, rather than the one-off encounter of the marketplace; the relationship is established on holiday and continued on return home. In this way home box delivery schemes have also grown in recent years, along with the growth in farmers' markets. A long-term virtual link facilitating home deliveries alongside real place visit events may prove a more sustainable business model, more accessible to local and tourist alike. Such a system would strengthen the relationships upon which authenticity and sustainability are founded, facilitating a more open and 'honest' platform of social construction. Ideally they must maintain the best of both the old world and the new, and so it is interesting now to move onto a consideration of a more 'new world' case: the example of specific place and space development of farmers' markets within New Zealand.

Farmers' markets in New Zealand: a new-world case study

Farmers in New Zealand have long had a tradition of direct sales, typified by an unattended farm gate stall with an honesty box for payment. Larger farms may support a farm shop, particularly in horticultural areas frequented by tourists, but otherwise farm direct sales are micro-scale food retailing. Unlike Europe and North America, home box delivery schemes from farms to the local community are in their infancy in New Zealand, typically small, localised and related to community-supported agriculture (CSA) arrangements (Lockie *et al.*, 2000). Like Europe and North America, however, farmers and the communities around them have increasingly embraced farmers' markets as means of direct interaction with residents and visitors of appealing locations.

Farmers' markets themselves are a relatively recent innovation in New Zealand, with the first established in Whangarei in 1998. As a result of their newness, the markets do not have the long-established spaces and connections of markets in Europe, and must instead create a space for the markets themselves, both in the urban/rural fabric, but also in the consciousness of consumers. The number of markets in New Zealand has grown rapidly, from one in 1998 to 16 in 2004 (Cameron, 2005) to more than 70 in 2011 (see Figure 6.5). This reflects similar

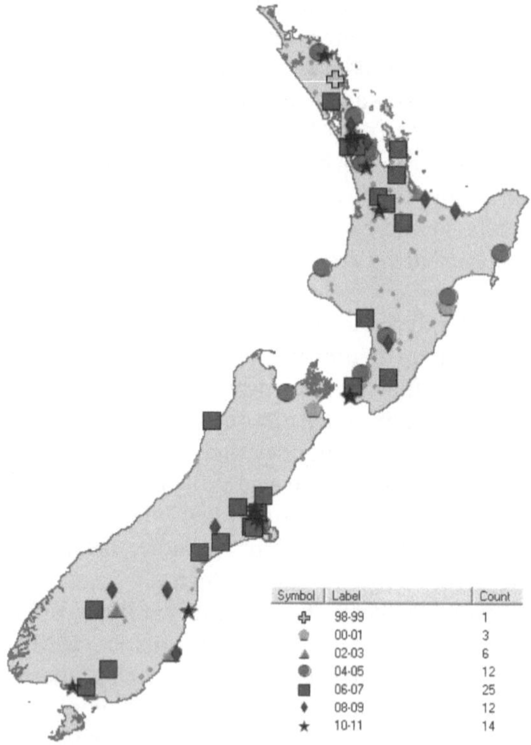

Figure 6.5 Diffusion of farmers' markets in New Zealand: 1998–2011 (source: author [Murphy]).

growth patterns in Australia, Britain, Canada and the United States (Guthrie *et al.*, 2006; Hall *et al.*, 2008).

Farmers' markets are a specific manifestation of ephemeral and experiential retailing, which also includes flea markets and garage/yard/car-boot sales (Gregson *et al.*, 1997; Sherry, 1990) plus craft markets and food festivals (Lewis, 1997; Littrell *et al.*, 1991; see Sherry 1990: 16 for a typology of marketplaces). Farmers' markets themselves can be divided into two groups: 'authentic' markets (Hall *et al.*, 2008) and mixed-use markets. Farmers' Markets New Zealand (FMNZ) specifies that an 'authentic' farmers' market:

> is a food market where local growers, farmers and artisan food producers sell their wares directly to customers. Vendors may only sell what they grow, farm, pickle, preserve, bake, smoke or catch themselves from within a defined local area. The market takes place at a public location on a regular basis.
>
> (FMNZ, 2008)

An 'authentic' market must comprise 'at least 80% local produce stalls', with what counts as 'local' up to the organisers of particular markets. This definition excludes mixed food and craft markets, plus markets which include retailers. Markets in New Zealand thus deliberately prohibit stalls selling woollen or wooden crafts, while permitting flower and plant sellers and derivative products, such as lavender oil.

Studies of producer interest in New Zealand farmers' markets suggest the primary importance of economic motives. Lawson and colleagues (2008) queried why producers sold through farmers' markets using unprompted open-ended questions. Coding the responses, Lawson and colleagues (2008) determined ten motives for stallholder participation, as in Table 6.2. In addition to economic drivers, there are clearly also aspects of the sociability of the market here: interaction with customers and each other. These are also held to be powerful motivations for customers, along with other social motives, such as supporting small, local, artisan suppliers and producers (Hughner *et al.*, 2008). Farmers' markets themselves publicise such reasons for visitor patronage, with the Hamilton Farmers' Market (2008) proposing '10 reasons to shop at your local farmers' market' as in Table 6.2.

For outdoor markets the attraction may be related to the weather and taking in the local environment: mingling, lingering and imbibing in the great outdoors, at least during favourable conditions. As an example, the Matakana Village market, north of Auckland, features around 40 stalls under permanent canvas cover, on sawn-plank tables propped up by wine barrels (Figure 6.6). Unlike most, this market is on a permanent site on private land, acting as a regular drawcard to the other permanent retail premises that surround it. Visitors are invited to linger through the provision of live music and seating tables to sample the variety of raw and cooked food and drink options on offer, and to take in the scenery of the nearby estuarine river. As featured in a *New York Times* travel review of Matakana, 'This is no dusty-radishes Birkenstock scene. With uniform chalkboards, resort-style

Table 6.2 Ten producer and consumer motives for farmers' market participation, as promoted by the producers

	Producers	*Consumers*
1	The desire to obtain a fair price	Know where your food comes from
2	The wish to avoid middlemen	Connect with the seasons through flavourful fresh produce
3	To obtain a supplementary income	Support local farmers and artisan producers
4	Convenience	Help promote responsible land use and preserve our cultural heritage
5	Market was well supported	Do the environment a favour, reduce food miles
6	Atmosphere of the market	Enjoy the regional bounty brought to you with love and care
7	To have contact with final consumer	Contribute to the local economy
8	To promote their products	Give your body a hug with healthy food – and the occasional treat
9	As a hobby	Get to know the best farmers, growers and food makers in the Waikato
10	Too small to trade elsewhere	Meet friends, enjoy the music and market fanfare

Sources: Lawson *et al.* (2008: 19); Hamilton Farmers' Market (2008).

Figure 6.6 Tourist farmers' market appeal (outdoor): Matakana Village Farmers' Market (source: author [Murphy]).

umbrellas and slickly packaged products, it's more like Dean & DeLuca in a country setting' (Klein, 2008). High-profile media coverage such as this leads to a tourist following, primarily from Auckland (either directly or from the nearby holiday home resort of Omaha), but also international tourists on backpacker and package tourist trails giving a *tourist farmers' market appeal* (Figure 6.6). In marked contrast to outdoor markets, smaller indoor events, such as at Albany in north Auckland (see Figure 6.7), are held in community halls, in which stallholders are responsible for decorating their own tables. These types of markets would seem to offer a more *local farmers' market appeal* (Figure 6.7).

The market scorecard research approach

A study of 11 farmers' markets across New Zealand (Figure 6.8; see also Murphy, 2011) aimed to determine what attracts producers and consumers (local and tourist visitors) to the events. A total of 353 customers and 111 producers were interviewed during 2008–9 using a structured questionnaire process, mostly completed face to face. Using a perceptual scale from 1 (not important) to 7 (important) for 31 possible influencing attributes, determined from prior literature and exploratory interviews, the questionnaire asked consumers and producers to rate the advantages/benefits and disadvantages/barriers of *visiting* or *participating in* farmers' markets. Producers were additionally asked to rate what they thought influenced customers, both positively and negatively, and both groups were asked to define what meaning a farmers' market represented to them.

Figure 6.7 Local farmers' market appeal (indoor): Albany Farmers' Market (source: author [Murphy]).

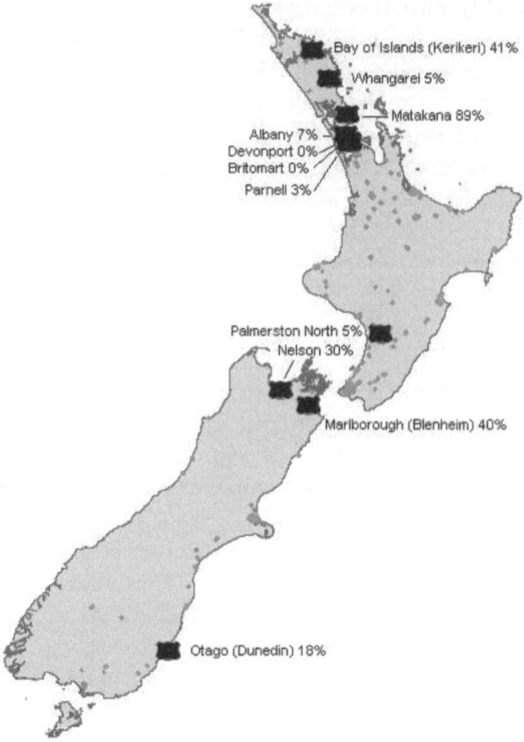

Figure 6.8 Studied New Zealand farmers' markets with percentage of surveyed non-local 'tourists' (source: author [Murphy]).

If we look at the breakdown of the total sample in Tables 6.3–6.11, it can be seen that most customers were fairly regular visitors, and had been coming for some time, with 69 per cent visiting regularly for more than one year. Most were female (63 per cent) and the socio-demographics were skewed towards those from predominantly well-off households (53 per cent from above median income of NZ$67,000), those with higher education attainments and higher age groups. There was a clear interest in organic food, although general food knowledge was not stated to be particularly high, and fewer than a third of respondents were regular purchasers of organic food (from any source). Interestingly, from a tourist point of view, although 57 per cent of customers came from within 10 km of the market location, this left over 40 per cent coming from further afield, including 20 per cent from over 50 km away (including 4 per cent from another country). For the purpose of analysis in this chapter, 'locals' are defined as those who live within 20 km of the market they were visiting, whereas 'tourists' come from further away.

When both customers and producers were asked to define what a farmers' market meant to them, using unprompted open-ended questioning, 'freshness' was

Table 6.3 Customer sample constitution from New Zealand farmers' market survey

Frequency of visit/purchase	*Visit markets (%; n = 353)*	*Purchase organic (%; n = 341)*
Every time	27	11
Most times	27	18
Sometimes	27	42
Hardly ever	10	20
First time	10	0.3
Never	0	9

Source: author (Murphy).

Table 6.4 Gender breakdown from New Zealand farmers' market survey (338 responses)

Gender	*%*
Male	37
Female	63

Source: author (Murphy).

Table 6.5 Age breakdown from New Zealand farmers' market survey (337 responses)

Age	*%*
Under 30	12
30–39	16
40–49	26
50–59	19
60 plus	26

Source: author (Murphy).

Table 6.6 Income breakdown from New Zealand farmers' market survey (316 responses)

Household income (NZ$)	*%*
Up to $10k	2
>$10–30k	8
>$30–50k	18
>$50–70k	19
>$70–100k	26
> $100k	27

Source: author (Murphy).

Table 6.7 Shopping history from New Zealand farmers' market survey (340 responses)

How long shop at farmers' markets	%
< 1 month	9
1–6 months	11
7–12 months	11
1–3 years	33
> 3 years	36

Source: author (Murphy).

Table 6.8 Educational backgrounds from New Zealand farmers' market survey (313 responses)

Highest education level	%
None	0.3
School	23
Polytechnic	12
University	64

Source: author (Murphy).

Table 6.9 Food knowledge breakdown from New Zealand farmers' market survey (347 responses)

Food knowledge	%
Low	61
High	39

Source: author (Murphy).

Table 6.10 Percentages travelling various distances from New Zealand farmers' market survey (338 responses)

Distance travelled to market (km)	*Local*	*Tourist*
< 10	59	
10–20	11	
21–50		6
51–100		15
> 100 and overseas		8
Unspecified		1

Source: author (Murphy).

Table 6.11 Spending patterns from New Zealand farmers' market survey (324 responses)

Average spend at farmers' market	*%*
< $20	37
$20–39	35
$40–59	20
$60 plus	8

Source: author (Murphy).

the most frequently mentioned defining factor (34 per cent), with other product-related constructs also featuring highly, including being 'home-made', realistically priced and free from chemical sprays (Table 6.12). However, measures relating to place, space and socio-cultural aspects also featured prominently here, including 'socialising' (mostly with other customers) in a 'relaxed atmosphere', eating food while there, and interacting with sellers. A *social responsibility* orientation was also evident, with customers interested in localness, environmental suitability and traceability. Although this last mention has food security connotations it also is a measure of *authenticity*, which also appears under 'being a food market only'. Producers in the study, whilst placing greatest emphasis on a functional definition of the market as a place where the grower can directly sell produce, also stressed elements of interactive (co-creative) meaning (Payne *et al.*, 2008), as reinforced by their fourth most popular mention being 'talking with customers'. When thinking of customer motives, producers were, in fact, quite in agreement with what customers themselves mentioned, rather different from their own motives.

That the quality of produce available at farmers' markets is the most highly rated attribute by customers (including the most frequent shoppers), as well as rated highly by producers, accords with previous findings on farmers' markets elsewhere (Payet *et al.*, 2005; Worsfold *et al.*, 2004). The benefits and costs of organic food and knowledgeable customers obtaining 'healthy' food often rated a close second. From a New Zealand survey comparing the highest-rated positive and negative rated factors separately, as summarised in Tables 6.13 and 6.14, we can see a definite split between perceived attractors to a market and the negative factors, along with variations in the ratings and ranking of these between customers, producers and producers' impressions of what customers ratings would be (with some of the wider variations highlighted).

Some more functional food factors for everyday shopping such as 'Low price' and 'Food on special', and even 'Organically produced food' appear low on the ratings of positive attractions, although 'Higher price' is listed as the number one factor for customers on the off-putting, negative factor list. This can be explained by the fact that customers already at farmers' markets could not readily identify reasons for coming less often, or spending less money, and thus disagreed with these potential negative influences (rated on the unimportant side of neutral). Of those negative influencers that did feature, price was the highest rated, but even this received a rather 'neutral' rating on a scale of 1–7.

Table 6.12 Visitor meanings of farmers' markets: unprompted definitions

Meaning of farmers' markets (unprompted mentions)	*Customer mentions (% of sample mentioning)*	*Producer mentions (% of sample mentioning)*	*Producer mentions of customer meanings (% mentioning)*
Fresh	119 (33.7)	28 (25.2)	53 (4.7)
Produce sold by growers	108 (30.6)	43 (38.7)	22 (19.8)
Local	99 (28.0)	29 (26.1)	34 (30.6)
Home grown/homemade product	52 (14.7)	2 (1.8)	3 (2.7)
Socialising	37 (10.5)	6 (5.4)	14 (12.6)
Relaxed shopping	26 (7.4)	1 (0.9)	2 (1.8)
Quality goods	26 (7.4)	9 (8.1)	11 (9.9)
Realistic price/cost	23 (6.5)	3 (2.7)	14 (12.6)
Spray-free/free-range product	20 (5.7)	1 (0.9)	2 (1.8)
Talking to producers/ knowledge	19 (5.4)	11 (9.9)	8 (7.2)
Variety of products	15 (4.2)	1 (0.9)	4 (3.6)
Support community	15 (4.2	4 (3.6)	3 (2.7)
Traceability of goods	11 (3.1)	4 (3.6)	6 (5.4)
Being food market only	10 (2.8)	3 (2.7)	1 (0.9)
Great place to visit	9 (2.5)	–	1 (0.9)
Place for breakfast on weekend	8 (2.3)	–	1 (0.9)
Different products from shops	7 (2.0)	2 (1.8)	2 (1.8)
Friendly	7 (2.0)	3 (2.7)	1 (0.9)
Interest	5 (1.4)	1 (0.9)	1 (0.9)
Reliable	1 (0.3)	1 (0.9)	1 (0.9)
Fun	–	5 (4.5)	3 (2.7)
Educational and informative	–	9 (8.1)	2 (1.8)
Good income	–	8 (7.2)	1 (0.9)
Total mentions	*617*	*174*	*190*
Sample size	*353*	*111*	*111*

Source: author (Murphy).

Bargain hunting did not tend to feature as an important positive attraction attribute for customers, who indicated they were not interested in seeking cheap products, with price specials and promotions rated low. This result concurs with other research that hypothesises that the general price level is a potentially negative influencer (Pan and Zinkhan, 2006), but in the case of farmers' markets existing customers did not find this to be particularly important. Customers also

Table 6.13 Importance ratings and rankings of positive influences/attraction motivators for farmers' market visits: customers, producers and producers' impressions of customer ratings, including most significant ranking variations

	Customers				*Producers*		*Producers' impressions of customers*	
Positive influences	*Rank all*	*Mean all*	*Mean tourists*	*Mean frequent visitors*	*Mean*	*Rank*	*Mean*	*Rank*
Quality produce	1	6.2		6.3*	6.6*	1=	6.5*	1
Healthy food	2	6.0		6.2*	6.2	5	6.2	3
Seasonal produce	**3=**	5.7		5.9**	5.4**	**11**	5.4	**10**
Support local community	**3=**	5.7	6.0*		5.6	**9**	5.2*	**11**
Locally produced food	5	5.6		5.7**	6.3*	4	6.1*	4
Having a good time	6=	5.5	5.9**		6.0*	6=	5.9**	6=
Customer service	**6=**	5.5		5.6*	6.6*	**1=**	6.4*	**2**
Lively atmosphere	8	5.3			5.9*	8	5.7**	8
Good looking food	9	5.2			6.0*	6=	5.9*	6=
Trying food on the spot	10=	5.1	5.4**	4.8*	5.3	12	5.6*	9
Slow pace	**10=**	5.1			4.8	**14**	5.0	12=
Talk producer/ customer	**12=**	5.0			6.5*	**3**	6.0*	5
More money to producers	**12=**	5.0			5.5*	10	4.3*	**16**
Low price	14	4.8	4.5*	5.0**	4.4**	15	4.7	14=
Organically produced	15	4.7	5.2*		3.9*	16	4.7	14=
Entertainment	**16**	4.4	4.8*		5.0*	13	5.0*	**12=**
Food on special	17	4.1			3.1*	17	3.8	17
Respondents		*350*	*95*	*191*	*110*		*110*	

Source: author (Murphy).

Notes
Bold if variance 4 or over: mean scorings of ratings 1 = low to 7 = high. Differences between high and low levels of customer groups */** significant (* = 0.05; ** = 0.01) for frequent vs tourist/infrequent visitors; customer and producer; producer-as-customer perceptions.

Table 6.14 Importance ratings and rankings of negative influences/attraction motivators for farmers' market visits: customers and producers' impressions of customer ratings, including most significant ranking variations

	Customers				Producers' impressions of customers	
Negative influences	*Rank all*	*Mean all*	*Mean tourists*	*Mean frequent visitors*	*Mean*	*Rank*
Higher price	1	4.1		3*6	4.6*	4=
Parking	2	3.8	4.1**	3.4*	5.0*	1=
Affected by weather	3	3.7	4.1*	3.4*	4.6*	4=
Limited range	4=	3.6			4.6*	4=
Unattractive looking	4=	3.6			5.0*	1=
Inconvenient location	6	3.5		3.2*	4.6*	4=
Low availability (seasonal)	7=	3.4			4.4*	10
Poor design/ organisation	7=	3.4		3.2**	4.5*	9
Lack of information dates/times	**7=**	3.4		3.0*	4.7*	**3**
Limited hours of operation	7=	3.4			4.0**	**12**
Lack of special offers (price)	11=	3.3			3.8**	13
Poor advertising	**11=**	3.3		3.1**	4.6*	**4=**
Don't enjoy myself there	11=	3.3		3.0*	4.2*	11
Takes too long to do the shopping	14	2.8		2.6*	3.3*	14
Respondents		*347*	*94*	*188*	*103*	

Source: author (Murphy).

Notes
Bold if variance 4 or over: mean scorings of ratings 1 = low to 7 = high. Differences between high and low levels of customer groups */** significant (* = 0.01; ** = 0.05) for frequent vs tourist/ infrequent visitors; customer and producer; producer-as-customer perceptions.

appeared to prefer that producers earned a decent income and provided quality rather than pursuing 'Low price' cheap food, and 'tourists' are even less interested in getting a bargain than locals (average rating of 4.5), although more frequent visitors are rather more interested in this (rating of 5.0).

In contrast, on the positive attractors list, many more visitor and tourist (or leisure shopping) factors appear as highly rated positive factors for consumers and producers alike (although the rating levels and specific order vary between them at times). Thus 'Having a good time', 'Trying food on the spot' and a 'Lively atmosphere' appear amongst many other attributes that seem to be around socio-cultural aspects, including aspects of locality. Visitors from further afield rate these attractors as even more important than locals. Customers at farmers' markets appear to value nostalgic elements of earlier modes of retailing, identifying the presence of a 'Slow pace' of browsing and shopping along with 'Talk[ing to] producer [or] customer'. These attitudes are also reflected in the negatively worded negative influencers, with 'Don't enjoy myself there' registering a low rating as a reason for minimising visitation and expenditure, whereas 'Having a good time' is placed relatively highly in the attractors. Likewise 'Takes too long to do the shopping' is not supported, whereas 'Slow pace' is.

The low rating for 'Entertainment' is, in the main, a function of the aural stimuli of bands playing (rating the second-lowest among the positive influencers), with producers who regularly attend differing in opinion here, commenting quite positively on bands as 'setting the mood' (and perhaps breaking the monotony of customer interaction). Interestingly, 'tourists' rated the importance of entertainment as significantly higher than locals, albeit still at a relatively low level of 4.8 out of 7.

Customers appreciated being able to try the food, and the interaction that activity entailed. Producers likewise placed importance on the more social aspects of the market environment – *both* with other producers and with customers. Producers also thought this interaction was more important from the customers' point of view, reinforcing their commitment to the market as a consumption experience in itself. For producers the influence of quality was closely followed by customer service and engaging with the customer, reflecting an interest in interactivity and co-creation (Payne *et al.*, 2008). Customers rated supporting the local community of greater importance than either producers or producers' perceptions of customers. In respect of this, one imagines, customers rated the earning potential of producers to be important (more so than what producers thought customers would value).

Retail design and other retail organisation influences were also presented as negatives (potential barriers to greater participation), as a lack of congruence in store atmospheric stimuli has been shown elsewhere to have a greater negative impact than the potential positive impact when stimuli are well coordinated (Parsons and Conroy, 2006). More frequent customers were even less concerned about these factors. Far-flung 'tourists' were more likely to be concerned about the ease of parking and the influence of the weather than locals, and much more so than frequent customers, reflecting a lack of commitment and perhaps involvement in the markets as a part of regular shopping activity. This may also be a function of alternative calls on the time of the tourist, with shopping outdoors in inclement weather not likely to be a priority. Conversely, the market at Matakana is only 7 km from the beach resort of Omaha, and 15 km from the golden sands of Tawharanui Regional Park; tourists may prefer the beaches to the crowded market on a beautiful sunny day.

Providing good customer service was rated as significantly more important by producers considering their own motives, and speculating about customers, than by customers themselves. However, customers rated supporting the local community as of greater importance than either producers or producers' perceptions of customers. Producers likewise did not think the generally higher prices found at the markets were a big problem for customers, rating parking as a larger problem, particularly in markets without plentiful nearby provision. This construct of inconvenience might reflect the difficulties producers experience in getting their produce and supporting infrastructure such as trestle tables to the market. Likewise, producers are more affected by the weather than customers because they have to remain in bad weather, whereas customers are more likely to stay at or return to home. Although this behavioural response might not adversely determine customer attitudes towards the weather, it is detrimental to producer takings. Lastly, customers did not appear to be negatively influenced by seasonality or vendor assortment decisions.

Conclusions: farmers' markets as tourist retail attractions

Farmers' markets are growing rapidly in number and influence in the retail scene in the UK, New Zealand and elsewhere. Their turnover may be small relative to the chain supermarkets, but their position in consumer behavioural patterns and in the public consciousness, particularly through food and tourist/travel media coverage, as well as in producer/small-farmer business plans is much more significant than even a few years ago. Because of their ephemeral and interactive nature, farmers' markets have marked points of difference from regular retail environments, and the aim of this chapter was to establish how farmers' markets may operate as retail and tourist spaces as part of place attractions. Many farmers' markets use variations on the 'meet the people who grow your food!' tagline in their marketing efforts, suggesting a perceived interactional and locality value in the form of a retail-based, co-creative and socio-emotive interaction between customers and producers (Payne *et al.*, 2008; Vargo and Lusch, 2004).

The study featured here on markets around New Zealand suggests that this notion of co-creation is of greater importance to producers than it is to customers, with the latter indicating preferences for broader, more social-emotional goals such as in supporting the local community and finding local produce. Detracting influences, such as market design and product range limitations, were not strongly supported by consumers, whereas producers were more concerned about these factors on behalf of customers.

Of course no two visitors to a farmers' market are exactly alike. In order to tease out some of the more important differentiating elements of customer perceptions, this chapter has considered the attitudes of customers that visit markets the most frequently compared with those that visit rarely, and those that live locally versus those that have travelled at least 20 km. The latter distinction might be considered as a rudimentary segmentation of farmers' markets into what has been termed *tourist farmer market appeal* and *local farmer market appeal*. Frequent visitors rate the most important attracting elements of markets as even more important (quality, seasonality, localism) and rate negative elements as closer to unimportant (price, parking, weather, location and enjoyment). For two elements the most frequent visitors portray their market experience, by being less interested in trying food on the spot, and being more interested in lower prices. Visitors who have come the furthest (here labelled 'tourists') are more interested in trying food, having a good time, entertainment and supporting the local community; and less interested in obtaining low prices. They also specify a greater concern with the impact of the weather, and in the ease of parking. This last concern applies particularly to Matakana, where cars can crawl for many kilometres approaching the village because of a lack of accessible parking in close proximity to the market.

In summary, standard retail concepts do apply to farmers' markets, but in varying ways from mainstream retail stores given the temporary and transitional nature of the spaces and places of the markets. Although these may appear to be disorganised and flimsy retail environments, some careful planning of assortment, promotion and product placement does occur, if only to placate the potential rivalries among producers. The lack of sophistication is often a drawcard for visitors, as they may inculcate a sense of 'authenticity' relating to a perceived bygone era 'dreamscape' of small-scale, local and interactive retailing that encourages visitation. Such customer nostalgia may be deliberate, as market organisers incorporate rustic and temporary elements into the market design, even for permanent sites (such as seen at Matakana), reflecting what S. Brown (2001) termed the 'retro revolution'. Should farmers' markets continue to proliferate, and constitute a greater proportion of shopper discretionary spending, then considering the retail marketing aspects of these *throwback* retail spaces that many markets present will assume greater importance in the future.

The food consumer, just like all other consumers, is a beast of change. There have been a series of recognisable eras of food consumption with specific characteristics of production, distribution and purchase. Most recently food consumers' behaviour has been characterised by concerns relating to healthy eating, food safety, the environment, quality and food culture – these all having relevance to food's significance to, and relationship with, 'place'. These issues affect the individual, whether at home or away. In response to this a series of initiatives have developed, farmers' markets being part of modern developments in responding to the needs to distinguish local food and its supply chain. Rather than being a simple source of functional nutrition, 'local' food of distinction can hopefully be recognised and reinstated as a fundamental part of an area and its inhabitants' heritage, thereby serving to identify individuals and their environment.

In terms of pursuing the authentic and the sustainable by attracting consumers back to connecting food with 'old world' notions of place and consumption space – in a construction between the food, society and the individual – new platforms can be more inclusive, if ultimately only representing an impression of the original that may be considered contrived or staged. Ultimately though, are not the arbiters of what is or is not authentic to a locality as likely to be the tourists as the locals, or both in partnership?

References

Alkon, A. (2008a) Paradise or pavement: the social constructions of the environment in two urban farmers' markets and their implications for environmental justice and sustainability. *Local Environment* 13(3), 271–289.

Alkon, A. (2008b) From value to values: sustainable consumption at farmers markets. *Agriculture and Human Values* 25(4), 487–498.

Andreatta, S. and Wickliffe, W. (2002) Managing farmer and consumer expectations: a study of a North Carolina farmers market. *Human Organization* 61(2), 167–176.

Ãseb, K., Jervell, A. M., Lieblein, G., Svennerud, M. and Francis, C. (2007) Farmer and consumer attitudes at farmers markets in Norway. *Journal of Sustainable Agriculture* 30(4), 67–93.

Atkins, P. and Bowler, I. (2001) *Food in Society.* London: Arnold.

Baber, L. M. and Frongillo, E. A. (2003) Family and seller interactions in farmers' markets in upstate New York. *American Journal of Alternative Agriculture* 18(2), 87–94.

Beer, S. C. (2001) Food and society. In Eastham, L., Sharples, L. and Ball, S. (eds) *Food Supply Chain Management: Issues for the hospitality and retail sectors.* Oxford: Butterworth-Heinemann, pp. 21–37.

Beer, S. C. (2008) Authenticity and food experience: commercial and academic perspectives. *Journal of Foodservice* 19, 153–163.

Beer, S. C. (2009) What is ethnic: reappraising ethnic food and multiculturalism among the white British. In Lindgreen, A. and Hingley, M. K. (eds) *The New Cultures of Food: Marketing opportunities from ethnic, religious and cultural diversity.* London: Gower, pp. 3–31.

Beer, S. C. and Redman, M. (1996) The relationship between post war cultural shift, consumer perspectives and farming policy. In Edwards, J. S. A. (ed.) *Culinary Arts and Sciences: Global and national perspectives.* Southampton: Research Machines, pp. 351–362.

Bellamy, R. (2005) *Food for All (Action for the Environment).* Monkato: Black Rabbit Books.

Belliveau, S. (2005) Resisting global, buying local: Goldschmidt revisited. *Great Lakes Geographer* 12(1), 44–53.

Bentley, G., Hallsworth, A. G. and Bryan, A. (2003) The countryside in the city: situating a farmers' market in Birmingham. *Local Economy* 18(2), 109–120.

Berger, P. and Luckmann, T. (1966) *The Social Construction of Reality.* London: Penguin.

Blythman, J. (2005) *Shopped: The shocking power of British supermarkets.* London: Harper Perennial.

Body, R. (1982) *Agriculture: The triumph and the shame.* London: Temple Smith.

Body, R. (1984) *Farming in the Clouds.* London: Temple Smith.

Body, R. (1987) *Red or Green for Farmers (and the Rest of Us).* Newport: Broadleys.

Boniface, P. (2003) *Tasting Tourism.* Aldershot: Ashgate.

Boynton, L. (1986) The effect of tourism on Amish quilt designs. *Annals of Tourism Research* 13, 451–465.

BPM (2010) *Barnstaple Pannier Market.* Online source: http://www.barnstaplepanniermarket.co.uk/ (last accessed 13 July 2010).

Brown, A. (2001) Counting farmers markets. *Geographical Review* 91(4), 655–674.

Brown, A. (2002) Farmers' market research 1940–2000: an inventory and review. *American Journal of Alternative Agriculture* 17(4), 167–176.

Brown, C. (2003) Consumers' preferences for locally produced food: a study in Southeast Missouri. *American Journal of Alternative Agriculture* 18(4), 213–224.

Brown, C. and Miller, S. (2008) The impacts of local markets: a review of research on farmers markets and community supported agriculture (CSA). *American Journal of Agricultural Economics* 90(5), 1296–1302.

Brown, S. (2001) *Marketing: The retro revolution.* London: Sage.

Bruner, E. (1994) Abraham Lincoln as authentic reproduction: a critique of postmodernism. *American Anthropologist* 96, 397–415.

Bryant, C. A., Dewalt, K. M., Courtney, A. and Schwartz, J. (2004) *The Cultural Feast: An introduction to food and society*, 2nd edition. Pacific Grove: Brooks/Cole.

Burr, V. (1995) *Social Constructionism.* London: Routledge.

Cable, V. (2009) *The Storm: The world economic crisis and what it means.* London: Atlantic Books.

Cameron, A. (2005) New generation farmers' markets: another option for small producers. *The Smallfarmer* 61, 8.

Carson, R. (2002) *Silent Spring.* New York: Mariner Books, Houghton and Mifflin.

Chhabra, D. (2008) Positioning museums on an authenticity continuum. *Annals of Tourism Research* 35(2), 427–447.

Chiffoleau, Y. (2009) From politics to cooperation: The dynamics of embeddedness in alternative food supply chains. *Sociologia Ruralis* 49(3), 218–235.

Clapp, J., and Fouchs, D. (2009) *Corporate Power in Global Agrifood Governance.* Boston: MIT Press.

Clunies-Ross, T., and Hildyard, N. (1992) *The Politics of Industrial Agriculture.* London: Earthscan.

Cohen, E. (1988) Authenticity and commoditization in tourism. *Annals of Tourism Research* 15(3), 371–386.

Cohen, E. (1989) Primitive and remote: hill tribe trekking in Thailand. *Annals of Tourism Research* 16 (1), 30–61.

Cohen, E. (2001) Ethnic tourism in south east Asia. In Tan, C. B., Cheung, C. H., and Hui, Y. (eds) *Tourism, Anthropology and China.* Singapore: White Lotus.

Cohen, E. (2007) 'Authenticity' in tourism studies: apres la lutte. *Tourism and Recreation Research* 32(2), 75–82.

Cole, S. (2007) Beyond authenticity and commodification. *Annals of Tourism Research* 34(4), 943–960.

Connell, D. J., Smithers, J. and Joseph, A. (2008) Farmers' markets and the good 'food' value chain: a preliminary study. *Local Environment* 13(3), 169–185.

Daniel, Y. P. (1996) Tourism dance performances authenticity and creativity. *Annals of Tourism Research* 23(4), 780–797.

DEFRA (2010) *Protected Food Names Scheme.* Online source: http://www.defra.gov.uk/foodfarm/food/industry/regional/foodname/index.htm (last accessed 20 July 2010).

FARMA (2009) *Certification.* Online source: http://www.farmersmarkets.net/certification2.htm. (last accessed 21 December 2009).

Festing, H. (1994) *Should Farmers Market Direct to Consumers? America says yes.* Ashford: Wye College Press – Food Industry Perspectives.

FMNZ (2008) Farmers' Markets New Zealand Incorporated website. Online source: http://www.farmersmarkets.org.nz/home.htm (last accessed 9 November 2011).

Gergen, K. J. (2009) *An Invitation to Social Construction.* London: Sage.

Germov, J. and Williams, L. (1999) *A Sociology of Food and Nutrition: The social appetite.* Victoria: Oxford University Press.

Govindasamy, R., Italia, J., Zurbriggen, M. and Hossain, F. (2002) Predicting consumer willingness-to-purchase value-added products at direct agricultural markets. *Journal of Food Products Marketing* 8(1), 1–15.

Govindasamy, R., Italia, J., Zurbriggen, M. and Hossain, F. (2003) Producer satisfaction with returns from farmers' market related activity. *American Journal of Alternative Agriculture* 18(2), 80–86.

Goyan Kittler, P. and Sucher, K. P. (2008) *Food and culture*, 5th edition. Andover: Cengage Learning.

Gregson, N., Longstaff, B. and Crewe, L. (1997) Excluded spaces of regulation: car-boot sales as an enterprise culture out of control? *Environment and Planning A* 29(10), 1717–1737.

Guthman, J., Morris A. W. and Allen, P. (2006) Squaring farm security and food security in two types of alternative food institutions. *Rural Sociology* 71(4), 662–684.

Guthrie, J., Guthrie, A., Lawson, R. and Cameron, A. (2006) Farmers' markets: the small business counter-revolution in food production and retailing. *British Food Journal* 108(7), 560–573.

Hall, C. M., Mitchell, R., Scott, D. and Sharples, L. (2008). The authentic market experience of farmers' markets. In Hall, C. M. and Sharples, L. (eds) *Food and Wine Festivals and Events around the World*. Oxford: Butterworth-Heinemann (Elsevier), pp. 197–231.

Hamilton Farmers' Market (2008) 10 reasons to shop at your local farmers' market. Online source: www.hamiltonfarmersmarket.co.nz/why.html (last accessed 30 January 2008).

Harris, M. (1985) *Good to Eat: Riddles of food and culture*. London: Allen and Unwin.

Harvey, G. (1998) *The Killing of the Countryside*. London: Jonathan Cape.

Higgins, D. (2006) Local flavour save. *Alternatives Journal* 32(3), 23.

Hinrichs, C. C. and Allen, P. (2008) Selective patronage and social justice: local food consumer campaigns in historical context. *Journal of Agricultural and Environmental Ethics* 21(4), 329–352.

Hinrichs, C. C., Gillespie, G. W. and Feenstra, G. W. (2004) Social learning and innovation at retail farmers' markets. *Rural Sociology* 69(1), 31–58.

Holloway, L. and Kneafsey, M. (2000) Reading the space of the farmers' market: a preliminary investigation from the UK. *Sociologia Ruralis* 40(3), 285–299.

Hughes, G. (1995a) Food, tourism and Scottish heritage. In Leslie, D. (ed.) *Tourism and Leisure: Cultural heritage and participation*. Brighton: LSA, pp. 109–128.

Hughes, G. (1995b) Authenticity in tourism. *Annals of Tourism Research* 22(4), 781–803.

Hughner, R., Robinson, J. and Nganje, W. (2008) Stated and revealed preference for locally grown produce: implications for food marketing systems. Proceedings of the 33rd Annual Meeting of the Macromarketing Society, Clemson, SC, 4–7 June, pp. 136–138.

Hunt, A. R. (2007) Consumer interactions and influences on farmers' market vendors. *Renewable Agriculture and Food Systems* 22(1), 54–66.

Jarosz, L. (2008) The city in the country: growing alternative food networks in metropolitan areas. *Journal of Rural Studies* 24(3), 231–244.

King, C. A. (2008) Community resilience and contemporary agri-ecological systems: reconnecting people and food, and people with people. *Systems Research and Behavioral Science* 25(1), 111–124.

Kirwan, J. (2004) Alternative strategies in the UK agro-food system: interrogating the alterity of farmers' markets. *Sociologia Ruralis* 44(4), 395–415.

Kirwan, J. (2006) The interpersonal world of direct marketing: examining conventions of quality at UK farmers' markets. *Journal of Rural Studies* 22(3), 301–312.

Klein, D. (2008) North Island coast of small wineries and big pleasures. *New York Times*, 13 January. Online source: http://travel.nytimes.com/2008/01/13/travel/13next.html (last accessed 9 November 2011).

Kneafsey, M., Holloway, L., Venn, L., Dowler, E., Cox, R. and Tuomainen, H. (2008) *Reconnecting Consumers, Food and Producers: Exploring alternatives*. Oxford: Berg.

Knudsen, B. T. and Waarde, A. M. (2010) *Re-investing Authenticity: Tourism, place and emotions*. Bristol: Channel View Publications.

Lang, T., Barling, D. and Caraher, M. (2009) *Food Policy: Integrating health, environment and society*. Oxford: OUP.

Lawson, R., Guthrie, J., Cameron, A. and Fischer, W. C. (2008) Creating value through cooperation: an investigation of farmers' markets in New Zealand. *British Food Journal* 110(1), 11–25.

Lewis, G. H. (1997) Celebrating asparagus: community and the rationally constructed food festival. *Journal of American Culture* 20(4), 73–78.

Littrell, M. A., Stout, J. A. and Reilly, R. (1991) In-home businesses: profiles of successful and struggling craft producers. *Family and Consumer Sciences Research Journal* 20(1), 26–39.

Lockie, S., Lyons, K. and Lawrence, G. (2000) Constructing 'green' foods: corporate capital, risk, and organic farming in Australia and New Zealand. *Agriculture and Human Values* 17(4), 315–322.

Long, L. M. (2004) *Culinary Tourism*. Lexington: University Press of Kentucky.

MacCannell, D. (1973) Staged authenticity: arrangements of social space in tourist settings. *American Journal of Sociology* 79(3), 589–603.

MacCannell, D. (1976) *The Tourist: A new theory of the leisure class*. New York: Schocken Books.

Marshall, D. (2005) Food as ritual, routine or convention. *Consumption, Markets and Culture* 8(1), 65–85.

McIntosh, W. A. (1996) *Sociologies of Food and Nutrition*. London: Plenum Press.

Mennell, S. (1992) *Sociology of Food and Eating: Eating, diet and culture*. London: Sage Publications.

Millinger, W. (1994) Towards a critical analysis of tourism representations. *Annals of Tourism Research* 21, 756–779.

Millstone, E. and Lang, T. (2003) *The Atlas of Food: Who eats what, where and why*, second edition. London: Earthscan.

Molz, E. (2007) Eating difference: the cosmopolitan mobilities of culinary tourism. *Space and Culture* 10, 77–93.

Murphy, AJ. (2011) Farmers' markets as retail spaces. *International Journal of Retail and Distribution Management* 39(8), 582–597.

Nellemann, C. (2009) *The Environmental Food Crisis: The environment's role in averting future food crises*. Stevenage: United Nations Environment Programme.

Nestle, M. (2004) *Food Politics: How the food industry influences nutrition and health*. California Studies in Food & Culture. Berkeley: University of California Press.

O'Connor, B. (2010) *The Law of Geographic Indications*. London: Cameron May.

Pan, Y. and Zinkhan, G. M. (2006) Determinants of retail patronage: a meta-analytical perspective. *Journal of Retailing* 82(3), 229–243.

Parsons, A. and Conroy, D. (2006) Sensory stimuli and e-tailers. *Journal of Consumer Behaviour* 5(1), 69–81.

Patel, R. (2007) *Stuffed and Starved: Markets, power and the hidden battle for the world food system*. London: Portobello Books.

Payet, J., Gilles, M. and Howat, P. (2005) Gascoyne Growers Market: a sustainable health promotion activity developed in partnership with the community. *Australian Journal of Rural Health* 13(5), 309–314.

Payne, A., Storbacka, K. and Frow, P. (2008) Managing the co-creation of value. *Journal of the Academy of Marketing Science* 36(1), 83–96.

Quan, S. and Wang, N. (2003) Towards a structural model of the tourist experience: an illustration from food experiences in tourism. *Tourism Management* 25, 297–305.

Reisinger, Y., and Steiner, C. J. (2006) Reconceptualizing object authenticity. *Annals of Tourism Research* 33(1), 65–86.

Richards, G. (2002) Gastronomy: an essential ingredient in tourism production and consumption. In Hjalager, A. M. and Richards, G. (eds) *Tourism and Gastronomy.* London: Routledge.

Ritzer, G. (1996) *The McDonaldization of Society*, second edition. London: Pine Forge Press.

Roberts, P. (2008) *The End of Food.* London: Bloomsbury Publishing.

Saili, A. R., Fay, M., Rola, R. and Batt, P. J. (2007) Review of farmers' markets. *Stewart Postharvest Review* 3(6), 1–6.

Schlosser, E. (2002) *Fast Food Nation.* London: Penguin Books.

Schneider, M. L. and Francis, C. A. (2005) Marketing locally produced foods: consumer and farmer opinions in Washington county, Nebraska. *Renewable Agriculture and Food Systems* 20(4), 252–260.

Schwartz, H. (1986) *Never Satisfied: A cultural history of diets, fantasies and fat.* New York: Free Press.

Seyfang, G. (2003) *From Frankenstein Foods to Veggie Box Schemes: Sustainable consumption in cultural perspective.* Working paper, Centre for Social and Economic Research on the Global Environment.

Sherry, J. F. (1990) A sociocultural analysis of a midwestern American flea market. *Journal of Consumer Research* 16(4), 13–30.

Silver, I. (1993) Marketing authenticity in third world countries. *Annals of Tourism Research* 20(2), 302–318.

Smith, V. (1977) *Hosts and Guests: The anthropology of tourism.* Oxford: Blackwell.

Smith, S. L. J. and Honggen, X. (2008) Culinary tourism supply chains: a preliminary examination. *Journal of Travel Research* 46(3), 289–299.

Smithers, J., Lamarche, J. and Joseph, A. E. (2008) Unpacking the terms of engagement with local food at the farmers' market: insights from Ontario. *Journal of Rural Studies* 24(3), 337–350.

Spiller, K. (2007) Farmer's markets. *Geography Review* 21(1), 40–41.

Stagl, S. (2002) Local organic food markets: potentials and limitations for contributing to sustainable development. *Empirica* 29(2), 145–162.

Stephenson, G., Lev, L. and Brewer, L. (2008) 'I'm getting desperate': what we know about farmers' markets that fail. *Renewable Agriculture and Food Systems* 23(3), 188–199.

Szmigin, I., Maddock, S. and Carrigan, M. (2003) Conceptualising community consumption: farmers' markets and the older consumer. *British Food Journal*, 105(8), 542–550.

Vannoppen, J., Verbeke, W., Van Huylenbroeck, G. and Viaene, J. (2001) Consumer valuation of short market channels for fresh food through laddering. *Journal of International Food and Agribusiness Marketing* 12(1), 41–69.

Vargo, S. L., Lusch, R. F. (2004) Evolving to a new dominant logic for marketing. *Journal of Marketing* 68(1), 1–17.

Wallgren, C. (2006) Local or global food markets: a comparison of energy use for transport. *Local Environment* 11(2), 233–251.

Wang, Y. (2007) Customized authenticity begins at home. *Annals of Tourism Research* 34(3), 289–804.

Warde, A. (1999) *Consumption, Food and Taste: Culinary antinomies and commodity culture*. London: Sage.

Weis, A. (2007) *The Global Food Economy: The battle for the future of farming*. London: Zed Books.

WI (2010) *The WI*. Online source: http://www.thewi.org.uk/ (last accessed 20 July 2010).

Worsfold, D., Worsfold, P. M. and Griffith, C. J. (2004) An assessment of food hygiene and safety at farmers' markets. *International Journal of Environmental Health Research* 14(2), 109–119.

Zukin, S. (2008) Consuming authenticity: from outposts of difference to means of exclusion. *Cultural Studies* 22(5), 724–748.

7 Entertainment retail tourism

Charles McIntyre and Daniel Ganly

Introduction: big store, little store – extant and extinct?

The aim of this chapter is to consider specific entertainment retail formats, large and small, and their roles as tourist attractions and experiences. It will focus particularly on the role of large department stores and entertainment product megastores in enhancing city-centre attractiveness – both being major tourist retail attractions in the last half of the twentieth century. However, whereas the earlier developed form – the department store – continues to the present day, a case study on the rise and fall of music-based 'megastores' is included as an example of a dying tourist retail format that featured widely across Europe, America, Asia and Australasia during this period. In contrast to these 'big store' tourist magnet formats, there is a consideration of the potential tourist retail attractiveness of small trader operations, with views upon their alternate effectiveness in competing for visitors (and co-existence) with the bigger players in the modern tourist retail cityscape.

Big store: department stores and tourist retail entertainment dimensions

In enhancing large town and city-centre experiences, where shopping tourism is an accepted mainstay, 'shopping events organised by big stores' have been ranked as a key entertainment activity, mentioned alongside cinema, theatre, fun-fair ice skating and festival attractions in visitor perception studies (Stachow *et al.*, 2009: 7). As the prime, long-term example of 'the big store', department stores have been described by their managers as being a 'part of show business' (Willans, 1997: 147), and from their inception have been associated with 'Grandiose architecture and theatrical forms of lighting and display' (Bowlby, 1985: 3). The department store emerged a few decades prior to Veblen's (1899) theorised rise of the leisure class, and were typified in Zola's societal writings as the place where:

> People could now come and go, to look and to dream, perchance to buy, and shopping became a new bourgeois leisure activity – a way of pleasantly passing time, like going to a play or visiting a museum.
>
> (Bowlby, 1985: 4)

The rise of telecommunications and efficient postal services at the time of the inception of department stores had already seen the advent of catalogue shopping, following on from street hawkers as an alternative to actively 'going' to shops at a time of an increased growth in consumer desires. Department stores, however, with their many product sectors under one roof for one-stop shopping, were designed to attract heavy footfalls and are the first retail format that truly focused on 'putting on a show' and inviting leisurely, 'just looking', 'scopic' or 'tourist gaze' leisure shopping activities (Bowlby, 1985; Urry, 1995; Falk, 1997). They used entertainment features and events to attract and retain customers into a dream world of desire, with social interaction and interpersonal display and promenading being noted as a key positive feature of such shopping trips (DEHCD, 1978; Glennie and Thrift, 1996; Tauber, 1972, 1995), providing sites of *détournement* and *dérive* for the designers and *flâneurs* respectively.

This theatrical consumer orientation of department stores was particularly of interest for personalised and recreational shopping behaviours of the urban leisured middle and upper classes, before the more broadly inclusive (largely suburban) shopping mall design developments in the second half of the twentieth century (Jones, 1999; Stone, 1954). The first noted large department store offering a similarly large cornucopia of delights to challenge catalogues is widely considered to be Bon Marché in Paris, opened in 1852, and the format has been heavily associated with the rise of post-industrial Parisian bourgeois city culture (Miller, 1981). Early development of department stores was also evident in other cultural locations, however, many of which have maintained a significant presence in their large towns and cities – notably in Britain, America, imperial Germany and, particularly strongly, in Japan.

The Japanese retailer Mitsukoshi showed that country's tendency towards department stores, linked to their notion of *classical shopping streets* and blocks with high levels of service, and offering a distinctive quality in the outward appearance or *Teisai* of both products and packaging (Coles, 1999a; Davies and Jones, 1993; Furihata *et al.*, 2004; Hobson and Christensen, 2001; Willans, 1997). Larke and Causton (2005), in their survey of the Japanese department store sector, classify the many remaining examples first into 'urban' and 'regional' forms, with the larger, city-centre 'urban' classification then being sub-divided into 'traditional' (often early kimono suppliers that expanded in the late 1800s) and 'railway' (established by railway companies for their travellers at their developing main stations). These larger, leading traditional department stores in Japan, although sometimes having many different types of outlets, have been shown to have a high proportion of their sales from their main outlet, of between about 20 and 60 per cent of total chain sales, thus making the main store a major visitor attraction, whereas the railway department stores, dependent upon 'casual' customer flow via stations, have been contributing to department stores' shrinkage in both total sales and numbers since the 1990s (Larke and Causton, 2005).

Larke (1994) has proposed that department stores have flourished in Japan thanks to their intrinsic involvement in traditional gift-giving of a high-status nature that has been embedded in the culture, aligned with a desire for 'a high degree of pampering' (p. 194). Possibly because of this, they also appear to have been the only large store format to have escaped Japan's Large Store Law, which aimed to protect small stores from too many large stores opening, but which seems to have had the effect of reducing retailer power as opposed to manufacturer and distributor power. Although now appearing to be suffering from some industry modernisation that is more encouraging to other large stores, nevertheless the Japanese department store is a good example of magnets for visitors from large areas of population, with many events organised within them in conjunction with traditional gift days.

The department store as an attractive tourist retail format

Relating to the nature of the 'high degree of pampering' that can be expected within a department store format, Willans (1997) contended that it should have at least four trading departments, one of which must be ladies'/girls' wear. However, in an earlier design definition by Pasdermadjian (1954: 12) the format was characterised as 'a gathering under one roof of a *considerable* number of selling departments, each of them corresponding to a speciality shop' (our emphasis). In support of this expanded notion, the provision of a speciality food offer often appears to be a key attraction of tourist-related department stores. This is evident in the grandly theatrical 'food halls' of the Harrods and KDV department stores in London and Berlin respectively as well as the current Parisian examples such as Printemps (2010) and Galeries Lafayette (2010), which offer six and sixteen food offers respectively, each targeted at different customer groups.

The essential nature and culture of department stores has been described as being overtly feminine in orientation (Albeson, 1989; Benson, 1986; Bowlby, 1985; Clarke, 2003; Laermans, 1993; Leach, 1984; Nava, 1997; Williams, 1982; Zola, 1995) and, in relation to this, has commonly featured prominent toiletry and cosmetics departments. This is noted as a key entrance floor feature of many department stores, and has specifically been described in a Swedish department store example as offering 'for young girls . . . a place of longing' (Fredriksson, 1997: 124) – should 'place' be 'palace' here?. The provision of a romantic and aspirational lingerie/undergarment department also stands as a particular female pampering treat – all such departments being essentially of a 'luxury' nature.

There are often, however, selections of other departments in major department stores, many of which would seem to be equally pampering for men or children, such as hardware, homeware and entertainment goods, including particularly grand toy departments which feature the almost mandatory Christmas grotto (and window) 'tourist' attractions. Santa's seasonal appearance alongside elaborate Christmas grottos (often with moving figures in a Disney-like fairy story telling form) is one of the earliest and most long-term entertainment retail marketing innovations generically associated with department store theatrics (Coles, 1999b), as can be seen in many Hollywood entertainment examples of the genre, often including Macy's Christmas parade through New York.

Some of the potential departments and features, although provided in many classic department stores including the Scala-Buda department store group in Hungary, are not an essential requirement for inclusion in a store format definition, as it is accepted that a sub-group of department stores are of a predominantly 'fashion' orientation, which would be where a chain store such as Marks & Spencer (M&S) may be considered to reside in the sector, as some classify it. One author has called the Scala-Buda store in Budapest 'the Marks and Spencer of Hungary' (Worthington, 1989), although it would seem that this is meant more in similarity of quality between both operations rather than similarity in their operational parameters. The Scala-Buda has one of the widest range offers possible of a department store, greatly in excess of all of the criteria stated above (and of any M&S store), and was once described as having 'a true department store range of products for sale' (Worthington, 1989: 28). All of this illustrates a continuing confusion in definition of department store product range characteristics, but there is a link between their attractions and entertainments and those of tourists and tourism in that they are generally associated with bringing a world of products to their customers. Neither total range of products nor extent of retail space in themselves, however, would make a department store. KMart or WalMart stores in the USA would surely not be considered as 'department' stores, their reduced 'femininity' dimension only being one objection. Rather they are more likely related to a variety/general store or 'big box' retail experience.

Although Timothy's (2005: 120) extended general store list of department store attributes includes 'low prices', central locations, 'cheap rents' and a wide variety of goods under one roof, the low price associations of department stores would seem more related to the lower-rent city-centre cultures during the first century of their existence – or in certain cash-strapped cultures or times (Bowlby, 1985; Fredriksson, 1997). Alternatively, in major tourist locations in France, Britain and Japan, department stores have been more related to premium quality, entertainment and enhanced co-creational value (Payne *et al.*, 2008).

Historically, department stores' multi-floor format development was due to the concentration of city-centre space and the resulting economics of urban space costs, necessitating building upwards into higher floors with lower corresponding individual floor space rents (Pasdermadjian, 1954: 10). It is particularly interesting, in respect of the multi-floor and high footfall criteria, to consider that the Japanese predilection for the department store format may be based upon Japan's city-based population densities and spatial restriction problems requiring more building upwards than outwards. The grand nature of the high block buildings often associated with the classic department stores gives them an architectural drawing power within the city, of a similar nature to classic theatre, gallery, museum and church buildings that can characterise and dominate the area in which they are sited. Their biophilic and vertical scopic drawing powers featuring high ceilings and atrium spaces, has drawn comparisons to the grand exhibition buildings at the end of the eighteenth century, the same time as the advent of the department store (Bowlby, 1985; Pasdermadjian, 1954).

The grand aspects of the design and experience of the department store, in fact, illuminates experiential similarities with the cruise ship experience, that other grand link to high living and the status aspirations and associations of the classical leisured (and promenading) lifestyle, within which to see and be seen (Quartermaine and Peter, 2006). Department stores have been described as being 'linked to the visual' in terms of imaginative display opportunities and the spatial display opportunities that the format offered, constructing in effect a narrative of lifestyle and aspirational aspects of status and self-image related to how the product is displayed as well as intrinsic aspects of the products themselves – a grandeur consisting of the 'spectacle' of internal display (Debord, 2009). The department store can be seen as a form of virtual tourism where the markets of the world are *brought to the customer*, themselves 'cocooned' in a luxury environment replete with grand, palatial surrounding and rococo restaurants; the cruise shop experience has a similar appeal, but instead *takes the customer to* the markets of the world (see Figure 7.1). The cruise ship experience design dimensions, at least in its classic, mythic form, consists of a perception of high personal service levels and indulgence (and high staff costs) in a visual spectacle environment, akin to that of the department store format, both being original products of glass and steel industrialisation processes (Dotson and Patton, 1992; Gilchrist, 1994).

Of course 'grandeur' is also displayed in shopping malls, and modern mega-cruise ships have often been compared in internal design to these manifestations

Figure 7.1 Advertisements for Galeries Lafayette department store in Paris (the two on the right), and the similarly 'classic' tourist event of a cruise, illustrating an experiential link, beyond spatial design characteristics of both (sources: Avellis and Guyon, 1996; Quartermaine and Peter, 2006; the authors).

of consumerist modernity (the cruise ships themselves often contain shopping malls). Much has been written about the spatial characteristics of the shopping mall relating to lifestyle shopping (Goss, 1992, 1993, 1999; Shields, 1989, 1992; Uzzell, 1995) and there is little doubt that they contribute to a postmodern culture of the spectacle and meaning in terms of a mythical/magical landscape of grandeur or power to explore (Venkatesh, 1992; Zukin, 1991), perhaps in this way attempting to supplant the classic city-centre department store of a past age? There is also a growing symbiosis and interdependency; wherein the mega-shopping mall's original, predominant locations on the peripheries of large cities have now stretched into inner cities, with department stores often serving as 'anchor tenants'.

The overwhelming *scopic* dimension, in relation to tourist-based gazing attractions in the atriums of malls, is the noted increased exploratory vertical orientation of tourists in a public realm, over the predominant horizontal gaze of non-tourist behaviours (Falk, 1997: 183). Department stores, arcades and malls present galleried and domed ceiling features and characteristics to facilitate promenading behaviours, often under weather-sheltering yet prismatic cover of glass and steel canopies (Benjamin, 2002; Bowlby, 1985; Galeries Lafayette, 2010; Printemps, 2010). Chain stores and 'big box' retailers in contrast often exclude daylight and have lowered, suspended ceilings to give and accent primarily on the products, thereby remaining somewhat distant from a 'big store', vertical tourist gaze orientation (Falk, 1997).

A spectacular element of the department store category, that would go against M&S being one in most cases, is the contention that department stores have a distinct role in the definition of place and that they have a specifically defined cultural form that is strongly likened to locality and local place distinction (Chaney, 1983; Timothy, 2005: 83). This would give distinctive appeal to tourists, and this attractive local distinctiveness effectively makes local people into tourists as they come into socio-cultural centres from the suburbanised surrounding areas (Bowlby, 1985). In this respect, the city centre has been described as being spatially 'no longer lived and . . . no longer understood practically. It is only an object of cultural consumption for tourists' (Lefebre, 1996: 148). Big box retailers and M&S stores in contrast are largely of a standardised, efficient and generically defined 'chain store' format; often blamed for the generation of modernistic, commoditised, homogenised shopping malls and 'clone town' public spaces of McDonaldisation, if not Disneyisation dimensions (Bryman, 2004; Carmona *et al.*, 2008; Guy and Bennison, 2007; Hollander, 1973, 1979; Ritzer, 1996).

Whilst there are a growing number of department store chains in modern retail, the department store format itself is, and has always been, very large and costly in relation to other retail formats and is 'anchored' physically to a specific locality. They are highly dependant upon an enhanced frequency of visitation by local residents and visitors alike. They are usually, of necessity, had to significantly adapt its offer to the needs of its local population, and this locality identification may be one of the secrets of their attraction to tourists. Macy's, Harrods and Galeries Lafayette effectively define New York, London and Paris just as adequately as the Statue of Liberty, Big Ben and the Eiffel Tower. This is where comparisons can be made with some of the experiential differentiation in localised branches of major tourist city theme restaurant chains. A consumer, in brand personification of image effects may thus be desiring to 'wear the T-shirt' or display the 'carrier bag effect' of locally significant 'I-was-there' retail outlets in the same way as they will go for the Hard Rock Cafe to signify their touristic experience of a distinct location.

For newer and chain branches of department stores this 'fitting in' with the local environment, or dominating in a way that enhances the surroundings, can be a tough job. In this respect Selfridges Birmingham is perceived as being, and needing to be, distinct from Selfridges London from a consumer point of view, but yet avoiding negative incongruity dominance with its local surroundings. Harrods, Knightsbridge, and Selfridges, Oxford Street, and many other traditionally long-standing department stores do not have this problem in that their external architecture has come to define the appearance of the area itself through organic acceptance. Selfridges Birmingham seems to have accomplished acceptance and place attractiveness by the creative building in of architecturally significant and distinct external fascia features to what was a new-build, generic shopping mall location; it effectively uses incongruity dominance to positive effect through pleasing and innovative design features that effectively redefine (or rebrand) the locality itself, contributing new location identity values (see Figure 7.2). This imagery has received much attention in the media for its attractiveness and distinctiveness, thereby coming to form a new symbol for the city's identity for visitors in much

Figure 7.2 Incongruity dominance overcome? Selfridges department store, Birmingham: using a creatively distinctive building design in terms of architecturally significant and distinct external fascia features to dominate the cityscape (source: Selfridges, 2010).

in the same way that the incongruous but exceptional design of the Sydney Opera House structure did for that cityscape's identification in the 1960s.

It is the Japanese department stores, including Daimaru, Isetan, Misukoshio, Seiyu, Sogo and Takashimaya, that have shown some of the greatest tendencies in the sector to move internationally (Davies and Jones, 1993; Williamson, 1986). This is possibly on account of a limited domestic space and expansion 'push' effect, as well as their obvious success in their home territory. It has also been suggested that there is a strong 'pull' factor in these stores appealing to Japanese tourists in cities with high visitation rates (Hobson and Christensen, 2001). The French Galeries Lafayette have also expanded as a major department store brand, but success in department store expansion has been limited and many dominant stores in particular countries or locations remain only of localised importance. The need to achieve distinctive qualities for a department store brand to exert sufficient trade in new regions has already been mentioned in comparison with chain stores' greater abilities to translate and 'fit in'. The much larger investment required for department store expansion is therefore an issue here. These difficulties may be considered in relation to Michael Porter's (1980) generic strategies for business orientation (Figure 7.3). Department stores, in this model, fall within the non-cost-based, wide scope and high differentiation quartile of this model. This position would seem to give problems in gaining establishment in new territories due to extremely high costs in operational terms, so making them dependent upon

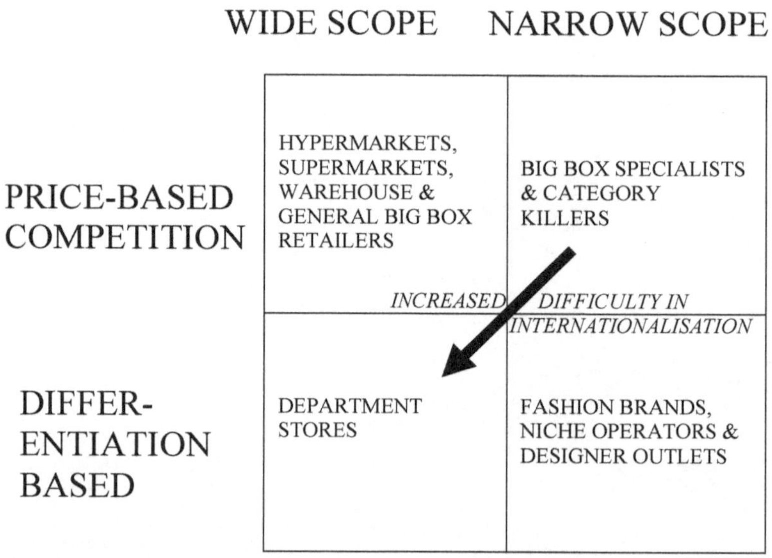

Figure 7.3 Amended version of Porter's (1980) generic strategies to show the potential difficulty in internationalisation of department stores. The arrow represents the orientation of increasing difficulty of international expansion. Wide scope differentiation-based is the most difficult to translate into local values as opposed to more narrow scope or price-based retail formats (source: the authors).

achieving consumer distinction to gain the necessary footfall and premium return on sales across a wide product base – a process that could take some (costly) time to achieve.

If, as seems to be the case, significant building architecture, prime location within a city destination and relevance to the local peoples and cultures are indicators of department store success throughout the history of the format, then one can see the link to tourism flow within the city location. Thus the major stores of Bon Marché, Galeries Lafayette and Printemps in Paris are significantly located in the tourist areas of the city and have buildings that are distinctive, having impressive features either externally or internally: galleried tiered floors with central atriums and/or domed, top-floor restaurant features. The same can be said of the KDV store in the central Kurfürstendamm of Berlin. A restaurant with a view, perhaps with a gallery or 'viewing deck' promenade, is a feature of many of these, with an impressive backdrop (and sometimes forefront) of surrounding scenic architectural grandeur and significance – a particular attraction of the department store, it would seem. 'If you haven't seen Galeries Lafayette, you haven't seen Paris' reads a promotional leaflet handed out to passengers on the great transatlantic ocean liners (Avellis and Guyon, 1996).

The tourist appeal of theme restaurants, in comparison, and their ability to achieve distinction rests upon their ability to fit out each internal environment with sufficient space signifiers in terms of mythical embodied artefacts. In the case of Hard Rock Cafe these are abundantly available in the market of rock'n'roll ephemera. The attached retailing of Hard Rock Cafe T-shirts, signifying that the wearer has visited specific global locations of the restaurant, shows a traditional 'I've been there' souvenir tourist appeal. In department stores local distinctiveness can also translate into high desirability of the characterising signifier, sometimes of the 'wearing the T-shirt' variety but more often in their 'carrier bag' effect denoting a lived experience status of Harrods of Knightsbridge, Macy's of New York and KDV of Berlin. There cannot be many visitors to these destinations who do not wish to be seen with these artefacts of their visit to the location in airport lounges – something that has been exploited by many of these big store city brands by the locating of outlets in the airports themselves (Harrods in terminal 5, Heathrow, London, for instance). Considering the analogy of the theme restaurant, the Harrods, Knightsbridge, carrier bag proves at least as effective a place experience differentiator for the holder as the Hard Rock Cafe, London, T-shirt. Given the comparisons and analogies made between the department store experience design dimensions and other tourist experience formats in this section, Table 7.1 summarises the 'Big format' department store as a theme restaurant or cruise shop, shown against a 'Big formation' shopping mall-like consumer experience, illustrating where defining characteristics of each may be similar – or not. These analogies, and the other definitive aspects that make up department stores, will be further considered in the next section, where the focus moves to small store formats and how they may compete with, or mimic, successful big store/big brand outlets as local population and tourist promenading 'magnets'.

Table 7.1 The department store as a theme restaurant, cruise shop or shopping mall-like consumer experience, covering functional, hedonic and humanic environmental cues?

Qualities [YES, YES limited (ltd) or NO]	*Department stores*	*Like theme restaurants*	*Like cruise ships*	*Like shopping malls*
Functional				
Integrated experience	YES	YES	YES	YES
Highly controlled and corporatised	YES	YES	YES	YES
Under one roof	YES	YES	YES	YES
Retail (gift) and food element	YES	YES (ltd)	YES	YES
Clothing element	YES	YES (ltd)	YES (ltd)	YES
Situated in a number of stratified floors	YES	NO	YES	YES
Premium service	YES	NO	YES	NO
Hedonic				
Visual signifiers of ambient difference	YES	YES	YES	YES
Would wear the T-shirt/carry the bag	YES	YES	YES	NO
Health/cosmetic element	YES	NO	YES	YES
Architectural elements of aspiration and grandeur	YES	NO	YES	YES
Non-everyday space	YES	YES	YES	YES (ltd)
Humanic				
Festive elements/ stagings	YES	YES	YES	YES
Culturally embedded	YES	YES	YES	YES
Historical associations	YES	NO	YES	NO
Tourist attraction	YES	YES	YES	YES (ltd)
Predominant feminine appeal	YES	NO	YES	YES

Little store: smaller retail formats as competing or complementary place signifiers to big stores?

Successful, established department stores in themselves have so much cachet that major proprietary brands, particularly of a premium or exclusive nature, see them as exceptional opportunities to showcase their own brand and add to its value, in terms of 'stocked at' or 'available in' tags, sometimes by the hiring of concession spaces within the stores. Luxury clothing and other brand-dependent products, such as cosmetics, see this as a most desirable place to present their products within an acceptable overall 'brandscape' or 'brand magnet' landscape (Kinleysides and Kinleysides, 2003; Sherry, 1998). This preference of established product brands for large formats and large company chains has contributed to the loss of smaller format experiential competitiveness, contributing towards and given a small store versus large store orientation to retail attractiveness (Hollander, 1973, 1979). In examining the characteristics and analogies of the department store experiential qualities raised in the last section, it can be asked, how can or do smaller active retailers compete for the tourist and general city visitor attention?

The importance of prime location and distinctive aspects of a building's architecture and appearance have been mentioned in relation to the department store's appeal, both internal and external, in generating an aspect of grandeur or 'awe' in the consumer. Obviously small stores cannot compete in anything like these terms, although featuring exceedingly imaginative design concepts and locating within imposing buildings, even if they are smaller, can still generate a similar sense of awe or 'wonder' within a more restricted space. Smaller stores could also try to serve consumers by focussing only on more niche or focused consumer needs. This small store niche element, although decried in Zola's (1995) praise of the palatial new Parisian department store cathedrals of consumption, was alternatively somewhat eulogised in Louis Aragon's (1994) detailed descriptions of the disappearing small store arcades in Paris. There are therefore alternative perspectives that signify that all may not be lost for the small trader – in the city at least!

Department stores, for all their grandeur (or possibly because of it), have been shown to be a precarious and vulnerable concept at times. The decline of many UK and US department stores in the 1980s, effectively making them potential retail 'dinosaurs' (Gilchrist, 1994; Raunch, 1991; Willans, 1997). This was very much linked to a decline of city-centre appeal compared with the new competition from shopping malls – themselves containing aspects of physical, 'built' grandeur in their internal design but more flexible in many operational aspects than the 'difficulty in turning' department store format. The one-organisation, 'cruise ship' operation of the big department store would seem to make it highly susceptible to changes in the macro-environmental, economic 'weather'. The format's lack of manoeuvrability or flexibility reminds one of the strategic inflexibility of large organisations in general, similar to large ships, not being able to change directions as quickly as smaller, more manoeuvrable 'ocean-going' craft, or the 'fleets' of individual retail outlets within a shopping mall. So, perhaps the flexibility in stocking and organisational aspects in relation to changing fashions could benefit small stores and leave them the winner in a 'David and Goliath' battle during changing or tough times.

Of course small stores could also compete with department stores if they located in shopping malls that conferred a sense of grandeur to the shopper in their overall design – the mall itself becoming a substitute department store format and the small retailer standing as an effective departmental, sub-brand concession within it. However, one of the drawbacks for smaller, independent retailers is that, unlike department stores and chain stores, they may be just as unlikely to be able to afford the high rents these malls demand in exchange for their offered grandeur and resulting footfall as they are to afford those in city central locations; rising rents and increasing parking difficulties contributed to 1990s city-centre decline. So the shopping malls, it would seem, simply transpose the big store and big brand culture of high street power into the location of the mall, offering little in the way of a competitive, alternative location to the independent or smaller retailer.

Apart from single-store niche specialisation, there has been a growing realisation that smaller retailers also have the distinctive and effective option of mutual cooperation in order to provide particularly attractive retail 'cluster' attractions or city 'quarter' effects to compete against the twin attractions of department stores and shopping malls. In many locations these can be formed in attractive lane locations with casbah effects, providing a selection of specialist and/or varied diversity across a large number of very small, lower-rent outlets near to a tourist or central location – the unit specifications not being something that chain stores could easily adapt their operations to. The Bath and Brighton 'Lanes' areas are good examples of this, offering distinctive localness, quirkiness and fashionability to compete with nearby city-centre high street big retailers. As a tourist attraction these can be seen as small-scale version of traditional casbah entertainments for travellers, such as Istanbul's famous Grand Bazaar, offering a variety of small-scale local enterprises as an explorative alternative to a large, grand (and vertically scopic) retail format such as department stores or megastores, as illustrated in Figure 7.4.

In a study on Manchester's alternative culture Northern Quarter, Bennison and colleagues (2007) follow Davies's (1976) cautionary line that the origin of specialised and niche, smaller store quarters cannot be planned but must arise organically or in a 'natural' arrangement, as planning favours chain stores over independently run outlets. However, this would seem to omit the need for non-independent small shops to also take part in quarters; book, music and niche clothing chains for instance would fit in easily and synergistically with an 'alternative' offer. It also downplays the fact that independents also 'plan' their location on the same principle as any other stores – will it work here and does it give me any competitive edge? Apart from contemplating the organic (or other) origins of such associations and clusters, there would seem to be no doubt that localised social and economic networks can form successful consumer attractions by various outlets working 'symbiotically so that the total is so much more than the sum of its parts' (Bennison *et al.*, 2007: 635). The description of an ideal retail 'cluster' agglomeration as a 'specialised functional area' of diverse activities which can also be said to 'share a common quality level or status' (Bennison *et al.*, 2007: 634; Davies, 1976: 148) has distinct parallels with a department store's appeal, as opposed to a shopping mall or a mainstream high street, but potentially representing a less corporately controlled or dominated shopping experience that any of these.

Figure 7.4 Big store/little store. Comparison of alternate horizontal/vertical scopic appeals of the Grand Bazaar casbah of Istanbul with the Paris Virgin Megastore, Champs Elysées: a choice between varied ‘quirky’ local, small-scale enterprises, similar to city lanes and markets, and grand, multi-departmental, company enterprises, with similarities to the department store – marbled halls, towers, balconies and grand staircase (source: the authors).

Retail partnerships can thus form marketing orientations of urban 'clusters' featuring collaborations of 'urban actors with potential responsibility for marketing the retail provision of towns and cities' (Warnaby *et al.*, 2004: 545). This urban zoning has largely been considered to have relatively local or 'neighbourhood' marketing effects, although the complementary groups that the retail agglomerations would be interacting with would include tourist attractions and tourist promotional agencies.

In terms of attracting tourist-retail consumers with their own distinctive consumer characteristics, the retail cluster if uncovered, in tandem with the main street, suffers the inconvenience of a lack of provision of an all-under-one-roof venue ambience and attraction – as can be provided by the department store or shopping mall. Unlike chain-store-dominated high/main streets, however, a suitable framed retail cluster can, if augmented by street cafés and other leisure entertainments, provide an element of integrated theatre or a festive or festival marketplace nature, while providing less corporate and more consumer-structured attractions – as noted in revitalised economic conglomerations in struggling downtowns in the USA (Maclaran *et al.*, 1999; Pryor and Grossbart, 2005) or various ethnic specialist zones in the multicultural cityscapes of Australia (Collins *et al.*, 1995). Thus they can offer an integrated lifestyle or 'lifespace' offer to mimic or challenge the appeal of a department store or mall, albeit in a focused niche manner for specific consumer needs. Old buildings of a grander age could also, if highlighted, effect an element of grandeur in the alternative shopping process. Many 'alternative' shopping areas are sited in older, more run down buildings that could provide an ambient advantage for less conventional consumer groups. It is also true that small stores may choose to operate their particular specialist niche and biophilic appeal in smaller tourist resort areas as opposed to city centres, where they will be less troubled by big business intrusion, Figure 7.5 illustrates a summary of the means by which it is proposed that small stores can compete and co-exist alongside department stores or shopping malls in and around modern city centres with positive tourist effect.

Entertainment retail evolution: the rise and fall of the megastore

> Unfortunately the large retail music store is a dinosaur.
>
> Virgin employee (Sisario, 2009)

In considering entertainment formats, it may be informative to consider the fate of a format whose entire basis was in the retail process of selling defined 'entertainment products' in malls and major high streets, often in their own 'grand' format of awe – the music megastore. These outlets grew to be key retail entertainment destinations in their own right in many major city locations in the past few decades. Unlike department stores in the recent past, the decline of these big store formats appears to have been terminal within only the first decade of the new century, although small formats in the same product sectors have shown almost

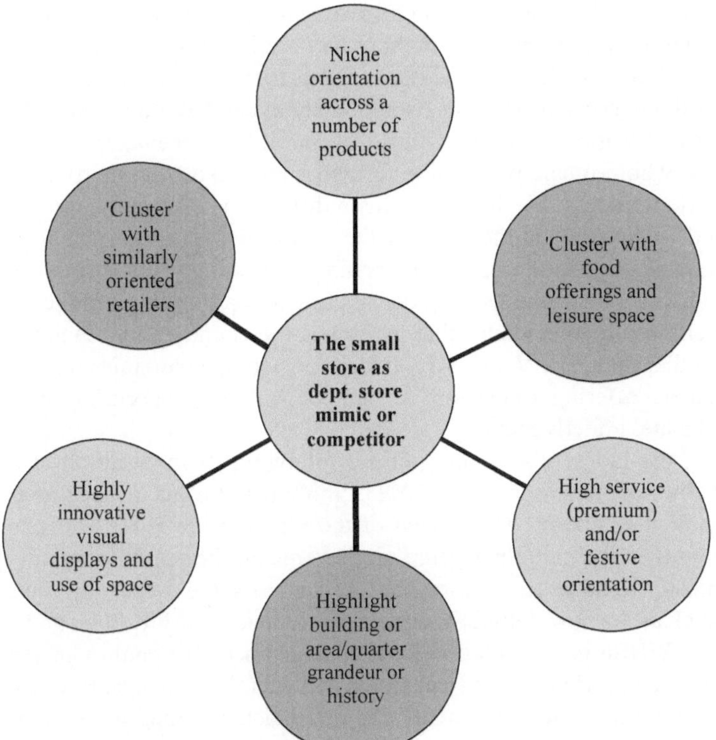

Figure 7.5 Suggested positive tourist retail dimensions for smaller retailers in competing with bigger and more corporate environments (source: the authors).

a similar decline. This has been because the previously tangible product-based entertainment sector has moved to an intangible form of supply in the form of computer downloading, leaving the entertainment sector with evident 'dinosaur' extinction characteristics (Jones, 2009; McIntyre, 2009).

The rise: the megastore age of big store, tourist entertainment retail

The 'potted' history of entertainment software stores follows the technological development of various encoded tangible entertainment carriers or product formats. Encoding intangible music into saleable tangible product forms, the manufacturing industry originally sold its wares via department stores, catalogue shops, musical instrument stores and radio set suppliers/homeware stores, as reproduction cylinders just over a century ago. This was in the age of limited transport and economically viable small town and neighbourhood shopping strips, as well as in grand city-centre store palaces of consumption.

With the expansion of music reproduction devices into more homes, specialist recorded music stores started to be seen where people could order, listen to and purchase a widening selection of available stock emanating from a number of recording organisations. The by now favoured format of discs (brittle shellac developing into more hardy vinyl) and various trends or fads of music both before and after the Second World War continuously expanded the market. This expansionary trend was aided by the 'birth' of the affluent teenager, in the post-war 1950s, for whom music purchasing formed a major socio-cultural and symbolic consumption process. By the 1980s this industry was extremely large and highly organised – controlled in the main by the suppliers who each owned specific artist's music reproduction copyrights, selling increasingly via a small number of large specialist music chains, thus distributing and promoting products en masse. It was perhaps no coincidence that in the UK the country's two major megastore brands at that time, HMV and Virgin, were owned by companies that also owned record labels, offering a means of further controlling and securing overall distribution channel effectiveness.

During the industry's 'boom' period, following the maturation in the 1960s of the baby boomers (McIntyre, 2011), 'the music business' became the 'home entertainment business'. The advent of the video in the 1980s (later to become DVD) and then the computer game markets meant the previous music specialist stores mostly became entertainment stores, as to some extent did many variety stores, such as the now defunct Woolworths chain and the UK book and stationery specialists WHSmith (which bought the music specialist chain Our Price in the 198s). By the late 1990s, electrical stores and chemists (such as Boots in the UK) also had entertainment departments opportunistically taking up ever-larger parts of their floor space to capitalise on the burgeoning more adult-oriented market, including mass-market, non-specialist music buyers who had taken to the convenient, new compact disc (CD) product format.

The market for audio CDs in the UK was around 200 million units by 2000, double the total market of around 100 million units for vinyl LPs and cassettes combined in the mid 1980s, when CDs were introduced (O'Sullivan *et al.*, 2003). Supermarkets were also to enter the fray for the consumer of these small objects of desire – CDs, videos, DVDs and games – in a major manner, offering discounts to consumers that only their levels of buying power and need for footfall loss-leaders could maintain. Thus entertainment retail developed flexible, grey or fuzzy parameters, largely set by software developments and their market lifecycles, and it took a lot of talent, foresight or luck to be able to make a living from products in a fast-shifting format, content and consumer mix.

In its heyday the specialist chains that grew out of the market included the companies of Tower (Records) and Sam Goody in the USA, HMV (EMI), Virgin and Our Price in the UK, WOM (World of Music) in Germany, FNAC in France (previously predominantly a bookseller), Fame in Holland and various other chains in most developed territories, as well as numerous independents to cover either territories or specialist genres too small for the larger companies to be bothered with (including a burgeoning second-hand collector market). Most of the big operators (apart from Sam Goody in the USA and Our Price in the UK) gradually increased their reliance on larger and lager store formats holding increasing levels of product inventories. As new technology entertainment formats arose, specialist entertainment outlets developed for games and video/DVD, many starting as hire outlets before targeting sell-through markets. An 'entertainment' retailer then became defined as a company or outlet that did not restrict itself only to one format but took in all aspects of home entertainment software, as well as books and magazines – increasingly in the form of 'giant' entertainment department stores, superstores or 'megastores' as featured in most high-traffic and tourist locations. Piccadilly Circus in London and Times Square in New York, and their surrounding streets, could be expected to have extremely large outlets of Tower, HMV and Virgin megastores, for example, often in central and prodigious buildings. Piccadilly Circus by the late 1990s featured a large Tower store as its most visible retail landmark. Only yards away from this was the large Piccadilly Circus HMV store in the Trocadero Building (along with Madam Tussaud's Rock Circus tourist attraction), and less than five minutes' walk up Regent Street was the major HMV superstore at Oxford Circus ('The largest music store in the world'). Then it was only another five minutes' walk along Oxford Street (the highest UK footfall location) to another two major HMV superstores and Virgin Megastore in one direction (towards Marble Arch) or alternatively to the largest UK Virgin Megastore in the other direction (at the Tottenham Court Road junction).

The megastores were often designed with stage areas for personal artist appearances, DJ booths, cafés and restaurant facilities and a vast array of listening and viewing merchandising units. To make the consumer choose one store over another (for products that were largely the same) these retailers were trailblazers in the field of putting on a retail show and experiential marketing – a true 'experience economy' (Pine and Gilmore, 1999). Banks of video screens were the norm, as were game-playing machines and zones in later years, and the whole aspect of entering one of these stores (originally termed megastores by the UK entrepreneur Richard Branson's Virgin organisation) was to enter a retail form of Disneyland. In fact it could be said that Disney stores learned their high street craft from the entertainment stores' arsenal – not the other way around. Further, their products being small objects of (easily transportable) desire, with music and books cited as amongst the top ten gift items, and music players (personal stereos) giving as much tourist appeal as other luggage-friendly, personal items such as jewellery.

Small outlets, often specialist in nature, continued to exist during the days of the giants, but the problems for smaller entertainment retail that made it hard to compete profitably with the big companies and megastores, even during the sectors heyday, were fourfold. First there was the need for uptake of new and arising technologies, often with large initial investment yet low initial sales. Second there was the copyright 'stranglehold' that legal protection gave to the product recorders, manufacturers and software license holders, which gave reduced bargaining ability to small retailers – one product could be obtained only from one supplier. Third there was the heterogeneity and variability of the fad-based and taste-led consumer base, leading to the need for ever greater stock investments and redundancy risk. Fourth there was the ability of specialist and non-specialist large retailers to 'cream off' the high-volume, non-specialist buyers with reduced pricing of major sellers. The city-centre domination effect of the megastores alone would make it seem that the appeal of the small, specialist music entertainment stores – definitely for tourist appeal – were truly numbered. But were they?

The Goliaths astride the world stage: megastore internationalisation

From the late 1980s onwards, many large entertainment retailers had stretched their home territory national boundaries and market shares to the limit, becoming effectively retail category killers. Thus the conditions were ripe for the most adventurous to try their hand at internationalising. Those that had been successful in their home markets, under the tough retail conditions where the a handful of producers maintained a tight control over product release and margins, could feel that they had the 'magic key' to capitalise in other markets, which seemed less well developed, to offer the consumer what they apparently wanted.

City-centre megastores proved to be extremely successful in many central locations in tourist city hubs since the early 1970s, with Virgin Megastores being particularly attractive destinations for many visitors. The chain's expansion followed a route of establishment of what might be considered the first truly modern big-city entertainment megastores or entertainment-based 'brandscapes' – in the 1970s preceding the development of NikeTown by decades. They have since been major features of some of the best-known global tourist locales of all in their time, including those of London (Oxford Street/Tottenham Court Road), Paris (Champs Elysées and the Louvre) and New York (Times Square).

Virgin, headed by its highly entrepreneurial founder Richard Branson, has long been seen as an innovative and pioneering company, consistently venturing into new business areas and transforming them in the process. The Virgin Group of companies has been highly involved in the tourist market as exemplified by Virgin Airlines and its holiday and hotel subsidiaries. Aligned with this focus and entrepreneurial spirit, Virgin achieved, along with the EMI-owned HMV chain, a UK-wide city-centre dominance in the entertainment superstore/megastore format since the format's genesis (Virgin 'Tottenham Court Road' Oxford Street store often being regarded as the first 'megastore'). The Virgin brand was subsequently developed by Branson into one of the few in an exclusive list that have managed to successfully stretch and extend their brand to encompass an increasingly diverse set of product and service categories, from financial services to travel, hotels, wedding services, alcohol, soft drinks and condoms. A key part of his strategy was that he was interested in building brand awareness in major markets across the world, particularly for his airline in the 1990s. Thus, the idea of flying the airline into a city with a Virgin megastore, where a customer was aware of the brand from a major high street presence, and the purchase of other Virgin products and services had strong brand-building appeal. Faced with the alternative of spending large sums on advertising programmes in any new airline territory, the investment into a chain of megastores, acting as 'brand cathedrals', offered a seductively synergistic investment opportunity. This, however, also made Virgin a big spender on prime, central tourist city sites, as the investment decision was more holistic than a simple single store, operationally financial pay-back one.

From the late 1980s and early 1990s both Virgin and HMV were trialling international chains and superstores/megastores across the globe including presences in Ireland, Canada, New Zealand and Singapore (HMV), Italy, Spain, the Netherlands, Austria, Japan, Belgium, Hong Kong and Dubai (Virgin) and France, Germany, the USA and Australia (both companies). This was in response to push and pull factors, including partly the 'invasion' of the British market by the American companies Tower, Sam Goody and Borders into highly visible and lucrative tourist sites, including Oxford Street and Piccadilly Circus in London. One particular international success story that illustrated the promise of high-profile tourist destinations for high tourist footfall locations outside the UK was the opening of Virgin's French operation with a major megastore in the Champs Elysées in 1987, which quickly became the highest-turnover specialist music/video/books outlet in the world. This opening was rapidly followed by major megastores in the French cities of Marseilles and Bordeaux. In 1991 Virgin commenced a five-year strategy, aimed at opening a further 25 megastores across the major territories of continental Europe, commencing with Milan in the later part of that year. During the two years following this, a further eight European stores were opened in Frankfurt, Berlin, Vienna, Amsterdam, Barcelona, Hamburg, Seville and Lisbon. They entered the US market with the opening of their Los Angeles megastore in 1992 in direct competition with the US giant entertainment store operator Tower Records.

By the mid 1990s Virgin and HMV found that national competitors in the territories that they had entered with their entertainment superstore/megastore concept were quickly copying them in a defensive response, launching their own large store formats where previously they had been content with smaller, more dispersed store formats across cities and territories. These competitive responses included extremely major large city-centre store investments by FNAC in France and Fame in the Netherlands as well as a globally renewed interest in larger store expansion by retailers in the major cities of other countries.

The fall: dinosaur extinction in under ten years!

Despite apparent overprovision in many tourist centres, the age of the battle of the dinosaurs in city centres continued until the advent of the new millennium, with superstores and megastores abounding in numbers relating to the city's overall market size and tourist traffic. By Christmas 1999 in Glasgow city centre, Scotland, for instance, within five to ten minutes' walking distance there were three major HMV superstores, two major Virgin megastores (one directly next door to the biggest HMV outlet in the old Lewis's department store building at the heart of Argyle Street, Glasgow's 'Oxford Street' equivalent), one major Tower superstore and a large Scottish independent chain's 'megastore' (Fopp) – both the last two by the city's Central Station (Fopp almost directly opposite that and one of the HMV superstores). This was complemented by a number of smaller stores in and around the city, some independent but some also owned by Fopp and HMV. Why these apparently thriving, large entertainment stores formats are now being referred to as dinosaurs takes us to the end of the story. As is apparent from their city-centre popularity and landscape dominance, their demise was not due to unpleasing or unattractive environments; rather it was a result of a major shift in 'product' form and an associated leisure consumption revolution (McIntyre, 2011).

Early in the decade 2000–2010, computers, the Internet and related technology started to allow mass-market uploading and downloading of music and video both onto home computers and for use with small, portable digital devices. A major consumer desirable that dominated this market for music (later incorporating video content too) was the Apple iPod, which could store thousands of tracks, most of which were available either on a pay-per-tune official basis (as from the Apple website iTunes) or from generally unofficial, free online sources. This revolution in how people listened to music, as well as exchanging and sharing the experience with others (through file sharing), occurred at the same time as a mobile phone and social networking revolution whereby the majority of the public were eagerly assimilating all aspects of small, mobile communication and computing devices into their everyday lifestyles. A large degree of the control on music's distribution – in particular the copyright owners' hold on the market – was now lost along with its tangibility as the new 'product' was digitally transferred 'data' in the form of digital files.

The effect of this shift upon entertainment stores was swift and damaging. This was particularly seen with the large superstore and megastore format retailers, their dinosaur status now being confirmed as month after month another went into extinction. The American Tower Records closed its 89 stores in 2006, one of the largest chains to vanish completely from city centres and high streets in a long line of closures covering individual stores and major companies. By 2009 Virgin Group retained a megastore presence only in France, Greece and the Middle East and Gulf territories, along with a store presence in Germany and Australia, these being joint ventures or owned by other companies as opposed to being under wholly Virgin ownership or management (Virgin.com, 2009). Its last US stores to survive were those of Los Angeles and Times Square, New York, which closed their doors in 2009 following HMV's exit from the USA in 2004. Thus Virgin was effectively out of the entertainment store business. Even the US-originating Borders chain, which had most of its space given to books and other merchandise, never managed to fill the gap made in its large entertainment superstores by the loss of its extensive music (and to some extent video/DVD) departments, commencing the closure of its UK stores during the Christmas sales period of late 2009.

Although predominantly based in the UK, with an extensive high street presence that Virgin had never matched across that country, HMV in 2009 was still extant and even retained a chain and store presence in Ireland, Canada, Hong Kong and Singapore (HMV Group.com, 2009). More and more, however, it seemed that their continued existence seemed to be due to 'mopping up' the business as other entertainment high street retailers and chains closed (Woolworths, Virgin, Andy's and Borders in the UK, for instance). Thus they would seem to be increasingly taking up a 'last man standing' position in the city-centre presence of entertainment superstores – an increasing share of a decreasing market being a dangerous place!

Final call for entertainment retail . . . or is small beautiful?

In terms of the experience and attraction of city centres for tourism and visitors, as well as local inhabitants, the loss of the megastores stores did appear to leave entertainment gaps in many locations, with consumers decrying the loss of social and meeting spaces as much as a location to purchase products. The physical store gaps were largely filled by fashion outlets, taking over their tourist retail role. Nevertheless the 'death of the music store' was, and continues in many quarters to be, sadly lamented, opposed or even questioned with the advent of both a 'Record Store Day' and a 'Vinyl Saturday' support event for remaining outlets, most of which are small and many of which still sell vinyl records in addition to CDs and other formats (Harris, 2003; McIntyre, 2009; Sisario, 2009).

And so the small stores would appear to have won, although it may be only a slight and pyrrhic victory for those that can survive through niche specialisation and closeness to their customers, as smaller chains and stores have also been closing at a steady and dramatic rate since 2002 in the UK. The surviving small store format experience dimensions can be contrasted with those to the megastore, as potentially offering a more creative and immersive experience for the heavily involved music buyer, as illustrated in Figure 7.6. Small music stores can thus be hypothesised as offering a form of creative retailing where the consumer is a co-creator *of* value, similar to small, casbah outlets rather than in the cruise ship, grand megastore experience where value was perhaps created *for* the customer, more akin to an entertainment mini-mall kind of magic (Goss, 1993). This small store process for the highly involved music store consumer can involve a personal construction of inner myths through immersion in meaningful dimensions of the products and personnel of the stores. The 'substance' of this 'artistic' consumption space (Sack, 1980, 1992) is therefore becoming a more niche, fashion one in a process that favours older, retro, vinyl products with their artistic sleeve designs and enhanced tangible elements (McIntyre, 2009).

Small music stores, like small stores in other sectors, with their lower costs and ability to quickly adapt, specialise and form parts of lifestyle clusters, thus are perhaps better fitted to survive a macro-environmental cataclysm, such as the music product substitution by downloading which brought down even the book superstore specialist Borders in the UK. By providing a personal and co-creative retail experience, some small stores may possibly continue in some form (although in vastly reduced numbers) in the same manner that smaller life forms were better able to survive and adapt to the cataclysm that killed the actual dinosaurs in an early global, biological macro-environmental event. However, the promenading megastore experience and appeal to tourists in city centres is

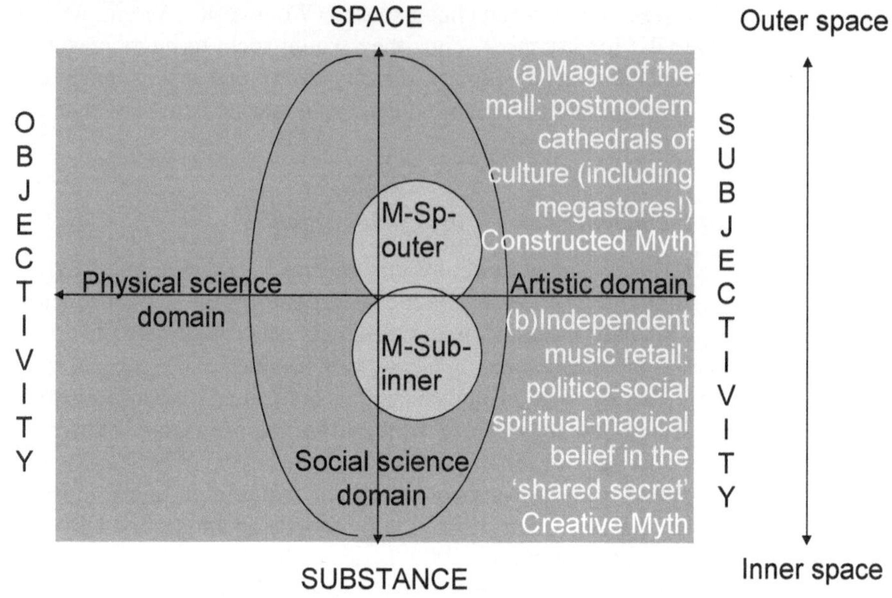

Figure 7.6 Big store/little store conceptual experience model. Cultural retail space framework proposing a creative (or co-creative) consumerist myth-building process for independent, small shops (here music stores) as opposed to shopping mall/megastore modernist shopping spaces, with both processes oriented towards the artistic mythical-magical view (M), but with varying orientations towards spatially outer-constructed (M-sp-outer) consumer mythology, and substance/produce elements in a small shop inner-(co-)creative (M-sub-inner) myth-building process (source: McIntyre, 2009, as adapted from Sack, 1980, 1992).

unlikely to be replaced by the very different appeal of small independent music stores in specialist locations. Perhaps fashion and mall environments, or a resurgence of department stores, can do this?

The four-decade adventure of entertainment megastores as major city-centre, experience-based retail attractions would thus seem to have ended in a dramatic and sudden manner – a fate that some had previously forecast for the department store format. During its rise even the department stores in cities whose cities were invaded during the 'megastore wars' seemed delighted by this retail format's appearance – in Austria, a major department store took out advertisements stating 'Hertzmanski welcomes Virgin to Vienna'. Yet it is the department store that has proved to be the more long-lasting entertainment and promenading attraction in the retail landscape. It has had the opportunity to adapt its extensive range over time whilst the major entertainment stores, despite borrowing the theatre of the department store, were limited by their dependency upon music and entertainment industry products. This leaves one to wonder in what form 'big store' entertainment retail could renew its role again as part of the city-centre entertainment retail landscape, or if that role is down to the shopping malls and department stores, balanced by some variety and innovation in niche 'festival retail' lane, strip or quarter developments – or will consumers disappear further into the realm of digital landscapes?

References

Albeson, E. S. (1989) *When Ladies Go A-Thieving: Middle class shoplifters in the Victorian department store*. Oxford: Oxford University Press.

Aragon, L. (1994) *Paris Peasant*. Boston: Exact Change.

Avellis, F. and Guyon, P. (1996) *The Century of Galeries Lafayette: 1896–1996*. Paris: Les Editions Stratégiques, Galeries Lafayette Publishing.

Benjamin, W. (2002) *The Arcades Project*, new edition. Cambridge, MA: Harvard Business Press.

Bennison, D., Warnaby, G. and Medway, D. (2007) The role of quarters in large city centres: a Mancunian case study. *International Journal of Retail & Distribution Management* 35(8), 626–638.

Benson, S. P. (1986) *Counter Cultures: Saleswomen, managers and customers in American department stores, 1890–1940*. Urbana: University of Illinois Press.

Bowlby, R. (1985) *Just Looking: Consumer culture in Dreiser, Gissing and Zola*. New York: Methuen.

Bryman, A. (2004) *The Disneyisation of Society*. London: Sage Publications.

Carmona, M., Magalhaes, C. de and Hammond, L. (2008) *Public Space: The management dimension*. Oxford: Routledge.

Chaney, D. (1983) The department store as a cultural form. *Theory, Culture and Society* 1(3), 22–31.

Clarke, D. B. (2003) *The Consumer Society and the Postmodern City*. London: Routledge.

Coles, T. (1999a) Competition, contested retail space and the rise of the department store in Imperial Germany. *International Review of Retail, Distribution and Consumer Research* 9(3), 275–289.

Coles, T. (1999b) Department stores as innovations in retail marketing: some observations in marketing practice and perception in Wilhelmine Germany. *Journal of Macromarketing* 19(1), 34–47.

Collins, J., Gibson, A., Alcorso, C., Castles, S. and Tait, D. (1995) *Shop Full of Dreams: Ethnic small business in Australia*. Sydney, NSW: Pluto Press.

Davies, J. D. and Jones, P. (1993) International activity of Japanese department stores. *Service Industries Journal* 13(1), 126–132.

Davies, R. L. (1976) *Marketing Geography*. Corbridge: Retailing and Planning Associates.

Debord, G. (2009) *Society of the Spectacle* (trans. K. Knabb). Eastbourne: Soul Bay Press.

DEHCD (Department of Environment, Housing and Community Development) (1978) *The Shopping Centre as a Community Leisure Resource*. Canberra: Australian Government Publishing Service.

Dotson, M. and Patton, W. E. (1992) Consumer perceptions of department store service: a lesson for retailers. *Journal of Services Marketing* 6(2), 15–28.

Falk, P. (1997) The scopic regimes of shopping. In Falk, P. and Campbell, C. (eds) *The Shopping Experience*. London: Sage, pp. 177–185.

Fredriksson, C. (1997) The making of a Swedish department store culture. In Falk, P. and Campbell, C. (eds) *The Shopping Experience*. London: Sage, pp. 111–135.

Furihata, T., Uchino, A., Takahashi, Y. and Tanaka, N. (2004) Hierarchical destination choice and retail agglomerations: a simulation. *Journal of Japan Society of Business Mathematics* 26(2), 151–163.

Galeries Lafayette (2010) Company website. Online source: http://www.galerieslafayette.com/ (last accessed 13 January 2010).

Gilchrist, S. (1994) Dinosaur of the retailing age stages a comeback. *The Times* (London), 18 February, p. 38.

Glennie, P. and Thrift, N. (1996) Consumption, shopping and gender. In Wrigley, N. and Lowe, M. (eds) *Retailing, Consumption and Capital: Towards the new retail geography*. Harlow: Longman, pp. 231–237.

Goss, J. (1992) Modernity and post-modernity in the retail landscape. In Anderson, K. and Gale, F. (eds) *Inventing Places: Studies in cultural geography*. London: Longman, pp. 159–177.

Goss, J. (1993) The magic of the mall: an analysis of form, function and meaning in the contemporary retail built environment. *Annals of the Association of American Geographers* 83(1), 18–47.

Goss, J. (1999) Once upon a time in the commodity world: an unofficial guide to Mall of America. *Annals of the Association of American Geographers* 89(1), 45–75.

Guy, C. and Bennison, D. (2007) Planning guidance and large store development in the United Kingdom: the search for flexibility. *Environment and Planning A* 39(4), 945–964.

Harris, J. (2003) The day the music shop died. *The Observer* (Manchester, UK), 7 December. Online source: http://www.guardian.co.uk/print/0,3858,4813722–111491,00.html (last accessed 4 June 2008).

HMV Group.com (2009) *About Us: History*. Online source: http://hmvgroup.com/aboutus/history.jsp (last accessed 5 December 2009).

Hobson, J. S.P. and Christensen, M. (2001) Cultural and structural issues affecting Japanese tourist shopping behaviour. *Asia Pacific Journal of Tourism Research* 6(1), 37–45.

Hollander, S. (1973) The American retailing scene. *International Journal of Retailing and Distribution Management* 1(1), 35–38.

Hollander, S. (1979) Large v. small retailers in the USA. *International Journal of Retailing and Distribution Management* 7(2), 25–28.

Jones, G. (2009) *Last Shop Standing: Whatever happened to record shops?* London: Proper Music Publishing.

Jones, M. A. (1999) Entertaining shopping experiences: an exploratory exploration. *Journal of Retailing and Consumer Services* 6, 129–139.

Kinleysides, J. and Kinleysides, C. (2003) The rise of the brand magnet. *Marketing* (London), 6 February, p. 27.

Laermans, R. (1993) Learning to consume. *Theory, Culture and Society* 10, 79–102.

Larke, R. (1994) *Japanese Retailing*. London: Routledge.

Larke, R. and Causton, M. (2005) *Japan: A modern retail superpower.* Basingstoke, Hants: Palgrave Macmillan.

Leach, W. (1984) Transformations in a culture of consumption: women and department stores, 1890–1925. *Journal of American History* 7(2), 319–342.

Lefebre, H. (1996) *Writings on Cities* (trans. and ed. E. Kofman and E. Lebas). Oxford: Blackwell.

Maclaran, P., Brown, S. and Stevens, L. (1999) The utopian imagination: spatial play in a festival marketplace. *European Advances in Consumer Research* 4, 304–309.

McIntyre, C. (2009) Diminishing varieties of active and creative retail experience: the end of the music shop? *Journal of Retailing and Consumer Services*16, 466–476.

McIntyre, C. (2011) News from somewhere: the poetics of Baby Boomer and Generation Y music consumers in tracking a retail revolution. *Journal of Retailing and Consumer Services* 18, 141–151.

Miller, M. B. (1981) *The Bon Marché: Bourgeois culture and the department store.* London: George Allen and Unwin.

Nava, M. (1997) Modernity's disavowal: women, the city and the department store. In Falk, P. and Campbell, C. (eds) *The Shopping Experience*. London: Sage, pp. 56–91.

O'Sullivan, T., Dutton, B. and Raynor, P. (2003) Case study: the music industry. In O'Sullivan, T., Dutton, B. and Raynor, P., *Studying the Media*, 3rd edition. London: Hodder Arnold, pp. 162–180.

Pasdermadjian, H. (1954) *The Department Store: Its origins, evolution & economics.* London: Newman Books.

Payne, A., Storbacka, K. and Frow, P. (2008) Managing the co-creation of value. *Journal of the Academy of Marketing Science* 36(1), 83–96.

Pine, J. and Gilmore, J. (1999) *The Experience Economy: Work is theatre and every business is a stage.* Boston, MA: Harvard Business School Press.

Porter, M. E. (1980) *Competitive Strategy: Techniques for analyzing industries and competitors.* New York: Free Press.

Printemps (2010) Company website. Online source: http://departmentstoreparis.printemps.com/ (last accessed 13 January 2010).

Pryor, S. and Grossbart, S. (2005) Ethnography of an American main street. *International Journal of Retail and Distribution Management* 33(11), 806–823.

Quartermaine, P. and Peter, B. (2006) *Cruise: Identity, design and culture.* London: Laurence King Publishing.

Raunch, R. A. (1991) Retailing's dinosaurs: department stores and supermarkets. *Business Horizons (USA)* 34(5), 21–25.

Ritzer, G. (1996) *The Macdonaldization of Society.* Thousand Oaks, CA: Pine Forge Press.

Sack, R. D. (1980) *Conceptions of Space in Social Thought.* London: Macmillan.

Sack, R. D. (1992) *Place, Modernity and the Consumer's World: A relational framework for geographical analysis.* Baltimore, MD: Johns Hopkins University Press.

Selfridges (2010) Company website. Online source: http://www.selfridges.com/index.cfm?page=1189 (last accessed 12 February 2010).

Sherry, J. F. Jr. (1998) The soul of the company store: Niketown Chicago and the emplaced brandscape. In Sherry, J. F. Jr. (ed.) *Servicescapes: The concept of place in contemporary markets.* Chicago: NTC Business Books.

Shields, R. (1989) Social spatialization and the built environment: the case of the West Edmonton Mall. *Environment and Planning* 7(2),147–164.

Shields, R. (ed.) (1992) *Lifestyle Shopping: The subject of consumption.* London: Routledge.

Sisario, B. (2009) Retail era closes with music megastore. *New York Times*, 15 June. Online source: http://nytimes.com/2009/06/15/arts/music/15virgin.html (last accessed 8 December 2009).

Stachow, G., Hart, C. and Rafiq, M. (2009) Exploring the formation of town centre image. EAERCD conference paper, University of Surrey, Guildford, July 2009.

Stone, G. P. (1954) City shoppers and urban identification: observations on the social psychology of city life. *American Journal of Sociology* 60(1), 36–45.

Tauber, E. M. (1972) Why do people shop? *Journal of Marketing* 36, 46–59.

Tauber, E. M. (1995) Why do people shop? *Marketing Management* 4(2) , 58–60.

Timothy, D. J. (2005) *Shopping Tourism, Retail and Leisure.* Clevedon, UK: Channel View Publications.

Urry, J. (1995) *Consuming Places.* London: Routledge.

Uzzell, D. L. (1995) The myth of the indoor city. *Journal of Environmental Psychology* 152, 299–310.

Veblen, T. (1899) *The Theory of the Leisure Class.* New York: Macmillan.

Venkatesh, A. (1992) Postmodernism, consumer culture and the society of the spectacle. *Advances in Consumer Research* 19, 199–202.

Virgin.com (2009) *Music and Entertainment Stores around the World.* Online source: http://www.virgin.com/company/virgin-megastore/ (last accessed 5 December 2009).

Warnaby, G., Bennison, D., Davies, B. and Hughes, H. (2004) People and partnerships: marketing urban retailing. *International Journal of Retailing and Distribution Management* 32(11), 545–556.

Willans, J. (1997) Department stores: an enduring retail format. *Journal of Fashion Marketing and Management* 1(2), 145–149.

Williams, R. (1982) *Dreamworlds: Mass consumption in late nineteenth-century France.* Berkeley: University of California Press.

Williamson, J. (1986) Department stores in Japan. *Retail and Distribution Management* 14(4), 14–17.

Worthington, S. (1989) The Scala-Buda department store: the Marks and Spencer of Hungary. *Retail and Distribution Management* 17(5), 28–29.

Zola, É. (1995) *The Ladies' Paradise* (trans. B. Nelson). Oxford: Oxford World Classics, Oxford University Press.

Zukin, S. (1991) *Landscapes of Power: From Detroit to Disney World.* Berkeley: University of California Press.

8 Fashion retail formats as tourist retail destinations and attractions

Corinna Budnarowska

Introduction

Globally, consumers appear to be in love with the concept of fashion, fashion shopping and fashion-related lifestyle activities. This chapter explores whether fashion destinations are tourist attractions in their own right, or whether they just form part of the 'package' or the 'attraction' of a holiday destination. The chapter is structured to examine the relationship between fashion and place, in terms of regional, national and international urban tourism. Although it is interesting to discuss the locations of fashion destinations, the discussion moves beyond this to examine the key attributes of generic fashion shopping destinations. Is leisure retail, especially fashion shopping, sometimes a primary element of tourism consumption and production? Another question raised is what type of fashion is attractive to potential tourists? Is it merely high-end fashion that serves as an anchor for a given destination, or can all types of fashion shopping opportunities, from designer to traditional markets, act as a 'hub' for a potential fashion destination? The chapter will consider relevant examples of fashion retailing destinations to determine their critical success factors and why consumers have apparently grown so fond of them, as well as considering the impact that the Internet and social networking sites (SNS) have had upon our global fashion awareness and interest.

Fashion destinations as a primary motivator for travel?

Building on the theme of 'retail as leisure' (Argyle, 1996), fashion retailing provides an accepted pastime to the general public worldwide and is often termed as a 'hobby' or even a 'sport' by some consumers. Fashion shopping routes have been developed as 'workouts', reinforcing this feeling of engaging in shopping as exercise with not many sectors of retailing being able to claim to absorb the consumer in an active leisure pursuit as fully as fashion can.

When considering consumer behaviour in the context of tourism, it becomes apparent that tourism academics often consider retailing to be a secondary consideration. Jansen-Verbeke (1986) considered tourism consumption and production within urban areas to be a 'leisure pursuit', but claimed that markets and shopping facilities were largely a secondary element of this consumption. Alternatively, Swarbrooke and Horner (2007: 266) claim that leisure shopping is a major element of the tourism market today, and that 'many tourists now spend more on retailing than they do on their flights or their accommodation' (Frommer and Frommer, 1996: 266). Swarbrooke and Horner acknowledge retail as a major contributor to the tourism economy, yet in their 'Quality Jigsaw in Tourism' they still cite retailing only in the context of 'shopping opportunities – designer shops to traditional markets' (a secondary reason for travel) (Swarbrooke and Horner, 2007: 266). Rarely have tourism (or retail) authors considered the two together to be of primary importance in the differentiation and selling of places, and even more rarely has fashion retail in particular been singled out for its tourism potential. So this poses the question: are fashion destinations a primary tourist attraction in their own right, or are they merely a secondary part of the bigger tourist attraction or 'package'?

Academic consideration of 'shopping tourism' has also historically considered the retail urban stakeholders to be of perceived secondary importance in their place-marketing programmes, but retailing is now becoming more widely considered to be important to urban economies and regeneration (Warnaby *et al.*, 2004). Fashion destinations are, in fact, at the centre of many urban developments, often defined by emergent suburbs or districts, but also 'manufactured' in the form of shopping centres or malls. Although centres and malls have seen a dip in visitor popularity since the 1990s, due to their 'clone' nature from selling only the large, recognisable brands (Timothy, 2005), there seems to be somewhat of a recent resurgence in creating mall environments primarily for fashion stores. The destination of these 'style' malls has shifted back from large, out-of-town developments towards the regeneration of inner-city suburbs. A good example of this is London's Westfield shopping centre, in White City, which opened in 2008. Westfield boasts a dedicated fashion area, named 'The Village', that plays host to all the top designer brands, from Prada to Versace. The shopping centre entered one marketing solutions company's 'Centres Futures UK 2008 Ranking' at number eight, knocking the more traditional out-of-town development of Bluewater in Kent (close to the M25 motorway) down to number nine in footfall terms in the UK (CACI, 2008). To put this into context further, the Trafford Centre in Manchester was ranked as the UK's twentieth in 2008, whereas the number one footfall spot was awarded to London's West End shopping area. Most of the top ten UK shopping locations, however, consisted of cities themselves as emergent fashion destinations, rather than man-made malls. This implies that fashion 'zones' are now generally preferred in terms of urban place, rather than built centres or malls – as is also a probable situation when considering fashion retail attractiveness on a global tourism scale.

A common problem with the marketing synergy of such urban destinations has historically been the relationship between the public and private stakeholders in agreeing how to market a place (Page and Hardyman, 1996; Warnaby *et al.*, 2002, 2004; Warnaby and Bennison, 2006). The need for place marketing within the developed retail trade in the UK was first proposed in the 1980s by the country's market-leading clothing and food retailer Marks & Spencer (M&S). M&S has always believed strongly in the concept of 'community' and in creating shopping destinations that provide more than just shops (Nobbs, 2010). The result of this began to emerge in the UK high streets of the 1990s with the introduction of both town centre and visitor management schemes under the banner of local Town Centre Management (TCM) that would manage the process more holistically, which had a varied success rate (Page and Hardyman, 1996).

London's Westfield is a more recent example of a successful synergy between private and public stakeholders, using a marketing company called Yellow Door led by an infamous UK media fashion retail consultant, Mary Portas, who successfully markets the destination as a total brand. Portas further exploited this relationship in July 2009 by persuading Westfield to host her own charity pop-up store for Save the Children called 'Living and Giving', getting it situated in the hub of the high-end fashion Westfield 'Village' quadrant.

Williams (1997) claims that tourism has become interconnected with all sectors of the economy, citing retailing as a primary example of this (p. 57). Within all the literature that discusses 'shopping tourism', shopping for fashion is considered to be one of the main sectors that tourists seek out, usually forming the 'hub' of many shopping centres and malls, alongside a wider experiential package (Snepenger *et al.*, 2003; Timothy, 2005). Interestingly, Yüksel (2007: 59) claims this form of tourist shopping means 'visitors may have an extremely fun filled and entertaining experience with or without making a purchase'. This statement is backed up by Babin and colleagues (1994), Bellenger and colleagues (1976), Bloch and Richins (1983), Bloch and colleagues (1989), Jones (1999) and Sherry (1990), who all consider the 'social' and 'experiential' aspects of shopping to be more important than the actual purchase; a tourist's experience of shopping, especially for fashion, proves to be as much about the experience itself as the purchase (Yüksel, 2007). Obviously, this experience is not exclusive to tourists and is often shared by local consumers, linking back to the fact that shopping for fashion is considered a general 'leisure pursuit' by many.

The differentiation between a distinct 'fashion destination' and mere 'places to buy fashion' may to some extent come down to the cultural experience on offer. Often tourists seek out markets or malls in order to immerse themselves in the perceived culture of a destination. This involves the seeking out of fashion items related to that culture (such as saris in India). This in itself rarely dictates the choice of holiday destination, whereas brand seekers (particularly high-end) may research potential destinations based primarily on the fashion availability.

Exploring the relationship between fashion and place

Both 'local' and 'tourist' consumers can enjoy a potential fashion destination as a leisure attraction, with Ashworth and Tunbridge (1990) identifying four potential users of urban leisure destination shopping, two of which are highly relevant to describing the 'local' and 'tourist' of a fashion destination. They describe the 'local' shopper as an 'intentional user from inside the city' or a 'leisure seeking resident', and the 'tourist shopper' as an 'intentional user from outside the city', for example a 'holiday maker' (p. 125). In terms of the relationship between fashion and place, both these consumer types must be considered as potential co-existing primary users of the destination. The 'tourist' consumer can further be divided into tourists from the domestic market and those from an international starting point who have 'sought out' the fashion destinations of a given country. Needless to say, it is important for place marketers to understand where a potential tourist or visitor comes from in order to market a destination to them effectively.

Stakeholders are also now aware of both the historic and economic value that consumers can give to destinations, such as can be seen from Turkey's economic success with cotton fashion products or France's connection to the post-Second World War re-establishment of designer luxury fashion. This is particularly capitalised upon in destinations where fashion design and/or manufacturing is entrenched in the heritage of a place, for example Scotland for its wool industry or Italy for its reputation for high-quality workmanship and design.

As a new researcher considering fashion destinations as a concept, I began by asking people to describe their vision of a fashion destination. The answer that generally came was the common fashion brand tag line of 'London, Paris, Milan, New York . . .' In terms of fashion and place as a concept, these places are the obvious choice, but then I began asking if place in fashion is defined only by high-end designer locations. People's relationship with the major fashion capitals of 'London, Paris, Milan, New York' perhaps stems from their hosting the twice-yearly designer fashion shows that go some way to defining the spring/summer and autumn/winter looks of the coming fashion seasons. There is a strong argument to link fashion and tourism together in this context, as the fashion shows attract large numbers of fashion tourists, ranging from industry insiders on somewhat of a 'working holiday', to the 'hangers-on', celebrities and glitterati who follow the shows for the associated glamour perception or to pick up a designer bargain from the various designer sales attached to the main event. London Fashion Week (LFW) also advertises 'London Fashion Weekend' for the public, which it organises as an extra revenue stream that invites paying guests to enjoy a ticket-only party and designer fashion sale, usually alongside an overnight stay in London. This serves as the perfect tourist package deal for fashion lovers seeking a piece of the action, and a major business has grown in designing package holiday breaks. These include tickets to the sub-events surrounding the major fashion shows, although not many people can obtain tickets to the big-name designer shows, as they remain 'invitation only'. Interestingly, fashion week shows in 2010 populated the sought-after front-row seats with fashion bloggers, who now appear to be the official 'opinion leaders' (Goldsmith and Clark, 2008) of the global fashion market. These seats were historically reserved for the media and celebrities, who were thought to set the trends, but the fashion world is now seeking its fashion tips from unknowns who have been catapulted to fame by expressing their opinions of fashion online. This shows that a democracy in fashion can exist (Jackson and Shaw, 2001) and that the 'trickle-up' (Field, 1970) effect on fashion through social media can be very powerful in the modern world.

Obviously some longevity is attached to fashion and tourism in the renowned fashion capitals. The designers have long been capitalising on the fashion show locations by opening stores in the fashionable and high-end locations of these cities. These, in themselves, serve as tourist 'hubs' for fashion shopping trips, but one must also not forget the other businesses that benefit from such fashion destinations, ranging from small designer labels, private boutiques, restaurants, hotels and entertainment businesses. Associated businesses tend to 'spill out' from the primary locations into further secondary locations that are found by roaming tourists or informed locals and can in themselves form 'hubs' that make them a potential destination in their own right. The 'fashion-forward' consumers will tend to gravitate towards these lesser-known extensions of the main hub, seeking out 'the best kept secrets' of a destination, whereas the 'fashion-follower' will look for familiar designer names. The fashion hierarchy dictates that well-known, high-end fashion appeals to both the wealthy and the 'wannabes'. True fashion enthusiasts pride themselves on steering away from well-known labels in pursuit of discovering 'the next big thing'.

It must also be acknowledged that the accessibility of such cities thanks to low-cost travel companies (for travel *and* accommodation) has extended the potential destination marketing of cities for weekends and shopping trips in general. In considering how far consumers would be willing to travel for fashion shopping, Frommer and Frommer (1996) argue that considering leisure shopping to be a tourist activity stems from the need to find new ways to visit old destinations, and that consumers are now seeking out new experiences in places that they are in some way familiar with, giving way to the opportunity for retail and leisure opportunities. These include the building and branding of locations as fashion destinations. Tourist guides now have extensive shopping sections dedicated to serve consumers seeking out fashion destinations from high-end to traditional markets (Swarbrooke and Horner, 2007). There is also now the expectation that shopping will be offered alongside other entertainment and leisure facilities, providing a total packaged entertainment attraction (Page and Hardyman, 1996). This suggests that many stakeholders may still hold the belief that retail alone cannot sustain a destination, and that other key service elements are required to make it one.

Coming back to the question of whether fashion destinations are only defined by high-end designers, it would seem, from the literature that the answer would certainly be 'no!' For instance, Timothy (2005: 43) claims that shopping as a motivation for travel either whilst on holiday or specifically going on holiday to shop is based upon three factors – the merchandise sought, the destination selected and/or the price advantages gained. Swarbrooke and Horner (2007: 60) have also stated that the motivators for visiting a leisure shopping complex are threefold – in their case concerning escapism, the search for a bargain and/or shopping for status (as in designer label shopping). In the specific context of tourist fashion shopping, Crippin (2000), meanwhile, offers four main types of fashion destination that motivate someone to consider fashion shopping as their primary or secondary reason for travel, these being for:

1 High-end designer fashion, sought out both by those that can afford it and also those aspire to afford it (essentially 'window shoppers');
2 Fashion that rides on the back of this, in the form of designer or outlet villages, selling essentially 'end of line' branded fashion at cut price;
3 Low-end fashion that creates its' own 'buzz', such as street fashion and vintage fashion (serving a consumer seeking out individuality rather than fashion conformity);
4 Fashion bought from a destination that is linked to it by traditional manufacture or heritage, often referred to as 'textourism'.

(Crippin, 2000: 271)

I have chosen to discuss this last typology in more detail in the following section, in terms of defining them as high-end or low-end, branded or customised retailers.

Fashion in stores, lanes or markets: high end or low end, branded or customised?

I have outlined an adaptation of Crippin's (2000) four types of fashion destination in Figure 8.1. The fourth type, identified as 'textourism', perhaps requires little initial discussion here. Although it is important to acknowledge that some fashion tourism stems from seeking out locally made, traditional and heritage fashion termed as 'textourism', nevertheless this would seem to be a very customised form of cultural retailing. Seeking out such 'authentic' crafts is not so much considering the location of a fashion destination as considering fashion 'by-products' of a destination's history and peoples, so I will not include this nature of destination in my further discussion but will instead focus on the other three types of destination.

Seong-Seop Kim and Crompton (2000) have postulated that understanding the key attributes of a destination that motivate consumers to visit will aid a business operationally. Essentially, fashion consumers will be attracted to a number of different types of fashion destination, purely for the love of fashion shopping, but it is essential for marketers to understand the different attributes of the types of destination identified. I will now go through each of the other three fashion destination types in more detail.

1. High-end designer fashion destination

High-end designer fashion is how many people define fashion destinations, as discussed earlier in this chapter. The fashion capitals of the world generally fall in line with where the main global fashion shows take place. Below is a list of the main global fashion shows:

- London, UK
- Paris, France

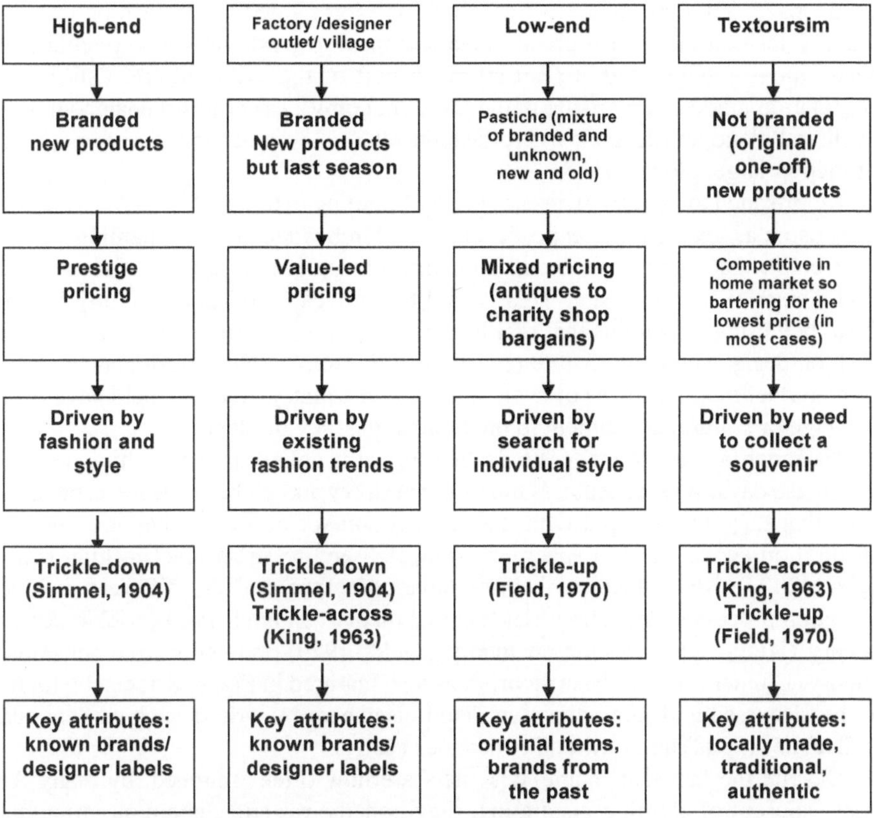

Figure 8.1 The key attributes of the four types of fashion shopping destinations (adapted from Crippin, 2000).

- Milan, Italy
- New York and Los Angeles, USA
- Madrid and Barcelona, Spain
- Sydney, Australia
- Dubai, UAE
- New Delhi, India
- Tokyo, Japan
- Moscow, Russia

The number of destinations has grown over the years, with the original shows, such as those of London and Paris, dating back to the 1960s and 1970s. These destinations will continue to shift and grow, following a pattern of economic development, but also depending on where the latest fashion 'hot spot' is considered to be. There are new fashion destinations emerging all the time, with the current example of the Dubai Mall development, having 12 million square feet of retail space, 850,000 square feet of which will form a dedicated 'fashion island'. Luxury fashion labels still predominantly appeal to westerners who populate or visit Dubai, though, and are not so much part of the local culture. Other new destination markets are arising in the 'new economy', eastern European countries such as Poland and Russia, where fashion retail is now becoming very popular, attracting large, global brands.

Moore and Doyle (2010) discuss luxury branding in terms of the five Es, which they name as 'exclusive', 'expert', 'elusive', 'embedded' and 'enchanting'. They also claim that in order to be an authentic luxury brand that you also need to add a sixth 'E': 'European'. This is said to be because of an apparently 'snobbish' belief that maintains that real luxury fashion stems from a deep heritage of fashion design and manufacture (e.g. Italy and France). 'New' designers tend not to manufacture themselves or even in their own country, so consumers have little heritage or cultural attachment to the brands that they produce.

Designer fashion no longer holds the title as the only source of fashion inspiration these days. With consumers more media savvy and globally aware, especially now that they are engaged with the Internet and social media, they are seeking inspiration across the full spectrum from high-end to street-level fashion (Law *et al.*, 2004). Many fashion theories have contextualised the different fashion adoption processes, including trickle-down theory (Simmel, 1904), trickle-across theory (King, 1963), trickle-up theory (Field, 1970) and 'collective selection' theory (Blumer, 1969). These theories, as also featured in Figure 8.1, can be found to be discussed and summarised in detail elsewhere by writers such as Kim and colleagues (2008) and Law and colleagues (2004).

Despite the fact that 'name' designers are now often 'snubbed' by many for other sources of clothing inspiration, they nonetheless still remain an important source of inspiration to the average fashion consumer. This sector of fashion retailing attracts the affluent consumer who buys into couture fashion, but it also has to cater for the 'window shopper' through its flagship stores by producing *diffusion lines* and affordable accessories for the less affluent consumer. Designer stores remain high-end in appearance, and serve to fulfil an aspirational shopping trip for the majority. Nobbs (2010) argues that flagships now need to be 'epicentres' or 'mega flagships' that encompass head offices and 'third spaces', such as cafés and entertainments, thereby serving as destinations that meet the objectives and key performance indicators (KPIs) of a company (not necessarily set to break even quickly).

The format of designer stores varies somewhat from city to city. In the UK, designers are found in their own stores in trendy suburbs or shopping centres, and also within department stores. Flagship stores are often large and innovative in their architecture, aesthetics and merchandise. Nobbs (2010) discusses how Diesel has rebranded its stores as 'style labs' in an attempt to stress its design process and the consumer experience that a flagship store should seek to provide. Popular streets for flagships in the UK are Oxford Street and Regent Street, with the surrounding suburbs providing space for smaller brands (such as Seven Dials in London's Covent Garden). Within central Europe, although designers can be found in the same broad format, the stores are generally smaller, more boutique-like and individual in nature. The UK follows a more US store formation, in general, than a European one, the US stores also favouring larger format and a more consistent brand image formats, whereas Asian markets adopt a mixture of huge, impressive buildings for stores, through to smaller, concept-like store formats.

Popular UK fashion-based department stores include Harvey Nichols, Selfridges and the tourist-infamous Harrods. Harrods is supposedly investigating the feasibility of adding a hotel to the top floor of the department store, to fully encompass the 'tourist experience' (Alexander, 2010). Likewise, the USA boasts department stores that are sought out by tourists, namely Saks, Macy's and Barney's. These large, high-end stores continue to dominate the rankings for city fashion destinations worldwide, with one major London newspaper (Finnigan, 2007) citing a top global fashion destination as Villa Moda department store in Kuwait City, although both department store formats and fashion zone 'hubs' continue to serve as popular tourist destinations globally.

A major problem that high-end fashion faces globally is the flood of cheap copies of sought-after designer fashion, sourced through the grey market. The typical customer is often in search of the 'look' rather than the authenticity. This is why global destinations boast tourist trips to their markets, which is predominantly where copies of designer brands and designer seconds can be bought at a fraction of the original designer price tag.

2. Designer and outlet villages

Designer and outlet villages have seen a rise in popularity in the last 20 years, being particularly popular in the USA and the UK. The UK has adopted an end-of-line, discount mentality since its acceptance of US retailers such as TK Maxx that feature this format. The natural drive of many consumers to seek out a bargain means that fashion can be sold as end-of-line, ex-factory, seconds or simply surplus stock and consumers readily buy in to this sector. Although this retail format is not exclusive to the fashion sector, fashion does appear to dominate the marketing of these 'outlet' shops. Success stories in the UK are the Clarks Village in Street (Somerset), Bicester Village, Oxford, and, by far the largest, the Freeport chain of designer outlets situated across the UK. As a global concept it appears to be readily accepted across Europe and the USA, also promoting travel and destination shopping over sometimes large distances, although mainly with domestic tourists in the past. However in recent years a fashion-based website has published a 'Top 10 Global Outlet Shopping Destinations' ranking, with Woodbury Common, New York, USA, taking the number one position and village outlets from all over Europe featuring in the rankings, with the UK's Bicester Village ranked at number eight (Handbag.com, 2009). There is some kudos now being associated with outlet shopping for fashion bargains, and it was recently featured within *The Guardian* (Fox, 2010) as a 'must-do' activity.

3. Low-end fashion

In accordance with the theories surrounding where consumers seek fashion inspiration, the trickle-across (King, 1963) and trickle-up (Field, 1970) theories postulate that consumers will seek out styles from their peers and from the street level. Low-end fashion has been popularised by such younger focused consumer behaviour that seeks to find fashion that does not conform to the high-end, designer image of fashion.

This has been fuelled by the popularisation of fashion on the Internet; the use of fashion blogs by companies and consumers, and the entrenchment of social networking into most peoples' lives has had a huge impact on how people view and learn about fashion. Online fashion word of mouth (WOM) is now controlled primarily by consumers, not companies, so little-known labels and destinations are experiencing surges in popularity with often little to no input from the product originators themselves.

Low-end fashion may be a style statement or an economic necessity. Nevertheless, low-end fashion hubs exist en masse, based on this youth following. Low-end fashion tends to focus on second-hand vintage or antique clothing and accessories, or reproduction fashions. This sits comfortably alongside street fashions sold in independent retailers in these low-end retail quadrants. London's Brick Lane and Seven Dials (Covent Garden and Carnaby Street districts) serve as examples of low-end fashion that have achieved cult status for the tourist market. Alongside established retail stores in and around these locations there may also be fashionable street markets, such as Portobello and Camden markets in London. These locations boast a stimulating and tourist-friendly mix of high- and low-end retail stores amidst mostly low-end market stall offerings. The eclectic mix attracts fashion shoppers from all social classes and fashion cycles (Rogers, 2003). Most towns and cities will now have such areas for low-end retail or a marketplace that is sought out by stylish fashion consumers.

This low-end retail enables smaller brands and designers to showcase their fashions as rents are more affordable, but the location needs to be carefully considered. Low-end does not always mean 'stylish' and the branding of these fashion destinations often takes time to build up in an organic manner (unless fast-tracked by online WOM), unlike that of the high-end, larger brands that populate the already established fashion destinations. Larger brands have a guaranteed audience whereas smaller brands need to work harder to build brand awareness as a fashion destination. Global and mass-market awareness from the Internet, however, has meant that small brands now have a fighting chance to compete alongside well-known, larger brands, which is an exciting opportunity for new fashion retailers. Low-end retail particularly interests the author, myself having been an owner of a fashion boutique in the independent fashion market until 2005. Having this focus of interest, and considering this area one of the most dynamically developing one for fashion tourist retail, I will present a case study fashion destination from this sector for consideration in the following section.

Case study: low-end fashion at Afflecks Palace, Manchester

I have chosen to consider a low-end fashion destination for the subject of further discussion, as I believe that it defies the traditional view of what a fashion destination is; the fashion destination under study is Afflecks Palace in Manchester, UK. This attraction was established in 1982 in Manchester's Northern Quarter, in a disused, run-down, five-storey building. The creator, James Walsh, wanted to create an 'Aladdin's cave' and 'a novel buying experience', reminiscent of the 1960s and 1970s fashion scene (Manchester, 2002). It primarily served as a second-hand market that specialised in 'experimental fashion' and unusual items. The website for Afflecks Palace describes it as 'an emporium of eclecticism, a totem of indie commerce . . . a fantastic place to shop for anything from top hats to tattoos' (Afflecks, 2010).

The image and branding that it has established (see Figure 8.2) attracts independent retail of new fashions and fashion-related retail products, alongside the traditional second-hand fashions and retail. The management allows fashion students and young designers to 'set up shop' and sell their brands alongside like-minded retailers, to stylish consumers. The idea of visiting Afflecks Palace is to seek out individual styles and fashions that provide alternative-minded consumers

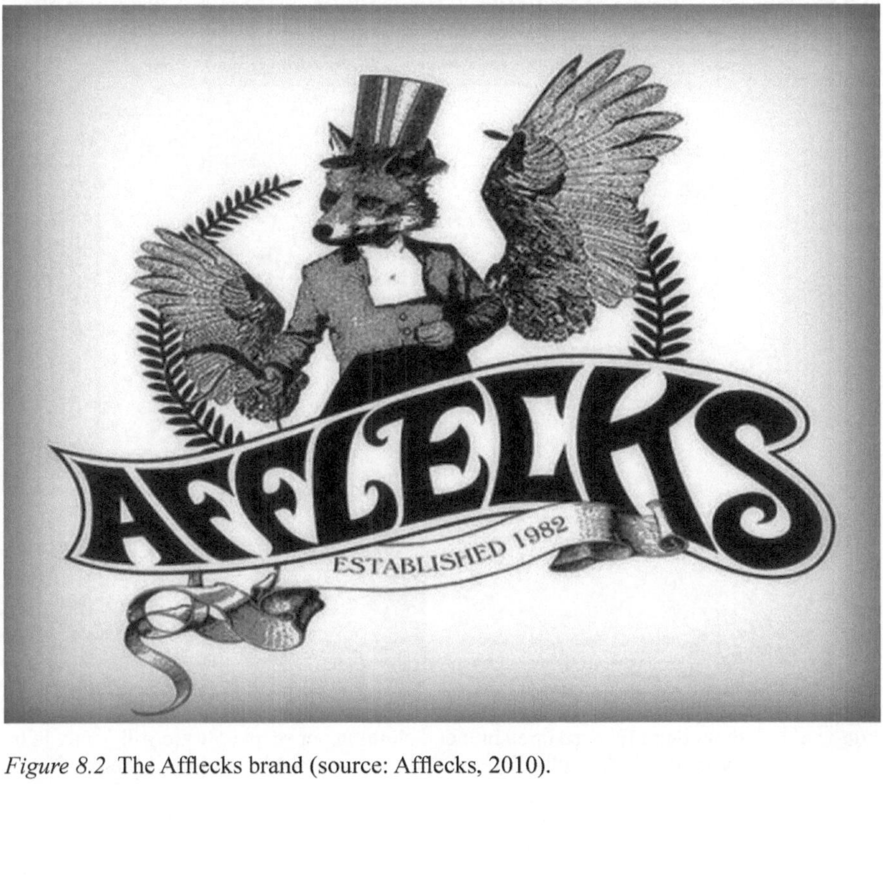

Figure 8.2 The Afflecks brand (source: Afflecks, 2010).

with a much-needed outlet to form an intended backlash against fast-fashion and value-fashion mainstream branded outlets in their choice behaviours. Consumers travel from around the UK and from global destinations to visit Afflecks, and its reputation has built up a global fashion following of customers happy to 'wear the outlet T-shirt' and sample its many attractions (see Figure 8.3).

Despite all of its continued success and augmentation since its creation, Afflecks Palace seemed to fall victim to the recession in 2008 and temporarily closed on 31 March 2008, only to be saved and reopened one day later, on 1 April 2008. The property manager of Afflecks Palace, the Bruntwood Company, had bought it in the interim and promptly rebranded it as simply 'Afflecks'. At the time there was a core consumer fear that the market would be sold on to property developers and cease to exist, but the current owners are quoted as saying:

> Never in our 30 year history have we bought one of our customer's businesses but Afflecks is a Manchester icon that we wanted to protect. We aren't however experts in managing markets, so will look for a suitable long-term owner.
>
> (Wikipedia, 2009).

Since the take-over, Afflecks has been revamped to return it to its former glory, and perhaps beyond this. The exterior of the building has been given a make-over, and the businesses inside continue to thrive and grow. The business mix has stayed

Figure 8.3 Although not focused upon branded clothing per se, people are still happy to be associated with the 'place' brand and wear the T-shirt (source: Afflecks, 2010).

true to the original ethos, though: cool, independent retail that attracts the fashion-alternative consumer who is seeking out individuality amidst the overproduction of mass market fashion. Afflecks is promoting the destination through word of mouth, its website and the use of social media, and has successfully established a customer 'community' that embraces the Afflecks brand (Afflecks, 2010).

Fashion destinations can come in very different formats, from high-end to traditional markets, but the key to their success is in knowing the motivations of their potential consumers. Afflecks Palace worked because it served as a destination in itself, having to be sought out by locals and tourists in a large old 'warehouse' type of building with plenty of local 'colour' and 'authentic' personality, as exhibited by those who frequent it as well as those who run it (see Figure 8.4). Its description of itself as an 'Aladdin's cave' of retail was probably most relevant to these consumers' searching, eclectic tastes. It was the innovation and originality that made it a unique global fashion destination, and that which is hoped to preserve it in the future by continuing to attract fashion tourists in great numbers. It is now entrenched in the culture of Manchester's fashion shoppers and serves as part of their history, and hopefully their future.

Figure 8.4 Local personality relating to 'authentic' people and locations (source: Afflecks, 2010).

Marketing a fashion destination: lessons from Afflecks Palace

It is important to consider how all of the different potential fashion destinations should be marketed. It has been stated that large city centres and shopping malls now employ a marketing company to manage this, towns and cities in particular employing TCM schemes to market a 'place' (Page and Hardyman, 1996). Smaller, low-end fashion destinations meanwhile build customer loyalty through word of mouth, and trade on their innovation and originality, with the added modern advantage of the Internet being used in this approach: a medium which has been very effective in spreading the word about Afflecks. Social media are cheap, and they reach the primary fashion audience, including particularly the key one for future viability: young people.

It should be remembered, though, that a destination is not merely a 'product' but is there to be 'consumed' (Buhalis, 2000; Morgan *et al.*, 2004). Destinations are, however, inevitably branded like a product for their easy sale to the tourist market. In this process Timothy (2005: 44, 48) claims that branding a destination should consider the image and the environment that is to be marketed and in doing this even shopping malls can become 'tourist destinations in their own right'. Shepherd (2009) specifically claims that fashion destinations need to be 'relevant' and 'contemporary', continuously reinventing themselves and carefully considering the retail aesthetics. In considering such developments and how global word of mouth and relevance can be communicated to a travelling audience, one thing is becoming very clear: in order to market a global destination these days, a good starting point is to have an attractive website and be involved in creating word of mouth through social networking. Consumers now want to experience as much about a destination as they can virtually before they commit to visiting it physically.

A tourist's search is increasingly beginning on the web, particularly for niche fashion audiences, and a web presence is a necessity for any size of business. Tourism is a sector that has been transformed by the Internet (Shaddick, 2007), in the forms and formations of its operational structures and value chains (Morosan, 2008), and also in terms of consumer expectations and usage. In line with this, fashion is a sector that has proved to be very popular on the web, changing the way that people search for information (Law, 2000). Because of this, the Internet has an increasingly important role to play in destination management (Feng *et al.*, 2003), and short city breaks are among the most searched-for tourist activities online (Shaddick, 2007).

A good website can be a 'virtual customer service representative' for a destination (So and Morrison, 2004) and, according to Gretzel and colleagues (2000), should provide 'information representation, collaboration, communication, interactivity, and transactions', in a different way from how traditional media do. This said, despite many authors, such as Buhalis (2003), proposing in the early part of the 2000s that online marketing would greatly reduce the need for offline marketing, others, such as Morosan (2008), have suggested that there still needs to be a mixed approach of both online and offline marketing to be truly successful in tourism and destination management. Even so, there are clear advantages for destinations to adopt a strong online presence: global reach, increased visibility (Buhalis, 2000), richness of information (Bender, 1997; Buhalis, 2000), customisation opportunities (Bender, 1997; So and Morrison, 2004), low cost (Buhalis, 2000; Gretzel *et al.*, 2000) and enhanced local cooperation (Buhalis, 2000). For consumers it represents a 'pull' medium (So and Morrison, 2004), rather than marketing that is 'pushed' upon consumers; they can actively seek out the information that they actually want about destinations, opening up retail destination opportunities. Consumers frequently consult visitor review sites, such as Trip Advisor, and value 'real' consumer opinions of a destination. Interestingly, though, much like the predominant academic view of retail as a secondary consideration of travel, Trip Advisor is yet to have a section dedicated to retail- or fashion-related tourist trips. With the rise in city breaks, it seems to be an obvious area of expansion for it.

Chapter conclusions: fashion destination developments for the future

At the outset of this chapter I posed two questions to consider in particular:

- Are fashion destinations a potential tourist attraction in their own right or are they merely one part of a bigger tourist attraction 'package'?
- Are fashion destinations only defined by high-end designers?

It has been accepted that fashion destinations exist readily in four sectors of fashion tourism: high-end, designer outlets, low-end and textourism (Crippin, 2000; Timothy, 2005). Within this typology, apart from possibly textourism, it is proposed that fashion retail provides the main basis for a fashion destination at all levels because of the attractive nature of the goods it sells to prospective customers of the fashion scene. The 'wow' factor of fashion means that it has followers at all stages of the fashion lifecycle (Rogers, 2003). The early adopters of fashion aspire to high-end fashion retailing, the fashion innovators to both high-end and low-end, and the fashion followers are content to buy fashion at a discount from designer outlets.

The global fashion marketplace serves all of these sectors in abundance and fashion retail now needs to be acknowledged as a primary motivator for tourism in order to be fully capitalised upon. Fashion destinations are still readily accepted to be major fashionable cities, but increasingly there are large and small, high-end and low-end, branded and customised fashion retailers globally that have achieved the cult status of being a fashion destination to discerning audiences of tourists and visitors, and will probably increasingly do so in a very active, growing and fragmenting market.

Fashion industry stakeholders need to acknowledge the following points in determining the success of potential fashion destinations and elevating them to a primary element of tourist consumption (Jansen-Verbeke, 1986):

1 Consider third place requirements, as in 'the city as a theme park' (Hannigan, 1998). This relates to the need for experience of shopping, like visiting a theme park, to encompass other forms of entertainment. In order to attract customers to fashion destinations, the retail provision needs to serve as somewhat of a 'fashion resort', offering a mix of activities that are dominated by shopping.
2 Utilise online and offline marketing of destinations, including customer reviews, the use of social media, mobile applications and blogs. The fashion audience is engaged in these media, so businesses should be too, in order to reach customers and appeal to them. This should work in tandem with offline campaigns, though, as traditional marketing methods are far from dead.
3 Remember heritage. A brand can be built and marketed on its heritage. Fashion thrives on the associations that consumers make with a brand, particularly in the luxury sector.
4 Consider shopper typologies. Know your audience. Stakeholders need to appeal to the fashion consumer who is at the appropriate stage in the fashion lifecycle. Early adopters want innovation and prestige, whereas fashion followers want acceptance from wearing established trends and fashion labels.

There is no doubt that fashion is big business globally, whatever customer you are seeking to attract. I personally believe that fashion can come to dominate the motivation of a tourist to visit a particularly relevant destination. To do this, the fashion destination needs to provide an all-encompassing experience of shopping and lifestyle activities that aim to actively and vibrantly promote positive 'conspicuous consumption' of fashion goods (Goldsmith and Clark, 2008).

References

Afflecks (2010) Website. Online source: http://www.afflecks.com/ (last accessed 9 November 2010).

Alexander, E. (2010) Harrods Hotel. *Vogue*, 15 October. Online source: http://www.vogue.co.uk/news/daily/101015-harrods-considers-opening-a-hotel.aspx (last accessed 9th November 2010).

Argyle, M. (1996) *The Social Psychology of Leisure*. London: Penguin.

Ashworth, G. J. and Tunbridge, J. E. (1990) *The Tourist Historic City*. London: Belhaven Press.

Babin, B. J., Darden, W. R. and Griffin, M. (1994) Work and/or fun: measuring hedonic and utilitarian shopping value. *Journal of Consumer Research* 20, 644–656.

Bellenger, D. N., Steinberg, E. and Stanton, W. W. (1976) The congruence of store image and self image. *Journal of Retailing* 52, 17–32.

Bender, D. E. (1997) The online marketer: think globally, market locally. Marketing applications of the Internet and the World Wide Web. *HSMAI Marketing Review* 14(2), 10–11.

Bloch, P. H. and Richins, M. L. (1983) Shopping without purchase: an investigation of consumer browsing behavior. *Advances in Consumer Research* 10(1), 389–393.

Bloch, P. H., Ridgway, N. M. and Sherrell, D. L. (1989) Extending the concept of shopping: an investigation of browsing activity. *Journal of the Academy of Marketing Science* 17, 13–21.

Blumer, H. (1969) Fashion: from class differentiation to collective selection. *Sociological Quarterly* 10, 275–291.

Buhalis, D. (2000) Marketing the competitive destination of the future. *Tourism Management* 21, 97–116.

Buhalis, D. (2003) *eTourism: Information technology for strategic tourism management*. Harlow: Pearson Educational.

CACI (2008) Westfield London enters the British retail hierarchy at number 8. Online source: http://www.caci.co.uk/302.aspx (last accessed 9 November 2010).

Crippin, K. (2000) The threads that tie textiles to tourism. In Hitchcock, M. and Nuryanti, W. (eds) *Building on Batik: The globalization of a craft community*. Aldershot: Ashgate, pp. 271–284.

Field, G. A. (1970) The status float phenomenon: the upward diffusion of innovation. *Business Horizon* 13(4), 45–52.

Feng, R., Morrison, A. M. and Ismail, J. A. (2003) East versus West: a comparison of online destination marketing in China and the USA. *Journal of Vacation Marketing* 10(1), 43–56.

Finnigan, K. (2007) The ten best fashion destinations in the world. *The Telegraph* (London), 18 March. Online source: http://fashion.telegraph.co.uk/columns/kate-finnigan/TMG3359596/The-10-best-fashion-destinations-in-the-world.html (last accessed 9 November 2010).

Fox, I. (2010) Outlets are the in thing. *The Guardian*, 6 April. Online source: http://www.guardian.co.uk/lifeandstyle/2010/apr/06/outlet-discount-shopping (last accessed 10 November 2011).

Frommer, A. and Frommer, P. (1996) *New World of Travel*. New York: Macmillan.

Goldsmith, R. E. and Clark, R. A. (2008) An analysis of factors affecting fashion opinion leadership and fashion opinion seeking. *Journal of Fashion Marketing & Management* 12(3), 308–322.

Gretzel, U., Yuan, Y. L. and Fesenmaier, D. R. (2000) Preparing for the new economy: advertising strategies and change in destination marketing organizations. *Journal of Travel Research* 39, 146–156.

Handbag.com (2009) Top 10 global outlet shopping destinations. Online source: http://www.handbag.com/fashion/top-10-global-outlet-shopping-destinations-intro/gallery (last accessed 9 November 2010).

Hannigan, J. (1998) *Fantasy City*. London: Routledge.

Jackson, T. and Shaw, D. (2001) *Mastering Fashion Buying & Merchandising Management*. London: Palgrave Macmillan.

Jansen-Verbeke, M. (1986) Inner-city tourism: resources, tourists and promoters. *Annals of Tourism Research* 13, 79–100.

Jones, M. A. (1999) Entertaining shopping experiences: an exploratory investigation. *Journal of Retailing & Consumer Services* 6, 129–139.

Kim, H., Rhee, E.-Y. and Yee, J. (2008) Comparing fashion process networks and friendship networks in small groups of adolescents. *Journal of Fashion Marketing & Management* 12(4), 545–564.

King, C. W. (1963) Fashion adoption: a rebuttal to the 'trickle down' theory. In Greyser, S. A. (ed.) *Toward Scientific Marketing: Proceedings of the American Marketing Association, December 27–28*. Chicago, IL: American Marketing Association, pp. 108–125.

Law, R. (2000) Internet in travel and tourism: Part I. *Journal of Travel & Tourism Marketing* 9(3), 65–71.

Law, K. M., Zhang, Z.-M. and Laung, C. (2004) Fashion change and fashion consumption: the chaotic perspective. *Journal of Fashion Marketing & Management* 8(4), 362–374.
Manchester (2002) Shopping in Manchester: Afflecks Palace. Online source: http://www.manchester2002-uk.com/shops/afflecks.html (last accessed 9 November 2010).
Moore, C. and Doyle, S. (2010) The evolvement of the luxury fashion retailing business model. Conference presentation at 17th Recent Advances in Retailing & Services Science Conference (EIRASS), Istanbul, Turkey. 2–5 July.
Morgan, N., Pritchard, A. and Pride, R. (2004) *Destination Branding: Creating the unique destination proposition*, 2nd edition. Oxford: Butterworth-Heinemann.
Morosan, C. (2008) DMO websites and the role of complementary media in tourism advertising. *Journal of Hospitality & Leisure Marketing* 17(1–2), 216–236.
Nobbs, K. (2010) Luxury fashion brand strategy: the role of the flagship store. Conference presentation at 17th Recent Advances in Retailing & Services Science Conference (EIRASS), Istanbul, Turkey. 2–5 July.
Page, S. J. and Hardyman, R. (1996) Place marketing and town centre management: a new tool for urban revitalization. *Cities* 13(3), 153–164.
Rogers, E. M. (2003) *Diffusion of Innovations*, 5th edition. New York: Free Press.
Seong-Seop Kim, J. L. and Crompton, C. B. (2000) Responding to competition: a strategy for sun/lost city, South Africa. *Tourism Management* 21, 33–41.
Shaddick, C. (2007) Sun, sea, sand and surfing. *Marketing Week*, 11 January.
Shepherd, K. (2009) *Lifestyles as Destination: Retail design today*. London: Fashion Group International.
Sherry, J. F. Jr. (1990) A sociological analysis of a Midwestern American flea market. *Journal of Consumer Research* 17, 13–30.
So, S.-I. and Morrison, A. M. (2004) Internet marketing in tourism in Asia: an evaluation of the performance of East Asian National tourism organization websites. *Journal of Hospitality & Leisure Marketing* 11(4), 93–118.
Simmel, G. (1904) Fashion. *International Quarterly* 10, 130–155.
Snepenger, D. J., Murphy, L., O'Connell, R. and Gregg, E. (2003) Tourists and residents use of shopping space. *Annals of Tourism Research* 30(3), 567–580.
Swarbrooke, J. and Horner, S. (2007) *Consumer Behaviour in Tourism*, 2nd edition. Oxford: Butterworth-Heinemann.
Timothy, D. J. (2005) *Shopping Tourism, Retailing and Leisure*. Clevedon, UK: Channel View Publications.
Warnaby, G. and Bennison, D. (2006) Reciprocal urban place marketing and co-branding? Retail applications. *Place Branding* 2(4), 297–310.
Warnaby, G., Bennison, D., Davies, B. J. and Hughes, H. (2002) Marketing UK towns and cities as shopping destinations. *Journal of Marketing Management* 18, 877–904.
Warnaby, G., Bennison, D., Davies, B. J. and Hughes, H. (2004) People and partnerships: marketing urban retailing. *International Journal of Retail & Distribution Management* 32(11), 545–556.
Wikipedia (2009) Afflecks. Online source: http://en.wikipedia.org/wiki/Afflecks (last accessed 9 November 2010).
Williams, C. C. (1997) *Consumer Services & Economic Development*. London: Routledge.

Conclusion

Tourist retail and the purpose of psychogeographical study: a cautionary tale!

Charles McIntyre

The potential value of the present text can possibly be considered by thinking forward to how the shopping environments of the future may change and be effectively constituted to meet the changing needs of society, as they seem to be in a state of dramatic change at the time of its compilation. The potential significance of the work herein can also be related to a backward glance at the statements expressed in the early twentieth century by Louis Aragon, who tried to elaborate upon his specific pleasures in the Parisian shopping arcades:

> I shall never cease to be astonished by the degree of man's disdainful indifference towards his pleasures, and his consequent failure to extend their domain . . . Even those people who appreciate the delights of chance make no apparent efforts to reproduce them. No system, no attempt at codifying pleasures. It is a miracle that they are still occasionally capable of giving way to what they so quaintly call vices . . . As far as I know the geography of pleasure has never been taught, although proficiency in this subject would constitute an effective weapon against life's tediums. No one has assumed the responsibility of assigning its limits to the frisson, of drawing the boundaries of the caress, of charting the territories of ecstasy. All that man has exceeded in extracting so far from the individual experience is a series of vulgar localisations. One day, perhaps, scholars will divide the human body up among themselves in order to be able to study the meanderings of pleasure: certainly such a study is as worthy of absorbing a man's activity as any other.
>
> (Aragon, 1994: 44)

Although that was written in 1926, one could contend that progress in this particular field of study remains at a limited level and therefore is as worthy of a person's activity as it was then – if not more so given our apparently ever-increasing assignation of importance to the realms of leisure experience. None of the contributors to this volume would, I am certain, lay claim to have arrived at a comprehensive theory of tourist retail spatial pleasures, they nevertheless reach some interesting way stations by such research by expanding upon certain findings within a discrete number of examples across the field. Their contribution rests in attempts to codify specific spaces of personal and social reward within liminal, or transitional, cultural-commercial consumption experiences and, by so doing, moves us towards an increased understanding of the dimensions needed to support them.

The types of space and the supporting attributes optimal for supporting these leisure consumption processes can also be considered relative to the following statement:

> The human being by his mere presence imposes a schema on space. Most of the time he is not aware of it. He notes its absence when he is lost. He marks its presence on those ritual occasions that lift life above the ordinary and so force him to an awareness of life's values, including those manifest in space.
>
> (Tuan, 1977: 36–37)

The provision of the music store case in Chapter 7 is perhaps one that I can offer as a cautionary tale in the study of tourist (and leisure) retail, as it tended towards a position that such a popular sensory-spatial leisure variety must have offered consumption processes of value that encouraged beneficial 'out-in-the-world' behaviours. Thus, the music retail revolution towards downloading substitution, despite the attraction of convenient or 'easy' modernist lifestyle advantages, could be read as a loss in retail varieties of 'active' experience of a 'real', localised nature in high streets and other physical shopping locations. This loss in *retail social capital* is therefore equivalent to a reduced diversity of cultural ecology and diminished varieties of sensory-spatial leisure consumption. It was not lost, in the writing, that this may simply be regarded as a process of inevitable change due to technological process and a nostalgia for the 'old' ways, as aptly stated by Blake:

> The Child's Toys and the Old Man's Reasons
> Are the Fruits of the Two seasons.
>
> *Auguries of Innocence*, 1803 (Blake, 1958: 70)

However, even giving allowance for the 'old man' status of the editor, many younger authors have contributed herein. In its mapping of selected experiential space dimensions across various parts of a cultural-commercial, tourist retail continuum, the 'final' destination of this body of research has implications for users of these varieties of leisure spaces. The study implies a prevalence of socially and culturally relevant artistic, creative (or co-creative) consumption events to be operating in this area of human experience – of immersion within communal and symbolically laden space and place. The transactional processes involved include ones featuring tribal searches for social capital (Bourdieu, 1984) whilst being 'out-in-the-world'.

Holistically differentiated spatial types in support of such searches appear to have artistic and/or creative consumption effects for the experiencer *in situ* that contribute towards a diversity of cultural ecology that they can openly explore through a process of psychogeographical *dérive*, or drift through various ambiences – with overall beneficial effects for individual and social enhancement.

This may encourage 'out-in-the-world' place and space identity, behaviours and satisfactions through immersion and investigation.

By the study of such realms it is hoped that we can ultimately improve and preserve some physical areas for tourist retail promenading and continue to explore the psychogeographical meanderings of pleasure; to ensure that a range of evolved human satisfactions experienced whilst being out-in-the-world, in times of great technological change, remain 'essentially a spatial activity – (in that) we still "go shopping"' (Goss, 1993: 18).

References

Aragon, L. (1994) *Paris Peasant* (trans. S. W. Taylor). Boston, MA: Exact Change.

Blake, W. (1958) *William Blake* (ed. J. Bronowski). Harmondsworth, Middlesex, UK: Penguin Books.

Bourdieu, P. (1984) *Distinction: A social critique of judgement and taste* (trans. R. Nice). London: Routledge.

Goss, J. (1993) The magic of the mall: an analysis of form, function and meaning in the contemporary retail built environment. *Annals of the Association of American Geographers* 83(1), 18–47.

Tuan, Y.-F. (1977) *Space and Place: The perspective of experience*. Minneapolis: University of Minnesota Press.

Index